Advance Praise for *Rhythm in the Rain:*

"Lynn Darroch has put together a great resource for musicians, listeners, and history buffs, compiling what seems to be the most comprehensive resource about the history of jazz in the Northwest. This book will do the important job of keeping the memories and stories alive of musicians and venues that, while they may be immortalized through recordings, have important history that may otherwise be lost to the murkiness of time. Darroch has done the community and the music a great service by dedicating himself to telling these stories." —John Nastos

"Lynn Darroch illuminates the rich history of jazz in the Pacific Northwest from the early twentieth century to the present. Interweaving factors of culture, economics, politics, landscape, and weather, he helps us to understand how the Northwest grew so many fine jazz artists and why the region continues to attract musicians from New Orleans, New York, California, Europe, and South America. He concentrates on the traditions of the big port cities, Seattle and Portland, and underlines the importance of musicians from places like Wenatchee, Spokane, Eugene, and Bend. Darroch has the curiosity of a journalist, the investigative skills of a historian and the language of a poet. His writing about music makes you want to hear it." —Doug Ramsey

"With the skills of a curator, Lynn Darroch brings us the inspiring history and personal stories of Northwest jazz musicians whose need for home, love of landscape, and desire to express, all culminate into the unique makeup of jazz in Portland and Seattle. Thank you Lynn for a great read and its contribution to jazz. Truly world-class. Just like the players." —Dave Averre

"Rhythm In The Rain is a compelling must-read for anyone interested in the cultural history of the Pacific Northwest. Lynn Darroch brilliantly captures the creative, can-do spirit of Cascadia, chronicles several generations of the region's leading musicians, and explores the secret of why so many of us—mystics, misfits, and vagabonds—choose to live and work here." —Dmitri Matheny

RHYTHM IN THE RAIN

RHYTHM IN THE RAIN

JAZZ IN THE PACIFIC NORTHWEST

LYNN DARROCH

Ooligan Press

Rhythm in the Rain: Jazz in the Pacific Northwest
© 2016 Lynn Darroch
ISBN 13: 978-1-932010-81-7

All rights reserved. No part of this book may be reproduced or transmitted in any form or by any means, electronic or mechanical, including photocopying, recording, or by any information storage and retrieval system, without permission in writing from the publisher.

Ooligan Press
Portland State University
Post Office Box 751, Portland, Oregon 97207
503.725.9748
ooligan@ooliganpress.pdx.edu
www.ooliganpress.pdx.edu

Library of Congress Cataloging-in-Publication Data
Names: Darroch, Lynn A., author.
Title: Rhythm in the rain : jazz in the Pacific Northwest / Lynn Darroch.
Description: Portland, Oregon : Ooligan Press, [2016] | "2016 | Includes
 bibliographical references and index.
Identifiers: LCCN 2015043329 | ISBN 9781932010817 (trade paper : alk. paper)
Subjects: LCSH: Jazz—Oregon—History and criticism. | jazz—Washington
 (State)—History and criticism. | Jazz musicians—Oregon. | Jazz
 musicians—Washington (State).
Classification: LCC ML3508.7.O66 D37 2016 | DDC 781.6509795—dc23
LC record available at http://lccn.loc.gov/2015043329

Cover design by Erika Schnatz
Interior design by Ryan Brewer and Olenka Burgess

Full image credits listed on page 218
References to website URLs were accurate at the time of writing. Neither the author nor Ooligan Press is responsible for URLs that have changed or expired since the manuscript was prepared.

Printed in the United States of America

CONTENTS

Foreword	ix
Preface	xi
Acknowledgments	xiii
We Live Here	15
From Frontier to Jazz Mecca	23
Jackson Street and Williams Avenue: 1940–1959	37
The Dark Ages: 1960–1972	55
The Renaissance: 1973–1982	77
Coming of Age: 1983–1993	97
A Rising Tide: 1994–1999	125
Riding the Wave: 1999–2007	145
Freedom on the Margins: 2008–2015	169
An Uncertain Future	199
Endnotes	213
Image Credits	218
Index	222

FOREWORD

I moved to Portland in the summer of 2011, after spending nearly two years in Winnipeg, Manitoba, smack-dab in the middle of Canada. My teaching position at the University of Manitoba had been a good one, but neither I nor my wife was fond of the area's six-month winters, during which temperatures can drop as low as -40°F. So, when I was offered a position at Portland State University, we jumped at the opportunity, packing our things and setting off on a twenty-eight-hour journey to the fabled city of Portland.

After recovering from the trip, I wanted to check out the Portland jazz scene. Before relocating, the only thing I knew about Portland and jazz was pianist Darrell Grant. I had met him very briefly in the early 2000s, and I had of course heard his great Criss Cross recordings. But I wanted to see what else was happening. I went out to hear Mike Prigodich's fusion band at a southeast Portland pizza joint, Javier Nero's group at a restaurant in northeast Portland, Damian Erskine's group at the Goodfoot, David Friesen's trio at the Camellia Lounge, Greg Goebel's trio at Wilfs, Ron Steen's jam at Clyde's, and Dan Balmer's trio at Jimmy Mak's. That was all in my first WEEK!

You will quickly realize while reading Lynn Darroch's *Rhythm in the Rain* that he is a die-hard Pacific Northwest resident and jazz fan. He knows the history of the music, he knows the history of the scene, and he insists that this region is a unique place for jazz artists to develop their craft. He writes with diplomatic honesty and a genuine love for the musicians, and he describes their techniques without so many technical terms as to bog down the uninitiated. Darroch has a thorough understanding of how this region's musicians are connected to the past, present, and future of jazz, and he is able to focus on the Pacific Northwest while keeping the global context in view. Darroch's book is a great companion to Robert Dietsche's *Jumptown: The Golden Years of Portland Jazz,* and I believe in time it will be considered as valuable a historical resource.

The thing I like most about Darroch's book is how evident it is that he knows how to roll with the punches of the jazz life. Jazz comes from blues, and blues came out of extreme hardship. Jazz musicians from whatever walk of life are no strangers to hardship. Sometimes you have a gig, and sometimes you don't. Oftentimes you don't! Still, you never lose hope and you just keep on playing, no matter what. We play because we have to, not because we have gigs, or because we make money, or because people come to see us play. We play because we love it.

Darroch's history lesson is honest, but he never loses his optimism. The cities of the Pacific Northwest are going through some serious growth, and with that growth come growing pains. The jazz scene is changing. Some of the changes are good; some are not. Still, we keep playing, keep practicing, keep listening. Hopefully, reading this book will inspire you to get out and be a part of the continuing evolution of the region's jazz scene.

George Colligan, July 2015

PREFACE

I live here.

I was born and raised in the Pacific Northwest, and though I've lived and worked elsewhere, most of my life's been spent right here. My heart belongs to this landscape and the communities shaped by it. This story is told from the inside.

And it's by no means a complete chronicle. I leave out most of the region's smaller cities. Many excellent and important musicians don't appear; Seattle alone is home to so many jazz artists it would take a chapter to simply identify them all. I hope those I've included adequately represent their colleagues.

There is no one "true" story of jazz in the Pacific Northwest. The record of human events can be used to tell many different tales. This is one of them, an account of particular people and what they've done in this place. To make sense of it, I've looked at political, social, and economic forces, as well as jazz made in the region. Mostly, my information and analysis come out of the many conversations I've had with musicians during almost forty years as a journalist. Thus that information is subject to the errors of memory that are inevitable in oral histories, despite fact-checking. My apologies for any details we may have missed.

And because history does not develop in convenient decade-long units, I've divided the continuous story of jazz in the Pacific Northwest into eras that begin and end with significant events that signal changes that occur over time.

Here I call "jazz" any music that a significant number of musicians, listeners, and critics identify as such. A "jazz scene" includes performers of a variety of styles, owners and operators of venues where the music is presented, organizations and businesses that present and promote the music, various media that report on it, and of course listeners.

It's a sprawling, untidy world. Think of its people as members of the Jazz Tribe of Cascadia. It's an imaginary kingdom, for sure, but its story may be just as real—and fascinating—as the music that has inspired it.

Lynn Darroch, July 2015

ACKNOWLEDGMENTS

I'm just a middleman. First I must thank the artists whose music and insights I've listened to over the years for providing much of the material for this book. Second, music historians Kurt Armbruster *(Before Seattle Rocked: A City and Its Music)*, Paul de Barros *(Jackson Street After Hours: The Roots of Jazz in Seattle),* and Robert Dietsche (*Jumptown: The Golden Years of Portland Jazz, 1942–1957*) have provided indispensable information for the early years of this story. Beyond that, I must thank Paul de Barros for the enlightening hours he's spent discussing all eras of the Seattle jazz scene with me.

Of course those writers aren't the only ones who have contributed to my understanding of the region's jazz and those involved with it, from artist to audience. Especially useful have been the magazines *Earshot Jazz* and *Jazzscene*. And it's thanks to everyone who has given me the opportunity to write about jazz and related music for publication—and to broadcast it on radio at KMHD as well!—that I got an inside look at the music and its makers in the first place.

The complete editorial team at Ooligan Press, under the direction of publisher Abbey Gaterud, is named in the end matter, but here I want to give special thanks to Margaret Schimming, who first brought the book proposal to the press, recruited me, and led the team through May, 2015; Tyler Mathieson, who took over the job from there; and editorial lead Olenka Burgess.

And thanks to my wife Susan Gustavson, who has been there encouraging me all along.

INTRODUCTION

We Live Here

"Every day I can see the mountains—St. Helens, Rainier, Hood, Adams—and I want to climb. A lot of what makes a great climber is the same as what makes a great improviser: courage, strength, creativity, total awareness of environment, the ability to focus pin-pointedly and generally at the same time—and finally, to let go of all ambitions, inhibitions, thoughts... and play."

Alan Jones

Esperanza Spalding didn't want to waste any time after her surprise win for Best New Artist at the 2011 Grammy Awards. She'd grown up hard in Portland and knew how unlikely the award was for a young black woman playing jazz. So she was in a hurry to put her fame to use—and knew exactly what she wanted to do: "Help the pillars of my jazz community gain the recognition they deserve."[1]

It only took two years.

At the 2013 Awards ceremony, Spalding shared another Grammy—this time for Best Instrumental Arrangement Accompanying Vocalist(s)—with Thara Memory, her Portland mentor, for his arrangement of her song "City of Roses." From her multi-award-winning album *Radio Music Society*, the hometown tribute also featured students from Memory's American Music Program.

If a single moment can capture the story of jazz in the Pacific Northwest, this might be it.

At the podium to receive the award, Memory leaned on his former student's arm. He was sixty-five and had lost a foot and parts of two fingers to diabetes. The Grammy was the culmination of a path he'd been on since age twelve, when he fell in love with the music of Miles Davis and started hanging around backstage whenever the leading man of jazz played nearby.

One day, Davis approached.

"You're that trumpet player, aren't you?" His voice was challenging. "I bet you can't play worth a shit."

« Cape Alava, Olympic National Park, Washington.

Memory was stunned but quickly took heart—the man had sought him out, recognized him. His reply became a vow that determined the course of his life.

"Well, no, not compared to you I can't," he said. "But I can hold down my own thing; I can hold down my own thing and bring some people up with me."

He did, and there he was, fifty years later: an underdog African American musician and teacher, originally from the South, accepting a Grammy Award with a former student who shared her success with the folks back home.

It's a heartwarming image. And it does represent the way musicians work together here, an alternative to the star system that supported the likes of Miles Davis. It also reflects the wider culture of the region—a culture distant from centers of power and influence and as distinct from them as the landscape that shaped it.

Many other images could capture the scene just as well: an afternoon in 1959, when Bobby Bradford and Cleve Williams waited outside Washington High School to make sure teenage drummer Mel Brown got to a rehearsal of the Walter Bridges Big Band. Or young drummer D'Vonne Lewis playing a tribute concert in 2013 for his grandfather, Seattle organist Dave Lewis. Or the 2013 debut of Darrell Grant's *The Territory*, a jazz suite that depicts the region and its history in sound. Like many musicians from this region, Grant feels a deep connection to the jazz that came before him here—music that embodied an approach shaped in part by its distance from the mainstream.

Not everyone finds that distance useful to the scope of their ambitions, including jazz artists who, like Spalding, have left to become international stars: Bing Crosby and Mildred Bailey decamped before a full-fledged jazz scene developed in the region; Quincy Jones always had his sights set on leaving. They were followed by Larry Coryell in the late 1960s, Chris Botti in the 1980s, and Aaron Parks in the 1990s. But growing up in the Pacific Northwest did shape the musicians they became. As it did Ray Charles, who got his start in Seattle, where Jimi Hendrix

Downtown Portland with Mount Hood in the background.

Terroir: The Territory Shapes the Artist

Darrell Grant, *On the Territory* blog, June 19, 2013

In wine they have a concept called "terroir"—that mix of dirt, rain, sun, wind, and water that makes one vineyard's grapes taste different from another's.

It is possible the territory shapes its artists, too. Seeps into our tunes and our dreams, inspires us, connects us—whether we are native or transplant. It runs deeper than genre or musical style. When you love a place, its story can't help but make its way into your own, and you can feel its current in the work.

Part of it is Geography. It is the land, the rocks, the rivers. In the Cascade watershed the interface of land and water defines us. The verdant, fertile soil laid down over millennia, the great river Columbia that is the lifeline of our region. The peaks—Hood, Adams, Saint Helens, Rainer, and the others—stand as spiritual monuments grounding us and fueling our imaginations.

The Territory is ground, water, sky, and everything in between. It is what was here before you came and what will be here after you are gone. It is the bones, the sweat, the blood, the dreams, the blessings, the harvests, the floods, the tears, the rocks, the roots, the broken branches, fallen leaves, and forgotten paths. It is the songs of bug, bird, blizzard, wagon wheel, salmon, elk, beaver, and berry. It is the bank of the creek, the bed of the river, the stump in the ground, and the memories of the elders. The territory is the whole story—told and untold.

grew up and learned to play the blues and Kenny G the saxophone. But it's not big names that define jazz in the Pacific Northwest. Quite the opposite.

What has developed here was shaped by and reflects the environment, the economy, and a jazz community that grew up in a kind of isolation often found out West, where artists are aware of movements elsewhere but not always in step with them. This is no place to gain fame and fortune playing jazz. It's rare for artists who remain in the Pacific Northwest to establish a national reputation without first attaining it elsewhere.

Some of the established players who relocated to the Pacific Northwest did so because they value the very qualities that have given the local jazz community its identity. That's the key: the values shared by artists who choose the Pacific Northwest, whether native-born or immigrant, determine the character of the region's jazz scene, whether the style is gypsy swing or avant-garde, chamber, funk, or straight-ahead. The region some call Cascadia, that rainy country from the Southern Willamette Valley to Bellingham Bay, between the Cascade Mountains and the Pacific, has shaped its music just as the culture and landscape of Southern California or the Mississippi Delta influenced music made there.

This book tells the story of that happy wedding of people and place.

It's a tale of port cities on the Pacific Rim and kids from the hinterlands drawn to them, where small African American and Asian communities found a crucial niche and native culture filtered in almost unnoticed. It chronicles the impact of economic boom and bust and the powerful influence of the landscape. Most of all, it's the story of the artists themselves and the remarkably supportive communities they created.

Maybe it's something in the water. Or just all the water everywhere here in Cascadia—the land of falling waters.

"I wouldn't live anywhere else in the world," says bassist Phil Baker, who toured with Diana Ross early in his career and is a longtime member of the pop-jazz band Pink Martini. "No place better than Portland in all respects. It's a user-friendly size, but not too small to have a lot of cultural activities and a deep bench for every instrument.

"Nobody's getting rich here," he adds, "but there's really a sense of community and camaraderie."

That was evident immediately to Darrell Grant, who was raised in Colorado and came to Portland from New York. "When I moved here, I was impressed by the community nature of the music," he says. "It's very much an 'all for one, one for all' kind of feeling."

Even those who have moved on agree.

"The jazz scene in Portland is very nurturing for youngsters; the people are very open," says trumpet player Chris Botti, who was raised in the Willamette Valley, got his start in Portland, and went on to international success. "Part of learning music is having a good relationship with mentors when you're young—it makes you progress tenfold. That was what the wonderfully supportive Portland jazz scene provided me."

And that supportive community stretches back to the 1930s, when Floyd Standifer hitchhiked to Portland from the little town of Gresham to hear jazz on Williams Avenue. Years later, after he'd moved to Seattle, Standifer toured Europe with his friend Quincy Jones. Unlike Jones, Standifer chose to stay in the region.

"Among musicians, there was a kind of respect around here that you didn't run into in New York," Standifer recalled. In New York, he found, other players would undercut a fellow musician's fee just to get the job. "That was not the case out here," he explained, "because everybody knew each other. There was no such thing as anonymity, because Seattle was too small a community for you to alienate anybody...

"We all knew we were here in the Northwest because everybody's fiercely independent. How do you maintain your independence? You don't maintain it by separating—you maintain it by cooperating to an extent with those who have like causes to yours. And so, if you didn't cooperate, you weren't gonna get anywhere."[2]

Standifer, with many others like him, passed on those values to later generations of musicians who also chose to make their art distant from the centers of power. In fact, that distance makes the region more hospitable to artists who want to pursue, among like-minded peers, a vision more effectively shared on a smaller stage—or where the stage is small but the landscape grand.

That's certainly true for avant-garde saxophonist and composer Rich Halley. His albums have consistently received critical acclaim, yet he worked a full-time job outside music for years to support his art and stay in Portland. "He'd be a star on the avant-garde scene if he lived in New York," writes Bill Milkowski in *JazzTimes*. But in New York, Halley, who is an active outdoorsman, might not have become the player he is.

"There's an advantage [to living here] in that you don't necessarily get overwhelmed with whatever the current trend is," Halley says, "and you can just do

Rich Halley, avant-garde saxophonist and active outdoorsman. "He'd be a star on the avant-garde scene if he lived in New York," said *JazzTimes*.

what you do. You can still absorb things that you listen to, but in some ways, it gives you a little bit of freedom to create your own world."

Of course, artists in the Pacific Northwest are influenced by music made elsewhere and work within a tradition that originated in other places. While in his twenties, for instance, Halley played in Chicago with avant-gardists from the Association for the Advancement of Creative Musicians as well as with R&B bands. And musicians who migrated to the Pacific Northwest, such as Grant, renowned guitarist Bill Frisell, or legendary bassist Leroy Vinnegar, have also brought influences unrelated to the region.

But not everyone chooses to come. And those you work with everyday—who have chosen this place, too—leave the deepest mark. You are what you eat, they say—what you breathe, see, touch, and hear. So jazz in the Pacific Northwest naturally reflects its geography and the communities shaped by it. That may be more important in jazz than other music. Because in jazz, your approach—maybe even your sound and stylistic preference—is powerfully influenced by the company you keep.

That company is usually found where jazz has always been made—in urban areas. But even in the cities of the Pacific Northwest, the landscape is an inescapable presence. It colors ambitions and gives flavor to artistic visions.

"Music should always sound like a place," says Portland composer Gordon Lee. Waterfalls tumble over basalt cliffs throughout the Columbia River Gorge.

As Seattle grew, it climbed the hills from the mudflats of Elliott Bay, filling the narrow neck of land between Lake Washington, Lake Union, and Puget Sound. Today, the freeway cuts right through the middle, though it has been partly covered with green spaces, and the central core is dense with the office buildings and condo towers that replaced low-rise neighborhoods. But every street corner offers spectacular vistas.

To the southeast, massive Mount Rainier; to the north, rising above Lake Washington, are Mount Baker and the jagged peaks of the North Cascades. To the west, on a clear day, the Olympic Mountains stand above Puget Sound; and just beyond, the Straits of Juan de Fuca, Alaska, the Pacific, and all of Asia.

Portlanders need only look north and east to see the volcanic peaks of Mount Adams, Mount Hood, and Mount St. Helens—the mountain that erupted in 1980, filling the sky with ash and shearing off the peak in a blast that leveled forests and clogged rivers with debris. The chain of volcanoes in the Pacific Northwest is partof the Pacific Rim's "The Ring of Fire."

Communities from the Willamette Valley to the Canadian border are favored by such settings, and they are tied psychologically and economically to the region's icons: the Cascade Mountains with forests of Douglas fir, spruce, and cedar; broad valleys and the rocky coast of the Pacific; apples, mushrooms, blackberries; clams, oysters, Dungeness crab. And salmon, the totem animal of the Pacific Northwest. These are part of daily life, even in the major cities, where the system of public parks and tree-lined streets also contribute to the ambiance.

Quick Definitions

Adapted from "Jazz Glossary," Center for Jazz Studies, Columbia University

To describe a complex and diverse jazz scene as it has changed over time, it's helpful to talk about subgenres. Here are some brief definitions of the terms used in this book:

Avant-garde: A term applied to various forms of experimental jazz first heard in the 1950s and to their later offshoots, especially in the 1960s and '70s, including free jazz.

Bebop: A style developed in the early 1940s in which standard tunes or their chord progressions are used as springboards for rapid improvisations with irregular, syncopated phrasing based on chordal harmony rather than melody.

Blues: A form usually consisting of twelve bars, staying in one key; or the musical genre, ancestral to jazz and part of it.

Free jazz: A cluster of jazz styles that minimizes fixed beat and harmonic structure and emphasizes sound and texture instead.

Funk: A fusion of blues or gospel-based harmony, rhythm, and melody with a straight-ahead approach.

Fusion: A style developed in the late 1960s that incorporates elements of rock and is built on repeated figures and non-improvised passages, a harmonic language simpler than bebop, and straight-8 time with a strong backbeat.

Hard Bop: A style that emerged in the late 1950s, it's essentially bebop with a hard-driving rhythmic feel and harmony based on blues, R&B, and gospel.

Smooth jazz: A version of fusion in which elements of R&B and pop music are distilled and refined for a standardized radio format.

Soul jazz: Hard bop that has incorporated elements of funk and is often played by organ groups.

Straight-ahead: A term that emerged in the post-bop era, it covers a variety of approaches that employ elements of earlier styles such as swing and bebop.

Swing: A form of syncopation, based on a triplet rhythm, that puts emphasis just before or after an expected beat. It also refers to a style of jazz popular in the 1930s and '40s played by large dance bands.

"In addition to sounding like a person, music should always sound like a place," says Portland composer Gordon Lee. And pianist Steve Christofferson also considers the natural beauty of the landscape important to the music he makes. A Seattle native, he has spent his career in the area. For years, he'd drive along the Columbia River from his home in a small town on the Washington side to the RiverPlace Restaurant in Portland, where floor-to-ceiling windows framed his view of the Willamette River from the grand piano.

"This music was composed to give expression to the uniqueness and the natural gifts we have here in the Pacific Northwest," says outdoorsman Alan Jones about the compositions on his 2010 album, *Climbing*.

"Growing up in Portland," he explains, "I've always recognized how lucky I am that I can drive fifteen minutes and be at the foot of the rocks. Drive an hour and be at the foot of the mountains. Every day I can see the mountains... and I want to climb."[3]

In a *DownBeat* article about pianist Dave Peck, Paul de Barros suggests we look at the world Peck lives in to understand his work. "Seattle's reputation rests on rain," he writes, "but folks who live there know it for the gentle contours of its clouds and mountains, its soft mists and almost mystical sense of natural intimacy. All that comes through in Peck's playing—lyrical and pastel, swinging and bluesy, with a ringing, crystalline touch."[4]

Glen Moore, bassist in the pioneering chamber jazz group Oregon, grew up chasing salamanders in the woodsy canyon of Johnson Creek by day and listening to Stravinsky on the radio at night. He traveled the state in a high school swing band called the Young Oregonians with American Indian saxophonist Jim Pepper, who'd highlight the program with a dance in full tribal dress.

Ralph Towner, fellow founding member of the band Oregon, grew up on the east side of the Cascades in the little town of Bend, below the ten-thousand-foot peaks of the Three Sisters and Broken Top. NASA sent the band's recordings to the moon on the Apollo spacecraft in 1971; they named two of its craters for Towner's tunes. Towner and Moore's classmate at University of Oregon, the Grammy-nominated singer Nancy King, grew up playing drums on a Willamette Valley mint and wheat farm.

In Portland, they moved in the same cirles as African American club owner and pianist Sid Porter and his wife, Japanese American singer Nola Bogle. She started her career in little eastern Oregon towns surrounded by sheep ranches. Her accompanist was the American Indian Jack Lightfoot. As a child, she'd been interned during World War II in the Idaho prison camp Minidoka. She fell asleep to the sound of a swing band, carried by the wind across the prairie.

Out of that melting pot came jazz in the Pacific Northwest.

1

From Frontier to Jazz Mecca

"Vice could be a virtue. You take from the more-than-willing customers. You give a little to City Hall. You invest the rest and give some of it back to the community in loans. You employ hundreds of people and you get to play jazz all night long."

Bill McClendon

IN THE BEGINNING

Natural beauty has never been enough to sustain a jazz scene, let alone an American city. When it comes to musical entertainment, or any professional arts activity, it's money you need. And the landscape of the Pacific Northwest brought great riches to many immigrants of European ancestry. Even today, the region continues to be the source of the natural resources that first shaped its destiny as a shipping hub and processing center for ore, fish, and timber. And in Puget Sound, where the military is a powerful economic engine, submarines armed with nuclear missiles cruise the depths along with salmon and orcas.

Portland grew at the confluence of the Willamette and Columbia Rivers and, like Seattle, is a deepwater port more connected to San Francisco, LA, Anchorage, and Tokyo than to New York. Both emerged from frontier settlements: Seattle a cluster of wooden buildings, some piers, and a sawmill; Portland a wallow of muddy streets on a riverbank among felled trees.

There were telephones and newspapers, and fortunes to be made milling and shipping the great forests to San Francisco. But it was still the Wild West, with lynchings, black exclusion laws, and sewage that flowed back into Seattle on the tide. People came anyway, mostly northern European stock in search of opportunity.

They may have believed that the little guy had a better chance to realize a big dream out on the distant western edge. Enough of them succeeded to generate the

« "Seattle's reputation rests on rain, but folks who live there know it for the gentle contours of its clouds and mountains, its soft mists and almost mystical sense of natural intimacy," says Paul de Barros. A view of Mount Rainier from Puget Sound.

Portland began as a wallow of muddy streets at the confluence of the Willamette and Columbia Rivers. A view of the city in 1890.

work that lured others, including Asians and African Americans. Discrimination against people of color dominated the region, where laws kept African Americans from owning property and even spending the night in some Oregon towns, and anti-Chinese riots repeatedly swept through the Puget Sound area. It was only after World War II altered the racial makeup of the cities that some of the worst discriminatory practices began to change.

And into the cities of that early twentieth-century Wild West—along with the loggers, sailors, farmers, cooks, wranglers, bankers, and businessmen—came the musicians.

MINSTRELS AND PROTO-JAZZ

First to arrive were the brass bands and ragtime piano men who worked the saloons. Then, in the 1880s, traveling minstrel and vaudeville shows played theaters in Portland, Tacoma, and Seattle. Pacific Northwest theaters were ornate halls open only to white audiences. But they often presented African American orchestras like W. H. Mahara's Minstrels, whose musical director was W. C. Handy, composer of "St. Louis Blues." Even before the Jazz Age of the 1920s, many kinds of proto-jazz were heard in the region, though resident musicians were few.

Gradually, those minstrels began to stick around, if only by accident. In 1911, for instance, a vaudeville troupe ran out of money and broke up in Seattle, stranding Nora and Ross Hendrix, future grandparents of guitarist Jimi Hendrix.[1]

During the thirty years between their arrival and America's entrance into World War II, all the ingredients necessary for a vibrant jazz scene fell into place. How it all came together reflects the types of musicians who lived in the region and the diverse communities in which they worked. Night people, gangsters, cops, politicians, timber magnates, and even the president all played a role in how the story unfolded.

Oscar Holden: Patriarch of Seattle Jazz
from *Jackson Street After Hours* by Paul de Barros

Born in Nashville, Tennessee, Oscar Holden played on Fate Marable's famous Mississippi riverboat excursions, where Louis Armstrong and other young New Orleans musicians had also honed their craft.... Anxious to get away from the South, Holden moved to Chicago.... Jelly Roll Morton says he brought Holden to Seattle from Vancouver, British Columbia, where Holden played clarinet in Morton's band. Holden's daughter, Grace, says the year was 1919.

Holden was a powerhouse player with a deep classical background and a stride style similar to Fats Waller's. He could transpose tunes into all twelve keys, accompany singers sensitively, and work with a band or play solo all night long and keep it interesting. Recalls [Seattle pianist] Palmer Johnson:

"Oscar was my idol, man.... He had a wonderful musical education. He was one of the first ones up here. Oscar was real black and had a soft voice. He was a great, great performer.... He'd play 'Rhapsody in Blue' right off from the beginning to the end."

Like many musicians in the area at the time, Oscar Holden also held a day job...at Todd Shipyards. Grace vividly recalls her father racing off to catch the ferry after work to play a graduation in Kirkland, or switching from his pipe fitter's clothes to his tux for a job at the Clover Club downtown.

"He'd come home from swing shift," she recounts, "then go straight upstairs, take his bath, change his clothes, and he'd be right back out the door at twelve-thirty a.m. so he could be on the job at one o'clock. He'd play from one until four-thirty or five o'clock in the morning."

Ron Holden recounts: "One of the fondest memories was Friday and Saturday nights.... I can remember lying in bed with butterflies in my stomach because I knew any minute my mom would come in and kiss me goodnight...all dressed up for the gig, and Dad would be in his tux. Two glamorous people kissing me goodnight."

"There was a piano in the basement, and a parlor grand upstairs," Grace added. "We ate music, we lived music."

JAZZ ARRIVES

The first time "jazz" was officially heard in the Pacific Northwest was 1914, when The Original Creole Orchestra, with cornetist/trumpeter Freddie Keppard, played the Pantages Theaters. Though Keppard was a New Orleans native, he had been living in Los Angeles for the previous six years, and his band was made up of Californians. It seems likely that West Coast and New Orleans versions of jazz were developing simultaneously. In fact, Keppard was reportedly the first to use a handkerchief to hide his fingering from competitors, years before Louis Armstrong made it part of his act.

In Portland, Keppard and his seven-piece band always stayed at the Golden West Hotel at the corner of Northwest Everett and Broadway, in the center of the small African American community. The hotel was equipped with Turkish baths, a gym, a restaurant, pool tables, and a barbershop, as well as a gambling room and bar with live music. Purchased by African American businessman W. D. Allen in 1906, it was the largest black-owned hotel west of the Mississippi and helped fill the glaring need for public accommodations and other services for people of color.[2]

One of the hotel's guests in those days sported a diamond in his front tooth and claimed he invented jazz. Ferdinand "Jelly Roll" Morton was traveling the West Coast and was still an unknown when he stopped in Seattle for several months in 1920. Morton augmented his income from music by working as a pimp for the "boarders" at a house he and companion Anita Gonzalez rented north of Tacoma. He also gambled on pool and cards and lost almost everything in a high-stakes game just before he left town.[3]

But Morton left something more valuable than money behind: his clarinet player, Oscar Holden, who also played piano, stayed on in Seattle to become one of the most important figures in Pacific Northwest jazz. The contrast between the flamboyant Morton and family man Holden reveals some of the traits that define the character of the region's jazz community.

While Morton ran prostitutes and gambled, Holden, with a wife and five children, supplemented his income from music by working as a pipe fitter. He'd regularly swim two miles across nearby Lake Washington. Classically trained, Holden played Chopin and sight-read with ease. He constructed a stable, middle-class life while pursuing an outsider art.

That was never the aim of men like Morton or clarinet player Joe Darensbourg. A hard-drinking Louisiana native who ended up in Los Angeles when the Original Dixieland Jazz Band broke up, Darensbourg started hearing about a paradise for musicians up north. "When I was in Los Angeles, a lot of musicians would come back from Seattle and tell you how great it was, how much money you could make . . . So that's what I was looking for." He came to Seattle in 1928, traveling with the Freda Shaw Band on one of the steamships that ran up and down the West Coast. Gambling, liquor, prostitutes, and lots of music were on offer.

"We'd get in, just for two nights, and meet some broads, and when we got through we'd go down to Twelfth and Jackson." There Darensbourg and other traveling musicians could sit in with local players. "At these after-hours clubs we had a lot of the sporting class of people come in, like pimps and prostitutes . . . We would wind up sometimes making $200 or $300 a night."[4]

GODFATHERS

Top: Jelly Roll Morton brought early jazz to Seattle in 1920, augmenting his music income by working as a pimp.

Bottom: Mildred Bailey was known as the first white woman singer in jazz, but she was actually half Coeur d'Alene.

The wide-open atmosphere that Darensbourg and Morton found in the region's cities—tolerated by strait-laced politicians and business leaders who profited from it—was based at first in skid road districts that attracted sailors, railroad men, freebooters, and other itinerants. In the early twentieth century, those districts expanded or shifted to adjacent neighborhoods, and the organized vice that partially sustained them persisted into the 1950s, generating work for many musicians.

Those entertainment districts were controlled at the street level by entrepreneurs who financed the clubs and speakeasies that existed as a result of payoffs to the local power structure, from the cop on the street to the mayor and police chief. Within that hierarchy, businessmen such as Seattle's "Noodles" Smith and Portland's Tom Johnson exercised a great deal of power. Along with others like them, Johnson and Smith were in part responsible for establishing the foundations of jazz in the region.

A Family Affair: Women Bandleaders

The image of early jazz in many people's minds is almost exclusively male, except for a few prominent singers. But before World War II, a number of jazz bands in the Pacific Northwest were led by women such as Evelyn Bundy and Edythe Turnham. In fact, they ran the most popular jazz ensembles in Seattle in the 1920s. It wasn't easy, but it wasn't as rare as one might assume.

Music-making was viewed as "a man's job," and female musicians were often accused of taking work away from male breadwinners. That was true for women in most fields, and like their counterparts everywhere, women in jazz also had to overcome the widely held belief that men were superior in all endeavors.

Yet in the early twentieth century, women were emerging as a force in public life. The Progressive movement was fueled by women who helped secure the right to vote in Washington (1910) and Oregon (1912). Women led the Temperance movement. Indeed, the 1920s, despite being dubbed "The Jazz Age," was also at the time called "The Decade of the New Woman." Women were leaving the farm for the city, and canned food meant less time in the kitchen. "Girl Bands" were at the peak of their popularity too.

Despite the independence women were gaining, for Evelyn Bundy and Edythe Turnham music was a family affair. Turnham, in fact, led a family band called the Knights of Syncopation, first in Spokane, then for six busy years in Seattle before they began touring the Orpheum Theater circuit and settled in Los Angeles. In *Jackson Street After Hours,* Paul de Barros outlines what he learned from Turnham's son, Floyd Jr., who went on to become a jazz and R&B sax player and bandleader.

She got her start in the small towns of eastern Washington and Idaho with her sister in a vaudeville act featuring two blackface comedians. In Spokane, she often played solo, and there the family band got its start, with Floyd Jr. on sax, her husband, Floyd Sr., on drums, Edythe on piano, and her sister Maggie singing and dancing. When they moved west, the Knights of Syncopation grew to five pieces and played all of the major clubs on Jackson Street. Negotiating the shifting color line, they also played department store fashion shows as well as The Bungalow Club—downtown locations usually reserved for white musicians. Soon, their union protested, and Turnham's band could no longer perform there.

The family was prominent in the small Seattle black community, where Floyd Sr. worked as a tailor and drove the band around in a big Hudson. Once, he drove them through the neighborhood on the back of a truck while the band played.[9]

Family often extended beyond blood ties, and Evelyn Bundy's home with her husband, Charles Taylor, a plasterer who also promoted her band, "became a hub of the Seattle jazz world," writes de Barros. "When touring musicians would come to town, they would congregate in the basement music room and bar...Everybody would take turns singing songs and telling stories and laughing."[10]

In addition to piano, which she played in a manner more akin to Duke Ellington than the rough stride style popular at the time, Bundy played banjo, drums, saxophone, and sometimes sang. She got her start at age thirteen walking from table to table in nightclubs, singing through a megaphone, and accompanying herself with high-hat cymbal. Her five-piece band, The Garfield Ramblers, which she began right out of high school, played for black society affairs and in Jackson Street clubs. Bundy's band drove to their gigs in a hearse.

Bundy's son, Charles Jr., followed her into jazz and led a band in the 1940s that included Quincy Jones. Both came from Seattle's small African American middle class, which nurtured young musicians in a relatively protected, family-oriented environment.[11]

Bing Crosby, a native of Spokane, Washington, was turned down at an audition for Seattle's Butler Hotel before seeking fame in California.

Beginning in 1917, Smith and various partners ran a series of clubs, taverns, and two hotels for African American patrons in Seattle's International District, and he operated much like other flamboyant gangsters of the era. Count Basie saxophonist Marshall Royal, who married Noodles's sister-in-law, liked to say that Twelfth and Jackson belonged to Smith. "He was the ward boss," Royal said. "In those days, you couldn't open up a nightclub unless you passed by Noodles Smith." When someone applied for a business license in the neighborhood, City Hall would call for Smith's OK first. Smith and Johnson also made loans to other African American entrepreneurs, taking a cut of their profits and collecting their property if they couldn't make a go of it.[5]

Though their origins were in the often violent and dangerous skid road areas of frontier towns, the African American entertainment districts that evolved in the Pacific Northwest from the 1920s through the 1950s were relatively safe for black and white alike. That was due in large part to men like Smith and Tom Johnson. Known as the Vice Lord of Williams Avenue, six-foot-two and 220 pounds, Johnson was born in New Orleans to freed slaves and came to Portland as a railroad worker after World War I. He quickly managed to gain control of a portion of the bootleg liquor trade, which accounted for his first fortune.

In the 1930s, he opened Tom Johnson's Chicken Dinner Inn in Northwest Portland, some blocks from the Golden West Hotel. It featured live jazz, and one of the pianists performing there was Bill McClendon, who later became publisher of the Portland newspaper the *People's Observer* and a leader in the city's African American community. Johnson offered McClendon not only financial assistance but advice as well.

"He wanted me to remember that Portland had always been a rough-and-tumble city, going back to the time it was called 'Shanghai Town.' It was filled with scandal.... The playing field was always uneven for blacks."

That attitude informed Johnson's business practices, as McClendon describes them: "You take from the more-than-willing customers. You give a little to City Hall. You invest the rest and give some of it back to the community in loans. You employ hundreds of people and you get to play jazz all night long."[6]

Johnson lost his bootlegging fortune in the Depression, but he made it over again in the 1940s with Keystone Investment Co. Its office on Williams Avenue included a gambling lounge, jukebox, and, in the basement, a six-foot-tall, eight-foot-wide safe stuffed with hundred dollar bills. Every Thursday, according to jazz historian Robert Dietsche, a police car would retrieve a percentage for the vault in the mayor's office.

Johnson's partner was Walter Emmanuel Green, an attorney who passed for white and was thus able—at a time when African Americans could not get bank loans in most Portland neighborhoods—to buy and then rent properties for taverns and other unlicensed food and drink establishments, some of which offered live jazz.

Johnson also ran a twenty-four-hour gambling den across the Columbia River in Vancouver, Washington. McClendon believed the house take was $6000 a day. Thus Johnson financed many businesses, usually with loans made for no interest. And he was the liaison between City Hall and the Williams Avenue community in much the way Smith served in Seattle. African Americans entering Portland in those days had to check in with Johnson, who reportedly screened out drug addicts, thieves, and violent criminals. He also made sure prostitutes working the area were tested for STDs.[7]

Johnson and Smith functioned as godfather figures in the small but economically self-sufficient communities of color where an important part of the identity of jazz in the Pacific Northwest was being formed. They enabled nightclubs to open, regulated their arrangements with police and city officials, and kept the area safe for business. And those businesses were a crucial part of the pre–World War II culture of Portland and Seattle, despite the efforts of church and social groups that led to the passage of "Blue Laws" regulating nightlife.

In Seattle, the Landes Ordinance, for instance, required dance halls to have a license, hire police matron chaperones, and discontinue "taxi dancing" and suggestive lighting; a law followed that prohibited public dancing on Sundays. In 1929, Seattle's mayor closed all dance halls and called dancing a "public menace."[8]

SPEAKEASIES, CROONERS, AND THE ROOTS OF SWING

The white versions of the Jackson Street clubs were the speakeasies, located on the outskirts of town or in some cases even downtown. The Venetian Gardens, for instance, a swank nightclub in Seattle's Olympic Hotel, provided a perfect Roaring Twenties setting for "sweet" white bands such as those led by trombonist Jackie Souders. He grew up in Seattle and worked the hotel for forty years. Its late-night counterpart was the Rose Room in the Butler Hotel near Pioneer Square.

One day in 1925, two young entertainers from Spokane showed up at the Butler for an audition. Piano player Al Rinker and singer Bing Crosby hoped to find some work on their way to Hollywood. Their move had been inspired by the success of Rinker's sister Mildred, who had taken the last name Bailey. She got her start playing piano in Seattle silent movie houses and demonstrating sheet music for customers at Woolworth's, but then she had a child and a rough time trying to make it on her own. She retreated to Spokane for a while, then headed to Los Angeles, where she immediately got a job at the city's top blues club.

Crosby and Rinker were not hired at the Butler, reported Souders, who sat in on the audition. "We all thought they were pretty good," he said, "but the hotel owner said he didn't like all that 'vo-do-de-de-o' stuff and wouldn't hire them."[12]

That 'vo-do-de-de-o' stuff Crosby had learned from vaudeville performers passing through Spokane. It went over better in California—just a year later, they were discovered by New York bandleader Paul "The King of Jazz" Whiteman and recorded their first big hit. In 1929, Rinker helped his sister get on with Whiteman, who became the first national-level leader to feature a female vocalist. It was a historic moment; soon, other dance bands added female singers.

Then, in 1930, after a string of concerts in the Pacific Northwest, Whiteman fired Crosby and Rinker for always running off to play golf. Besides, while in New York, they'd been hanging out in Harlem with black stars Cab Calloway and Duke Ellington, and Crosby reportedly was smoking reefer with Louis Armstrong. It didn't matter. By then, Crosby was on his way to a milestone career.

Meanwhile, in 1932, Mildred Bailey, still with Whiteman, sang "Rockin' Chair" on a live radio broadcast. It was a national hit, and she was ever after known as "The Rocking Chair Lady," though Whiteman billed her as "The Queen of Swing." Bailey also gained notoriety by recording with the African American musicians who had backed Billie Holiday. She pushed the color line further when she began performing *live* with an African American band she called "Mildred Bailey and Her Oxford Browns." Then she married jazzman Red Norvo (they became known as "Mr. and Mrs. Swing"), and his combo backed her on a series of hits before her death in 1951.[13]

Bailey was known as the first white woman singer in jazz. Few knew, however, that she was not "white" but one-half Coeur d'Alene. Bailey spent her childhood on the reservation in Idaho, and she credited traditional native singing—which she'd learned from her mother—with shaping her voice.[14] That information, not widely reported until more than fifty years after her death, is crucial for the recovery of ties between jazz in the Pacific Northwest and its native people.

Monte Ballou, leader of the most popular jazz band in Portland for twenty years, challenged segregationist attitudes of the day by letting his friend Louis Armstrong stay at his home.

JAZZ AND RACE

In Portland, the Castle Jazz Band, led by banjo player Monte Ballou, was the top white band. They played in a New Orleans style and were the most popular jazz group in Portland from the 1930s through the 1950s. There were no saxophones in the Castle Jazz Band, nor guitar or string bass; instead, the group included trumpet, trombone, and clarinet with a rhythm section of tuba, drums, banjo, and piano. And though Ballou's band was all white, they played in the style made popular by black bands of the 1920s. Ballou was also a close friend of Louis Armstrong, who sometimes stayed at his home in Portland. It was a challenge to segregationist attitudes of the day, and Ballou was not the only white jazz musician who made it a practice.

Ballou's band took its name from one of its earliest venues. A roadhouse with turrets, arched windows, and a tower, The Castle was built of hand-cut stone by a French artisan brought over for the job. Located on the highway north of Oregon City, it was one of a number of roadhouses where jazz provided the ambiance. Portland theaters and ballrooms also presented some jazz, and many more such venues appeared as swing took over the airwaves and dance halls in the 1930s.

In Seattle, the enormous Trianon Ballroom boasted a capacity of five thousand and the West's largest dance floor. It booked big-name touring bands such as the Fletcher Henderson and Jimmie Lunceford orchestras. The Trianon was owned by John Savage, who believed African American patrons were bad for business.

Seattle's Trianon Ballroom boasted the West's largest dance floor.

He only allowed people of color on the dance floor once a week on what came to be known derisively in the African American community as "spook nights."

Smaller Jazz Age hot spots outside black neighborhoods usually hired only white ensembles. And local musicians of African descent were not only shut out of work downtown; symphony, theater, and radio jobs were also closed to them—except for the Seattle band led by Archie Jackson that featured the legendary African American saxophonist and teacher, Frank Waldron.

Big, baldheaded, and known for drinking gin, Waldron was born in 1890 and came to Tacoma during World War I to play dances for servicemen at Fort Lewis (now Joint Base Lewis-McChord). In 1918, he began his teaching career in Seattle, just in time for the saxophone craze that swept America in the '20s (Seattle even had a complete saxophone orchestra). In 1924, Waldron published *Syncopated Classics*, a saxophone method book that used his own compositions to demonstrate jazz techniques. According to musicians of that era, Waldron was an influence on Quincy Jones, Buddy Catlett, and others who came of age in the 1940s and helped define the sound of jazz in the region.[15]

Jazz in the Pacific Northwest has been powerfully affected by several influential teachers who gave students the theory and ear training necessary for improvisation before it was taught in schools. And they did it with the authority of master instrumentalists who passed on the importance of good craftsmanship, a quality held in high esteem by regional artists. In Seattle, Waldron was the first of those masters.

It's not clear why Archie Jackson's five-piece Odean Jazz Orchestra, with Waldron its star soloist, was able to play in downtown Seattle's high-class Nanking Cafe while other African American musicians were not—especially when it appeared to defy the segregated musicians union. But race relations were complex, and though the attitudes held by the majority of European Americans toward people of color in the region were deeply racist, the improvisational nature of life in the entertainment business in the rough-and-tumble cities of the Pacific Northwest sometimes made such accommodations possible—especially when there was money to be made. At any rate, African American musicians who were able to find their way in that social order tended to remain in the region and shape the character of its jazz scene.

In Portland, there was no black musicians union, and people of color were not allowed to join until 1945. Seattle's musicians unions remained segregated until 1956. That was the pattern across the country—white musicians, unwilling to admit blacks who would compete for their jobs, encouraged the formation of separate unions and limited their territories.[16] But in Seattle, that arrangement had some positive outcomes for those treated as second-class citizens: because of the vice allowed in the territory they were assigned, black musicians often outearned their white counterparts.

THE END OF PROHIBITION AND THE RISE OF JAZZ

Regardless of color, musicians suffered along with most people during the Great Depression that followed the Jazz Age. In 1930 alone, three million Americans lost their jobs; tent cities sprang up under the Ross Island Bridge in Portland, on Seattle's south waterfront, and in cities all over the region. Unemployment reached 26 percent, and lines formed outside relief shelters. Theater orchestras disbanded, and symphony players were busking on the streets. But in 1933, Congress ended thirteen years of Prohibition, and for many jazz musicians, opportunities were suddenly greater than ever before.

In Seattle's small African American community, a line of clubs opened that stretched east from Chinatown, then north on Twelfth Avenue. They included Noodles Smith's Ubangi Club. Said to be the largest black-owned business north of Los Angeles, it was Seattle's first floor-show nightclub when it opened in 1936. It was modeled after Harlem's Cotton Club and catered mainly to whites.[17] Those clubs, as well as roadhouses scattered around the region, provided steady work for more than one hundred musicians of color. An even greater number of their white counterparts were working as well, but it was a historic high for black players in the region. From them came pianist Al Pierre's Royal Knights, which historians say was the first African American swing band indigenous to the Pacific Northwest.

Pierre grew up in a rural area outside Tacoma, then left to work in Los Angeles in the 1920s. When he returned in 1932, he played the large third-floor ballroom at Portland's Frat Hall, operated by several black fraternal organizations. He also played downtown, in a speakeasy owned by Portland racketeer Swede Ferguson. His bands played summers out in the country at the pavilion at Blue Lake Park; and for twelve years, they played for dancers every weekend at Berg's Chalet west of downtown.

So despite official segregation and the legacy of Oregon's notorious black exclusion laws, Pierre's band worked traditionally white territory that included high school proms and golf club dances—another instance of the malleable color line in the region. Pierre's bands could play both sweet and hot, were well dressed and well rehearsed, and had the best musicians because Pierre paid the highest wages. He moved his operation to Seattle in the early 1940s and was equally successful with the same approach.[18]

Squatter's shacks on the Willamette River during the Great Depression.

As the swing dance craze grew in the mid-1930s, all the top swing bands, white and black, came through the Pacific Northwest, including those led by Duke Ellington, Benny Goodman, Count Basie, and Guy Lombardo. Those touring ensembles often picked up a player or two along the way, while other musicians dropped out and stayed behind, adding to the number of skilled players in the region.

New jazz musicians emerged from within the Pacific Northwest as well, playing in the modern swing style. In Seattle, one of the most important among them was young pianist Julian Henson, who later moved to Portland and became a powerful influence on jazz artists who were coming of age in the 1950s. When pianist Jimmy Rowles came to Seattle in 1937, he learned modern harmony from Henson. But he already had the foundation.

As a teenager in Spokane, Rowles had been the protégé of a Blackfoot Indian named Tom Brown, another influence that worked its way into his style and adds credence to the claim of some musicians of the era that swing was influenced by American Indian music. When Rowles moved to Seattle, he quickly found a developing jazz scene that influenced the approach that would make him a star accompanist for such notable singers as Sarah Vaughan. His compositions, such as the haunting ballad "The Peacocks," have become jazz standards.[19]

Freedom Ride through a Warm Valley: Duke Ellington in Oregon

I dreamed I saw Duke Ellington, alive as you or me, in his private rail car on a siding near Ivon Street.

"Hey Duke, what'd you find," I asked, "when you came to Oregon?"

"A warm valley," he answered, "and people who opened their hearts to me."

So every time I pass three old Pullman cars on that siding in Portland today, I remember all the times Duke was in a dangerous Oregon country, and the beauty in the song "Warm Valley"—his reverie of ease inspired by this landscape.

In 1934, he was "traveling like the president," he said, in two private sleepers and a seventy-foot baggage car, rented to tour with dignity a country segregated by race. "We commanded respect," he said, of the twenty black men traveling in private rail cars, just like the president.

Heading out of Portland along the Willamette River, Duke gazed at foothills of the Cascade Mountains and saw a woman reclining there, free and easy, her warm valley so welcoming, he said, that he sketched the contours of her body in sound.

In Spanish they translate the title as "Valle Amoroso"—valley of love, where he dreamed the sound of a woman's body. Duke was free to dream, you see, when he was traveling like the president, a private man in the majesty of a private rail car, where he was free to think of music only.

Three Pullman cars on a siding in Portland today evoke dreams of Duke Ellington: welcomed here by the community, sitting in with locals, and playing McElroy's Ballroom on his birthday, when the Duke Ellington Orchestra came to town with dancer Ann Henry. She later became a Broadway star, then moved to Portland, the city she first saw with Duke, to compose the music that Duke played at Mount Angel Abbey on his return to those Willamette Valley foothills in 1970, when he didn't need a private car to be treated like the president.

"Warm Valley," his reverie of beauty and ease in a dangerous country, captures in sound the soft afternoon light through the window of a private rail car, like those on a siding here today, evoking dreams of Duke Ellington, looking at the foothills of the Cascades and thinking of music only.

In the 1930s, Duke Ellington and his band traveled through the Pacific Northwest in private rail cars. "Just like the president," he said.

The Bonneville Power Administration spent two billion dollars on the region's electricity needs when it built two massive dams on the Columbia River in the 1930s—a key development for the emerging jazz scene.

DAMS, SHIPYARDS, AND MUSICIANS APLENTY

Even with all the musical action in the 1930s, it was outside forces—including the public works projects of the Roosevelt administration and the defense industry during World War II—that brought about the economic and population boom of the 1940s that made possible a golden age for jazz in the Pacific Northwest.

In the 1930s, the Bonneville Power Administration spent two billion dollars on the region's electricity needs when it built two massive dams on the Columbia River. The project employed thousands and resulted in cheap and plentiful electricity. With the onset of World War II, Henry Kaiser built three shipyards in the Portland area that employed 150,000 workers. And with the newly abundant electricity, Alcoa Aluminum opened a plant in Vancouver, Washington. Seattle's economy exploded, too, fueled in part by the growth of the Boeing Company and the military bases nearby.

So musicians first came to the Pacific Northwest for defense and government jobs, or to entertain those who had them. Later, they would come for the lifestyle. But not much later. As early as 1950, Warren Bracken moved to Portland from Los Angeles and found a completely different life in the small, isolated city. On tour with singer Billy Eckstine, Bracken passed through Portland, met a local woman, and found an escape from the heroin epidemic sweeping through the jazz community. He also found plenty of work in a market where he could become a leader.

While black musicians like Bracken, a Kentucky native, came to the region primarily from the South and Midwest, white musicians from small towns around the region came to the cities in the 1940s, too, intent on learning to play jazz. And there the essential American experience of negotiating racial and ethnic differences took a distinctly Pacific Northwest form.

2

Jackson Street and Williams Avenue: 1940–1959

"Seattle serves a unique purpose. It's one of the loveliest incubators you'll ever run into. Seattle always was a place to get it together, or come off the road and reassess yourself. But you can't stay here, if you're going to make it big. But this town will hook you. You'll always end up coming back. . . . You're looking for someplace where life can mean something, you come here."[1]

Floyd Standifer

"That was probably the best time in my life. We had the best of everything: best music, best food, best women; all the people on the Avenue coming to see us. Yeah, it was definitely the best time in my life."

Tim Kennedy

THE CRUCIBLE

It was more than a street, it was a village.

That's how historian Robert Dietsche describes the entertainment district along Portland's Williams Avenue in the 1940s and '50s. Located in the heart of the city's African American neighborhood on the east side of the Willamette River, its primary revenue sources were the sale of liquor and other drugs, gambling, and prostitution. The soundtrack was fast and hot, provided by scores of musicians who had swelled the ranks of the city's jazz, blues, and R&B scene. On Williams Avenue and Seattle's Jackson Street, white and black artists worked together on the bandstand and became more comfortable with each other on the street. It was the crucible in which many of the characteristics of jazz in the Pacific Northwest were formed, an exciting place at a pivotal time.

"You could stand in the middle of the Avenue," wrote Dietsche, "and look up Williams past the chili parlors, past the barbecue joints, the beauty salons, all the way to Broadway, and see hundreds of people dressed up as if they were going to a fashion show. It could be four in the morning; it didn't matter. . . . There must have been more than ten clubs in as many blocks, not counting the ones in the surrounding area."[2]

Seattle's Jackson Street was much the same, according to Paul de Barros. "Imagine a time when Seattle was full of people walking up and down the sidewalk after midnight . . . when limousines pulled up to the 908 Club all night, disgorging celebrities and wealthy women wearing diamonds and furs.

"Whatever a young sailor or soldier wanted... he could pretty much get on demand. There were clubs with full casinos upstairs.... Trumpet player Leon Vaughn says that in 1948, if he started walking up Jackson from First Avenue, by the time he reached Fourteenth, he had passed thirty-four nightclubs.... Many of these spots were full-fledged cabarets, with a floor show, fancy decor, doormen, and waiters. Others were simply joints set up as an excuse to sell bootleg booze."

Floyd Standifer was prominent in the after-hours scene during those years. "The weekend started on Thursday and it didn't stop until Monday morning about eight o'clock," he remembered. "There was the Sessions Club. A guy named Jimmy Linegan ran that.... He kept a pistol on top of the piano. Later, we'd go in there and play for people like Zenobia, or George Bernie, a cat who'd dance on tables. Pick tables up with his teeth."[3]

Those seminal entertainment districts that were centered around Jackson Street and Williams Avenue provided the conditions under which race relations evolved and a mix of blues, R&B, and modern jazz took root as the region's most prominent style.

ISLANDS OF TOLERANCE

Whether makeshift bar or classy restaurant, just about every one of those night spots had live music, and many featured mixed-race bands as well as a mixed audience. Jim Gilles, a white pianist who worked in both Portland and Seattle, remembers playing the Black Elks Club in the early 1950s: "Even though there was strict segregation, it was like this back-door thing that everybody understood and nobody paid attention to. On that particular scene, it was very harmonious." In Seattle, the band he worked with at the Black Elks, and after hours at the New Chinatown, was led by African American saxophonist Pops Buford. "The rest of the band there was white guys," Gilles added, "which was unusual, because this was a black joint."[4]

Ray Charles was there, too.

Arriving from Florida in 1947, he found himself in conditions not at all like he'd experienced in the South. "Seattle was very different," Charles says in his autobiography, "because when you went to the clubs, you saw everybody—white, black—it didn't make any difference, people were just there! In Florida... if you worked in a white club, it was a white club, and that was that. It was new to me to go someplace and everybody was just loose and free."[5]

Well, not everybody.

In the 1940s, the State of Oregon had more Ku Klux Klan members per capita than any state in the Deep South. Williams Avenue was an island of tolerance, as Al Hickey found when he strayed off it. "After work [at McElroy's Ballroom] we were looking for something to eat... but we soon found out that we couldn't eat downtown. Blacks couldn't even get a cup of coffee downtown or try on a suit, use the restroom, or even sit on the main floor of a theater."[6]

And yet, inside those entertainment districts, race relations were evolving.

In Portland, a partnership between two promoters, one black and one white, represented the racial cooperation that came out of the jazz community to challenge social

The Dude Ranch

from *Jumptown: The Golden Years of Portland Jazz* by Robert Dietsche

There never was and there never will be anything quite like the Dude Ranch. It was the Cotton Club, the Apollo Theater, Las Vegas, [and] the Wild West rolled into one. It was the shooting star in the history of Portland jazz, a meteor bursting with an array of the best Black and Tan entertainment this town has ever seen: strippers, . . . ventriloquists, comics, jugglers, torch singers, world-renowned tap dancers like Teddy Hale, and of course the very best of jazz.

In July of 1945, the Dude Ranch, with its tap-dancing MC and its celebrity clientele, was the hottest Black and Tan supper club west of Chicago. . . . An elaborately carved ceiling . . . overlooked an even more elaborate dance floor. The floor was mirrored and slippery and led to an elevated bandstand banked by rows of tables. Above and to the rear was an imposing balcony, and that is where you had dinner.

Photographers were everywhere. Folded cards in the middle of each table read, "You ain't nothing 'til you've had your photo taken at the Dude Ranch." There were hatcheck girls, cigarette girls, and cowgirl waitresses dressed to look like Dale Evans, cardboard six-shooters snug in their holsters. Huge hand-painted murals of black cowboys lassoing Texas longhorns covered the walls. . . . Pat Patterson, the first black ever to play basketball at the University of Oregon, owned and managed the Ranch with his pal Sherman "Cowboy" Pickett.

The Ranch was packed like every other place in this postwar boomtown. Thousands of servicemen were passing through, home from the islands of the Pacific and crazy for entertainment. The money was easy; the housing was impossible. All-night movie theaters were converted into sleeping lodges; restaurants were telling people to stay home. Portland, once thought to be the wallflower of the West Coast, had become a twenty-four-hour three-shift transport city going about 78 rpm. The fast-and-free-spending crowd at the Dude Ranch was a reflection of that.

Among the well-dressed shipbuilders, maids, and Pullman porters were Bugsy Siegel–like characters in sharkskin suits and broad Panama hats, . . . pin-striped politicians with neon ties, Hollywood celebrities, and glamour queens in jungle-red nail polish and leopard coats. There were feathered call girls and pimps in fake alligator shoes; zoot-suited hipsters and sidemen from Jantzen Beach . . . racially mixed party people who couldn't care less that what they were doing was on the cutting edge of integration in the city that had been called the most segregated north of the Mason-Dixon line.

norms. Cole "Pop" McElroy, owner of McElroy's Ballroom in downtown Portland, was a civil rights activist of Irish heritage. He teamed with African American promoter Stanton Duke, a former dining car waiter who had developed contacts with leading African American bandleaders when he worked on the railroad. Soon, he and McElroy were booking bands into the Ballroom and smaller dance halls in the area.

Duke's godfather was the bandleader Lionel Hampton, an outspoken advocate for civil rights himself. Because of Duke, Hampton played Portland annually for fifteen years straight. In 1949, two years after Pops McElroy died, his son Burt and Duke staged the first interracial dance at McElroy's Ballroom. Hampton's band played the show.[7]

The entertainment district centered around Jackson Street was the heart of Seattle's jazz scene in the 1940s and '50s.

In Seattle in the 1940s, two major dance halls reflected the segregation of the day—the Trianon was white-only, while the Savoy, on Jackson Street, was run by and catered to African Americans, though whites were also welcome. In general, whites patronized the black entertainment districts freely, but black patrons were not admitted to downtown clubs.

Nevertheless, young middle-class African Americans such as Quincy Jones grew up in those neighborhoods "thinking they could conquer the world," de Barros observes. "Bumps Blackwell assumed that success was his for the taking, that he could take his 'Junior Band' to an exclusive white district like Broodmoor, or to the Trianon Ballroom."[8]

BUMPS, QUINCY, RAY, AND ERNESTINE

Blackwell began to challenge past practices when he took over management of a big band that had been founded by the fifteen-year-old Quincy Jones and young saxophonist Charlie Taylor (1920s bandleader Evelyn Bundy's son). Known as a tireless promoter, Blackwell ran a taxi company, a jewelry business, and a butcher shop; he also worked nights at Boeing. Members of the band weren't allowed to use drugs or alcohol, either, Floyd Standifer recalled.

"That band was successful because Bumps was a total professional and knew what to do and, more importantly, what not to do. He always had his bands dressed well and taking care of business. Consequently, Bumps was able to open certain doors to us and get us before white audiences." Besides the band, those Blackwell shows included shake dancer August Mae, a pair of ballroom dancers known as "Chicken 'n Giblets," and the comedy duo "Dexedrine and Benzedrine" that starred Jones and trombonist Major Pigford.[10]

Blackwell went on to an important career in Los Angeles, where he produced a record by Little Richard when the singer was unknown, and the first "crossover"

Jump Blues and Jitterbugs

In the 1940s, the country's most popular styles were bebop, boogie-woogie, and jump blues, or jump swing, often intended to accompany jitterbug dancing, an exuberant and even acrobatic variation on swing dance techniques.

Louis Jordan's Tympany Five, one of the most successful small bands in the country, became the model for jump bands in the Pacific Northwest. "Jump evolved from big bands such as those of Lucky Millander and particularly Lionel Hampton," writes Robert Dietsche.

"Like the big bands they came from, these little bands used repeated phrases called riffs when they were backing up soloists. Jump tried to do with three horns and a rhythm section what a sixteen-piece band does—and for a lot less money, making them very popular with agents and ballroom managers during the shortages and rations of World War II."[9]

And tenor sax ruled in jump bands, a tradition inspired by the flashy Illinois Jacquet, whose solos with the Lionel Hampton Band were designed to energize dancers and bring the crowd to a frenzied pitch.

soul hit, Sam Cooke's "You Send Me." Most important to the character of jazz in the Pacific Northwest, he was responsible for empowering his young African American band members. "Music made me full," said Quincy Jones about those years, "strong, popular, self-reliant, and cool. . . . Jazz gave black men and women dignity."[11]

Born in Chicago in 1933, by all accounts Jones was a handsome young man who drew others to him, including Ray Charles. When Charles—known then as R. C. Robinson—met Jones, it was "one of the most important moments in the story of Northwest jazz," according to de Barros. "Quincy's first recollection of Charles is at the Elks Club: 'Ray seemed o-o-o-old. He was so mature. And he was only two years older than I was! He had his own apartment, his own suits, and everything. Oh boy, did I look up to him.'"

According to musicians on the scene, Jones and Charles were inseparable during those years. "Both were alive to the musical possibilities exploding around them, and both were extremely ambitious," writes de Barros. And both left the region. They collaborated several times in their later careers, and Jones went on to write movie and TV scores (including *Roots*) and earned nineteen Grammy Awards for a variety of projects, including Michael Jackson's "Thriller."

"I wanted to get away," Jones told de Barros. "That's all I cared about. I knew I would never be home again. Never."

But in Seattle, despite an unhappy home life after his parents divorced, Jones had the support of a strong black middle class, and given the racial imbalance in the Pacific Northwest, he was able to learn to operate comfortably in a mixed-race situation.[12]

The ambition that drove Jones from his hometown was fed in part by the success of his friend Ernestine Anderson, the first Blackwell band associate to achieve national recognition. Unlike Jones and Charles, however, Anderson kept coming back to Seattle, where she lives today.

The first time, she returned from a tour with Johnny Otis "in a shambles," reports de Barros. Then she went back to California for another try, only to come home to raise her first child. In 1952, Lionel Hampton offered her a job, and

City Hall Annex #1

McElroy's Last Ball

The City's favorite annex,
424 S.W. Main Street (Bureau of (X4253)
Planning), soon to be dust and
rubble under the merciless wrecker's
ball, offers a special salute to the
walls and floors of yesteryear, when
the building was once McElroy's Spanish
Ball Room.

Join us for McElroy's LAST BALL, in
nostalgic celebration with Big Band
Music by "Bobby Baker's Good Time
Band", Sunday, April 20, 1980...7:00 to
11:00 p.m.

In the McElroy's tradition, coca-cola and
7-up will be served. $5 per couple, $2.75
singles.

P.S. Shoulder pads and suspenders welcome.

Anderson spent the next fifteen months on the road before returning to Seattle again. She was soon back in New York, however, then moved to LA, where—with Quincy Jones as producer—she released her major label debut, *Hot Cargo*.

It was a hit, her picture was on the cover of *Time* magazine, and she was keeping apartments in both New York and LA, while her children and the developmentally disabled sister to whom she also felt a deep connection remained in Seattle. After five more albums, her popularity began to slide, coincident with the rise of rock 'n' roll, and Anderson retreated again to Seattle in 1969; she didn't tour again until 1977.

She felt "a profound ambivalence about pursuing the limelight," de Barros observes. "The issue for Anderson does not seem to be one of confidence, as it is with so many musicians who find the national scene frighteningly competitive, but rather some basic 'homebody' spirit that constantly pulls her back to the house where she grew up."

She did resolve that ambivalence when she returned to the limelight in 1978, but before, she agreed, "There was a war. I couldn't put the two together—the homebody and the show singer."[13]

Every artist in the Pacific Northwest faces a similar choice. But those who opted for the smaller stage found like-minded musicians and the same exciting new music that was being played everywhere in the 1940s.

THE POWER OF BEBOP

One of the main attractions in those entertainment districts, especially for the young, was bebop. It was new in the '40s, strident and compelling. Its fast, jagged lines reflected a sense of urgency, uncertainty, and the social energy unleashed during World War II. Bebop became the music of the hipster counterculture, distinguished by its complexity and dissonance from the relaxed sound of the swing era. Bebop was art, not entertainment, its spokesmen proclaimed; to understand it meant you belonged. From the inside, hipsters could look out at "squares" with ironic detachment. No wonder it attracted white renegades like Beat writer Jack Kerouac and the comic Lenny Bruce.

Bebop also heralded the rise of the African American musician as intellectual. "The period of World War II was a very impressive, hot, explosive, controversial time. America was in great turmoil," says french horn player and bassist Willie Ruff. "Bebop was an expression of a vibrant young group of black intellectuals finding their maturity.... Bebop required this tremendous kind of virtuosity, intellectual activity and knowledge and musical education that had never been required before."

It spread quickly. People were moving around the country during wartime like never before, carrying with them new records and new ideas. Soon, bebop had captured the imaginations of young white musicians from the hinterlands of the Pacific Northwest. Saxophonist Don Lanphere, one of the most prominent bebop stars to come out of the Pacific Northwest, was perhaps the youngest of them all when he moved to Seattle in 1944.

It all started in his hometown of Wenatchee, a farming community on the

« The owner of McElroy's Ballroom was a civil rights activist of Irish descent who partnered with former dining car waiter Stanton Duke.

"In Seattle, I became a man," said Ray Charles. He made his first record while living in Seattle.

eastern slopes of the Cascades. Every week Lanphere's father would drive him to Seattle for saxophone lessons and big band music at the Trianon. Like other regional jazz artists who have gone on to wider recognition, Lanphere received instruction from an unheralded local, Wenatchee pianist Jack Brownlow. Later, after Brownlow had moved to Seattle, he had the same kind of quiet influence on musicians who were coming of age in the 1960s as he had on Lanphere.

But Lanphere was also studying all the top players in jazz via recordings—by the time he turned sixteen, Lanphere had collected two thousand records, many of them by bebop pioneers, and his parents gave him permission to live alone in a downtown Seattle hotel.

"I got introduced to life there," Lanphere recalls. "The war was still going on, so the Club Maynard was servicemen all night long. And yet, walking there at one o'clock in the morning, carrying my horn with a smile on my face, nobody ever bothered me."

Lanphere graduated from high school while working the Jackson Street clubs at night, then left for Northwestern University near Chicago but soon showed up in Manhattan, where he worked with the legendary trumpeter Fats Navarro and began recording a series of albums considered bebop classics today. Lanphere's girlfriend at that time was Chan Richardson, who next moved in with Charlie Parker and later lived with Phil Woods—all three were bebop alto players. Lanphere was at the heart of the most exciting developments in jazz. The apartment he shared with other musicians became a hangout for many top artists of the day. He played with Woody Herman's big band and recorded several sessions with Parker. And in those days, many in Parker's circle, including Lanphere, were, like their hero, addicted to heroin. Its easy availability in most major cities, as well as the drug's effect—allowing its users to "stay cool," some said, in the face of humiliating treatment and police harassment—account in part for its widespread use among jazz musicians of the period, a list that includes Miles Davis and Sonny Rollins, among many others. Despite his addiction, at age twenty-two, Lanphere was on top of the world. And then he was arrested in Detroit for buying heroin.

That sent him back to Wenatchee, where he spent the next six years working in his father's music store. Finally, after he and childhood friend and future journalist Doug Ramsey produced a two-day jazz festival in their little town, Lanphere was inspired to head east again. He rejoined Woody Herman and made some recordings. Then, in 1961, he was arrested for possession of marijuana in Oklahoma. His parents bailed him out, he retreated again to Wenatchee, and he didn't perform publicly for nearly twenty years.[15]

A TOTAL CULTURAL EXPERIENCE

Some look back on this era as a golden age, and in terms of the sheer number of working musicians and the size of their audience, it was. But the jazz scene was not separate from the social, economic, and political realities of the day. In fact, the entertainment districts that began to boom on the eve of World War II were a product of segregation, police corruption, and the mortgage industry practice of redlining, which prevented African Americans, Jews, and Asians from buying

Ray Charles in Seattle

When Ray Charles looked back, it was the record he made in Seattle that made him most proud.

"I never had great dreams about winning Grammys, although I did. My dream was to one day have a big band. Of course, even before then I always wanted to record a record, because everybody I knew that was famous was on a record. 'Boy,' I thought, 'if I could just get on a record, maybe I could be something!'"

He made that record in 1948—"Confession Blues" on one side, "I Love You I Love You" on the other. He was eighteen years old. "It was not a hit," he said. "I was just glad to hear my voice being played back to me from a record. I was thrilled to death!

"The other things just sort of came," he added. "The biggest thrill in my life was when I was young and I was able to do the things I had dreamed of."

Those dreams drove Charles, who was raised in Florida, to get on a Trailways bus to Seattle at age seventeen. Blind as a result of untreated glaucoma since age nine, he followed his friend, Garcia McKee, as far away from Tampa as they could get—Seattle.

"The idea of heading west was enticing as hell, all mystery and adventure. I also liked the fact it was way on the other coast—real far away. That term—West Coast—was appealing to me."

His first job in Seattle was at the Black Elks Club, where he could duck behind a huge elk's head mounted near the piano to toke off a joint. He sang "Georgia" for the Elk's Club cook, Georgia Kemp. Everybody seemed to love him, and life was good. His girlfriend Louise even came out from Tampa.

The life he found on Jackson Street helped make him the musician he was to be. On Jackson Street, R. C. Robinson, as he was known, came of age.

"In Seattle, all of a sudden I had to become a man. I started keeping house, I had an apartment, a piano, a big radio, hi-fi set, telephone. Cookin'." He laughed. "There ain't no doubt about it. I became a man." And in Seattle, Charles discovered his power—after that, he said, "The other things just sort of came."

He brought a southern approach—rocking blues and music of the sanctified church—that appealed to the new audience of African Americans from the south and southwest who had recently moved to the region for wartime jobs or with the armed forces. He could slide easily back into the blues. And sometimes, just for fun among friends, he'd sing in a gospel style that gave them a glimpse of the sound that would later make him famous.

And then, after two years, R. C. left town in the middle of the night.

He'd been dropping hints, said Ernestine Anderson, ever since the police started cracking down on junkies in the neighborhood. Because in addition to donning sunglasses in Seattle, Charles also started using heroin.

"One of these nights, I'm just going to disappear. I'm going to get on a train and I'll be gone," he said.

When he returned to Seattle two years later, he had become the singer the whole world came to love—The Genius.

"It was like a whole different person," remembered Anderson. "I was just so awed! I knew he was going to be bigger than life."[14]

That transformation began in Seattle.

Boeing initially had a whites-only hiring policy, but by 1944 they employed 1,600 African-Americans.

homes in all but a few neighborhoods. Those areas—primarily African American in Portland, with more Asian immigrants in Puget Sound—became busy communities where many ethnicities and social classes came together. Accommodations with the police and city hall were necessary to serve liquor, the essential ingredient for any after-hours entertainment venue. Often, those accommodations came at a high cost in both dollars and dignity.

And the music wasn't all "jazz." During the heyday of those entertainment districts, jazz was just one piece of an inclusive cultural experience. Musicians shared the stage with comedians and strippers, and the music included R&B, the blues, and torch songs. Jazz may have been the jewel in the crown of those shows, but it was only part of a fluid whole. And it wasn't jazz that brought in the big money.

"Maybe this big pimp would have ten girls here and he'd be supporting the party," saxophonist Billy Tolles recalled. "One girl would want 'How Deep Is the Ocean,' and this one would want 'Poor Butterfly' or 'Stardust,' or 'Body and Soul.' [They] would be there at that table twenty or thirty minutes, just singing for them and getting three, four, five-dollar tips.... They come back and drop it in the big galvanized tub, sitting right here by the side of the piano player. And boy, in the middle of the night, man, Al Pierre would be taking his foot, stuffing that money down in that tub. They'd take home eighty, ninety, a hundred dollars a night apiece."[16]

PIMPS, GAMBLERS, AND "FOLK POETS"

Given the circumstances in which they lived and worked, performers in the 1940s and '50s were in many ways quite different from jazz musicians of the twenty-first century. From the '20s through the '50s, jazz artists—though their music education was often quite extensive—were more like "folk poets" than the college-educated players who fill the ranks today. And since patrons expected more than just music, the more flamboyant the act, the more popular the musician. Big Jay McNeely, who came through Portland frequently and often stayed for months, had teenage fans screaming in delight as he lay on his back, tenor sax honking, while he kicked his feet in the air and a band member stood over him holding a microphone.

To operate successfully in this system, many top musicians played more than one instrument, developed their singing skills, and worked to become "complete entertainers." The music profession was one of the few opportunities beyond manual labor open to African Americans, and the work was coveted.

"Musicians, they were the glamorous part of life in those days," remembered Seattle trumpet player Sonny Booker. "The peak of the jobs for the black community were like mailmen and porters and sky caps. So if you weren't a musician or a pimp, you were riding on the boats or a shoe shine or a sky cap, or on the railroad."[17]

Businesses throughout the Pacific Northwest displayed "whites only" signs in their storefront windows until the mid-1940s.

CHANGING LAWS, STUBBORN MORES

For African American jazz musicians who were taking a leading role on the Seattle scene right after World War II, 1946 was a watershed year. New arrivals were changing the music and the way musicians worked, and some of them stayed to become a bridge to the generation that came of age in the 1960s. It was also the year the bottle clubs were put out of business when the Washington Supreme Court legalized the sale of liquor-by-the-drink. As a result, a number of Seattle-based players moved to Portland, and several became key performers on Williams Avenue.

They included white players like Jim Gilles and the black singer and guitarist Clarence Williams. "When things started to go bad [in Seattle], we'd finish our gig at the Washington Club or wherever, all jump into a car and drive 170 miles at 90 miles an hour just to be somewhere that didn't close at one in the morning. And finally, some of us just moved to Portland. Hey man, it was the happening place in the late '40s and very early '50s."[18]

Williams was billed as "The Prince of the Blues" because he played guitar and sang in the style of 1950s blues star T-Bone Walker. He remained in Portland for the rest of his life, even though the city wasn't always an easy place for African American musicians—especially in 1949, when Dorothy McCullough Lee was elected mayor and promised to "clean up sin, gambling, and prostitution." She reorganized the police department, enforced city ordinances against vice, and forced removal of illegal slot machines.

Legal barriers weren't the only stumbling blocks Williams faced. "One night at the Savoy a couple of guys from City Hall came in and the next thing I knew, I was fired for singing dirty lyrics.... I got the Los Angeles union involved in this and they got me my job back at the Savoy, but what I later discovered was that

"Sweet Baby" James Benton (second from left) converted a garage into a musical gathering place, hosting barbecues and jam sessions for area musicians and visiting artists.

the problem wasn't the lyrics but the little Jewish girl I was going with. That was the thing that was rubbing everybody the wrong way. Mixed couples in this city didn't set well."[19]

Interracial marriage was illegal in Oregon, while Seattle was known for its tolerance of such unions, at least on Jackson Street. That tolerance didn't extend very far afield in the 1940s, however. Boeing had a whites-only hiring policy, and Seattle's Frederick and Nelson requested "white applicants only" for holiday temp jobs. That environment favored African American musicians like Floyd Standifer, who had grown up with it.

"In those days, I did not feel able to speak out publicly. We knew what we were up against, too, and we went about our business in more of a subtle way. Wherever I was, I had always been the only African American kid in school. Consequently, I developed the education that allowed me to go back and forth without feeling ill at ease."[20]

A more activist stance was required to bring change—African American community leaders appealed to the mayor and Seattle City Council, the governor and the courts, and eventually, with the help of a revitalized NAACP, jobs began to open up. By 1944, Boeing employed 1,600 African Americans.[21]

Sweet Baby James Benton: Williams Avenue, 1953

When I imagine Williams Avenue in the '50s, I hear the stories of Baby James. Stories about the Avenue and characters like Little Sonny, his inspiration, who jumped up on the piano in the middle of a song.

"That blew my mind," says James. "When I saw those girls pulling him up and down Williams, I said, 'That's what I want to be.'"

And then a street-wise guy called Sweet-Smellin' Eddie gave James the name that would shape his destiny.

"He was a seaman, a guy who really dressed," says James. "He'd walk down the street, turn, and there'd be thirty women smelling where he'd been. So one day Eddie says to me, 'Someone got to carry this name, so I'm appointing you "The Sweet Baby".'"

So James carried the name, playing the Desert Room for shake dancers and a midget named Miss Dynamite. He's one of few left now from a heroic age. And it all started for James when he was hanging with a bunch of street dudes who one day were hired to play ball by a guy just split from the Chicago Hottentots.

"We'd travel to these little towns, seven of us in the car singing; that's how I learned," says James, remembering those barnstorming days when he'd leave the basketball court to play a piano courtside.

Back on Williams Avenue, his hit record *The Body* was banned from radio. "Got me my fifteen minutes of fame," says James.

But he'll go down in history for his converted garage on Shaver at Williams called The Backyard, where musicians created a real community in the 1950s.

"Man, we expanded that garage with theater seats, filled the walls with cork, had two pianos and a drum set. Had a big barbecue out back and three golf holes; guys'd play all day.

"It was known all over, top musicians came. Some guys kinda lived out of there. And wives—Charlie Parker's wife, Sammy Davis's wife, they'd be out back, too. Lot of guys would hang around—pimps, hustlers, you know; they'd bring cases of ribs and neck bones. I'd cook up a buncha black-eyed peas, and if a musician wasn't doing too good—just come by, man, get something to eat."

The door was always open at James Benton's Backyard, the touchstone for jazz, blues, and R&B in 1953, remembers Mel Brown:

"During the summer months, every day religiously, the musicians would congregate around twelve o'clock, barbecue like crazy, do some putting, and if you felt like playing, you just went inside and played. They would stay around 'til like six o'clock, then everybody would go home, change, and then go to their gigs. When the gigs were over, everybody went back and we'd jam until like five or six in the morning.

"It was really a musical family. . . . If one musician was having a difficult month, or couple of months, all the guys would throw in five, ten dollars, whatever, and say, 'Hey man, take care of the bills, get some food in the house for your family.'"

There were some good years, too, until half the neighborhood was bulldozed to make way for a freeway. Oh, James kept busy with the Del Tones, playing Vegas for Hollywood stars; he even sang country-western with Bobby Bare and the Four Colored Cowboys—until they tried to make him dress the part, and James ended up out of music for almost thirty years. "I wasn't wearing no cowboy suit," he declared.

And now James is back, singing sweet as ever . . . thinking about those days on the Avenue, and another fifteen minutes of fame.

MAKING THE BEST OF A BAD SITUATION

In that segregated environment, people of color found ways to rely on their own community for services. Like African American businesses, the Negro Musicians Union in Seattle had to work within its community, too, since most jobs downtown were off-limits. That's why the opening in 1946 of the Seattle Black Musician's Union Hall and nightclub, The Blue Note, was critically important as a symbol of solidarity and a focus for the community.

"The Blue Note was a hub of fraternal camaraderie, hosting sessions on Friday and Saturday nights," Paul de Barros writes. "Name players showed up often, not only to jam but to hang out, relax, and meet the locals." And, as was usual in those days, white players were welcome as well.[22] Several white musicians quit their union and joined the black organization, a detail that again reveals the ease of white access to the black world compared to the obstacles blacks faced in crossing the color line.

In Portland, where few African Americans were admitted to Local 99 and there was no separate union for black musicians, James Benton's converted garage, called "The Backyard," played the same role the Blue Note did—in an unofficial way. It was community center, social club, and jam sessions central. Musicians down on their luck could even find a place to sleep and a hot meal there. It was also a training ground for aspiring jazz players, such as then-teenaged drummer Mel Brown.

One of Brown's informal teachers, in the decades before college and high school jazz programs appeared, was the pianist Julian Henson. He came south when the bottle clubs closed in Seattle and became, according to Dietsche, "the best unknown piano player in town." He worked steadily on Williams Avenue, often with Clarence Williams, and later played with Marianne Mayfield.

Also crucial to the development of jazz in the Pacific Northwest were men such as Portland's Bill McClendon, a sometimes-pianist and one of the entrepreneurs who got his start with the help of Williams Avenue vice lord Tom Johnson. "McClendon had his hands into everything," writes Dietsche, "and a lot of it had to do with jazz." In 1949, McClendon bought the Savoy and renamed it McClendon's Rhythm Room. He ran it for five years, and it became one of the most important jazz clubs of the era. He actively sought white patrons, and the place hosted national jazz stars such as George Shearing and Earl Bostic, whose band featured then-unknown saxophonist John Coltrane. McClendon's club became so popular he had to turn away hundreds of disappointed fans for Oscar Peterson's sold-out shows.

"Oscar played two shows every day for two weeks.... They were coming from everywhere—North California, Idaho—and I began to think how important all these big jazz names were in the area of human relations and about how folks from the West Hills and downtown saw that what we were doing here was valuable."[23]

That perception didn't translate to tangible benefit for the jazz community or the neighborhoods that sustained it during those years. And the national prosperity of the 1950s didn't filter down to the musician on the street. By 1960, jazz was still heard in a few remaining Jackson Street and Williams Avenue clubs, but it was moving out of the neighborhoods that had supported it for more than twenty years.

THOSE WHO STAYED

Despite social and economic changes in the late 1950s, as big bands died and clubs formerly sustained by illegal activity closed, jazz managed to maintain a strong presence in the Pacific Northwest because many of the musicians chose to stay.

Why does one turn to the road and another stay at home? "Issues such as family, economics, and temperament often lead excellent players to work on a local scene," noted de Barros. "In Seattle, several of the best musicians stayed put, including Floyd Standifer.... These musicians and others pioneered Seattle's modern jazz scene."[24]

Standifer came to Portland as a child in 1936. His father, an African Methodist Episcopal Zion preacher, bought a farm outside of Gresham, where Standifer grew up milking cows, slopping hogs, plowing with a mule, and clearing land with a hoe. In high school, he was class vice president and worked in a cannery for the cash to buy a record player. When a friend brought him a Charlie Parker record, bebop became his passion. When his father's church transferred him to Seattle in 1946, Standifer enrolled at the University of Washington. But his real education came just down the street, where he started to jam on Saturday nights and met Ernestine Anderson, Quincy Jones, and everyone else.[25]

Jitterbug dancing reigned supreme in the 1940s, but dance palaces began closing in the late '50s as rock 'n' roll became the music of a new generation.

Standifer did tour Europe and work in New York. But he didn't stay away long. And like him, other quality players who had the option to join top touring bands, such as trombonist Cleve Williams and trumpet player Bobby Bradford, continued performing in Portland. Their mentoring at home left a lasting legacy.

"They were like godfathers to us," recalls drummer Mel Brown. "Bobby Bradford and Cleve Williams would wait for me after school, and I'd go over to Cleve's house and they'd show me how to set up certain figures with the Walter Bridges Big Band."

Many of Portland's top players passed through the Bridges band in the 1950s, '60s, and '70s. "We had quite a few enthusiastic local players who were willing to work for excellence," explains Bradford. And that's often all they were working for, since the pay for local big bands was low.

Bridges had come to Portland to work in the Kaiser Shipyards during World War II, and in 1945, as he tells it, his small group The Ebony Five was the first racially integrated band in the city. It may be true; at any rate, he had to force the union to admit him and his bandmates, who became the first African American members of the Musicians Union Local 99 in Portland.

Among those who passed through the Bridges band on their way to more distant fame were Tonight Show bandleader Doc Severinsen, American Indian saxophonist Jim Pepper, Hollywood studio player and composer Bill Hood, and Count Basie saxophonist Kenny Hing—a racially and stylistically mixed crowd.[26]

BEATNIKS AND THE DIY ETHIC

Bill Hood's brother, Portland guitarist Ernie Hood, left for a career in LA that ended abruptly when he contracted polio. Confined to a wheelchair, he returned to his hometown, became a composer and arranger and—in one of the highlights of Beat Generation Portland—co-owner of The Way Out, where he led an orchestra playing original jazz compositions. Located under the east end of the Hawthorne

Louis Jordan's Tympany Five, one of the most successful small bands in the country, became the model for jump bands in the Pacific Northwest.

Jazz to Rock 'n' Roll with Billy Tolles

Jazz players moved from R&B and the blues into early rock 'n' roll as they adapted to changes in the market. Seattle saxophonist Billy Tolles offers a striking example of that evolution—and the impact of jazz on "the Northwest Sound" of early rock 'n' roll.

Tolles came with his family to Seattle right before the Great Depression when he was only five, and he grew up in its African American community. He led a band of high school mates at the opening of the Savoy Ballroom, then a few months later left town to attend college in North Carolina. When he returned after the war, he helped lead the Jackson Street scene to its zenith.

As rhythm and blues began to have more crossover appeal to whites and attract larger audiences, however, Tolles organized a funky, hard-driving R&B band. "That tight backbeat, man.... That's what set everything on fire!" he told Paul de Barros. "We kicked ass right from the beginning. We were playing those heavy shuffles.... We came on with that blues and that 'Flyin' Home.'... I was playing the style I learned from Louis Jordan."[29]

By 1955, Tolles had streamlined his group to a trio; a year later their wild shows were drawing groups of University of Washington students to the Jackson Street neignorhood. "I could just honk," Tolles recalled, "and walk through the joint, jumping from tabletop to tabletop, honking on my low B-flat, walk the bar, [go] outside and come back in the back door, and all that kind of stuff. Those white kids, they'd be in there clamoring for that." Tolles also promoted shows and hosted a TV show on Seattle's Channel 13 called *Rock 'n' Roll Party*. Among those white teenagers drawn to Tolles's early rock 'n' roll were those who played with Pacific Northwest rock groups of the 1960s such as The Wailers.

"What many people forget is that there was a strong continuity between the older generation of pro musicians and the first generation of rockers here," said Seattle jazz bassist and bandleader Pete Leinonen, who had come of age in the early 1960s. "Most of those [early rock] bands were highly sophisticated in both their material and presentation. A lot of us jazz players caught the wave, too."[30]

Bridge in a building formerly owned by a local racketeer (the upstairs rooms were still rented to prostitutes), the coffee house hosted visual artists like Louis Bunce who painted while listening to jazz, and poets reading along with jazz.[27]

Hood and his fellow artists produced a weekly TV show in 1961 called *The Jazz Arts* that featured a variety of multi-media collaborations with a ten-piece ensemble playing compositions by Hood and Quen Anderson, another composer and instrumentalist recently returned to the Pacific Northwest.

Anderson had come home to Vancouver, Washington after a career as a musician and arranger in New York and Los Angeles. Hood's ensemble had Portland's top white jazz artists, so Anderson began to compose for them. But Hood's band stayed together for only a few years, and by the mid-1960s, Anderson was writing arrangements for the Carl Smith Big Band. By all accounts, Anderson's arrangements elevated the band from good to great.

Pete's Poop Deck, which opened in Seattle's Pioneer Square area in 1957, filled the same function as the Way Out, but it was much more commercially viable, and the musicians who worked there reached a much larger audience than the small bohemian crowd in Portland. Pete's was the first self-styled 'modern jazz club' in Seattle, where people came primarily to listen rather than dance or socialize. And Pete's hosted painters and poets, too. For five and a half years, the club's 140 seats were filled nearly every night. At the time, eight other Seattle clubs also presented modern jazz exclusively.

One of those Seattle clubs was Dave's Fifth Avenue, where the Mastersounds were born in 1957. The quartet was started by bassist Monk Montgomery with his brother Buddy on vibes. In contrast to the looser format employed by the jazz groups of the region at the time, the Mastersounds' material was meticulously arranged and rehearsed. They drew full houses at Dave's for months, especially when the third Montgomery brother, Wes, joined in on guitar. The ensemble only stayed together three years, but they became the best-selling jazz group to ever come out of Seattle.[28]

Despite such notable successes, many jazz musicians in the region had to supplement their income with day jobs. That accommodation has become a hallmark of the jazz scene in the Pacific Northwest, where artists have maintained a career in music while also working in other fields. Hood, for example, was a broadcaster, graphic artist, and cofounder of the city's community radio station. And those day jobs were becoming more common as the work for jazz players dried up.

THE END OF AN ERA

The popularity of rock 'n' roll was growing, and dance palaces were closing. In 1958, bulldozers leveled many of the clubs along Portland's Williams Avenue to make way for a new freeway and the Veterans Memorial Coliseum. In Seattle, the system of police pay-offs and graft that had supported illegal booze, gambling, and prostitution was about to be exposed. Almost overnight, it seemed, jazz lost its place as the dominant sound in the region. In 1959, Floyd Standifer was playing hard bop to standing-room-only crowds at The Flame in Seattle; a year later, he was playing for go-go dancers at the Pink Pussycat.

It was the end of an era—a darker and in some ways more vibrant time when jazz and related music found ways to survive and even thrive amid injustice and corruption, while thousands of dancers twirled to big bands unaware. Drummer Tim Kennedy remembers those days fondly:

"We knew about the segregation in Portland, but to us, Williams Avenue *was* Portland.... That was probably the best time in my life. We had the best of everything: best music, best food, best women; all the people on the Avenue coming to see us. Yeah, it was definitely the best time in my life."[31]

It may be difficult to see clearly in the cities of the East and Midwest, where African Americans have been shaping the culture for generations, but their impact in the mid-twentieth century Pacific Northwest was dramatically evident. By 1960, its once nearly all-white cities had been irrevocably altered by a five-fold increase in the African American population whose influence—primarily through music—far exceeded its relatively small size. What happened on Jackson Street and Williams Avenue during those tumultuous years from 1940 to 1959 became an integral part of the culture of the Pacific Northwest.

The Kaiser Shipyards employed 150,000 workers and fueled a booming wartime economy that sustained the active jazz scene.

3

The Dark Ages: 1960–1972

"It wasn't that jazz was gone—it changed. Look, we got South American music, and rock, and pop, and bands like Weather Report. For somebody who was not adaptable, sure, it was bad; there's so many jazz players who don't know how to intersect. But lots of guys kept right on working, and jazz adapted itself to these gigs."[1]

Jay Thomas

AFTER THE DUST

In 1960, after the dust from the bulldozers had settled along Williams Avenue and the clubs at the heart of Portland's golden age were replaced by freeway ramps and the Veterans Memorial Coliseum, after the Jackson Street night spots had closed and the African American communities began to scatter, the story of jazz in the Pacific Northwest went on.

Quietly at first, though.

The music that had provided the soundtrack for nightlife in the region was reaching fewer people and feeding fewer musicians after 1960. At the same time, on a national level, the Dave Brubeck Quartet, the Modern Jazz Quartet, and Miles Davis were selling millions of records, and jazz in New York City was at its peak. But social and technological changes were eroding its viability in the rest of the country. Sustained economically in the Pacific Northwest for decades by official corruption and illegal activities as well as the swing dance boom, jazz struggled to find its place in a new environment, where cities were cracking down on "vice" and the mood of the country had turned conservative. Television and growing families at the height of the baby boom kept adults home, while rock 'n' roll became the music of a new youth culture.

In addition, jazz in the Pacific Northwest lost its geographic base in African American communities after the mid-1960s. In part this occurred because it was driven out by anti-vice campaigns, and in part because black musicians were now working in what had previously

Bassist and singer Marianne Mayfield was known affectionately as everybody's surrogate mother. She played jazz by night and taught fifth grade by day.

been white territory. Perhaps more important, practices that had hindered the rights of African Americans to buy property were relaxed or ruled illegal, and people of color could choose to reside in many other neighborhoods. The first to leave was the middle class, and though the outflow was gradual, it soon undermined the viability of small businesses. Over time, those neighborhoods fell into poverty and disrepair.

The ways in which musicians in the Pacific Northwest adapted to those conditions in the 1960s and early 1970s left their mark on the character of the jazz community. The do-it-yourself approach and support from volunteer organizations that developed during this era helped prompt new venues for jazz and brought in new audiences. And younger players began to establish jam sessions where new musical directions emerged. A "jazz infrastructure" was being built that would set the stage for a renaissance to come in the late 1970s.

A WOMAN'S CHOICES

Jazz continued to be passed along from one generation to the next, and that created some degree of continuity. One of the informal mentors vital to that process in Portland was bassist and singer Marianne Mayfield. Known affectionately as everybody's surrogate mother, Mayfield's career offers one example of the ways in which women's choices shaped the Pacific Northwest jazz community.

Mayfield grew up in Oakland, California, where she received classical training and played briefly with the Oakland and San Francisco symphony orchestras. She also played jazz, and her circle of young colleagues included saxophonist Sonny

King. He later lived in Eugene, where he formed a common-law union with vocalist Nancy (Whaley) King. Sonny King's light burned bright for a few years as a teacher and performer, until his death from a drug overdose in 1983—a fate not at all typical in a community represented by the likes of Mayfield.

She came to Portland in 1960, on tour with The Three V's, an all-woman vocal harmony group; met the man who became her first husband; and decided to settle down. "That was that," she said. "No more touring." Within a year she was working at the Mural Room (later called the Jazz Quarry), with Williams Avenue veteran Julian Henson on piano; the band also accompanied strippers. It was seventeen-year-old Mel Brown's first steady job in music. "I'd have to go back to the kitchen between sets," he remembered, "and she'd come in, check my homework, and buy me a hamburger."

Two years later Mayfield had a son, and in 1965 Reprise Records offered her a contract and tour, but said there'd be no room for her three-year-old to come along. "That's when I decided I had better learn to do something else for a living," she said, "because he wasn't going to a boarding school—that was out."[2]

Although she divorced (and later remarried), that commitment and the abundant jazz work she found locally convinced Mayfield to stay in Portland. She put herself through college while raising her son and playing clubs at night, began teaching fifth grade in 1972, and didn't stop until she retired twenty years later. There were days she felt it was all too much; often, she threatened to quit. But Mayfield kept it up, leading trios at Portland clubs that included the Prima Donna downtown, a casual east-side tavern called Parchman Farm, and DJ's Village Jazz in the affluent suburb of Lake Oswego. "Everybody loved her," said Ron Steen, another drummer she mothered. Shortly before her death in 2004, the Mount Hood Festival of Jazz staged a tribute in her honor that included several of the Portland singers Mayfield had mentored.

"A light has gone out," said Marilyn Keller, one of those vocalists, "but she made her statement in this world." And that statement was especially powerful for Keller and other African American women. When Mayfield began performing in the early 1950s, she couldn't enter through the venue's front door, nor could her mother sit in the audience. She saw that change, and in addition, her success as an instrumentalist (who also sang) made a statement about the increasing role of women. "I'm grateful for the fact that I have enjoyed the respect of my contemporaries, the musicians, the guys," she said, looking back. "Not as a woman but as a musician and as a person."[3]

Keeping a family together while performing regularly was fairly common for women in jazz in those days. But it was always a difficult choice, as it had been a decade earlier for Ernestine Anderson. Others, such as Olympia singer Jan Stentz, chose family over career and dropped out, while some women followed a more maverick approach. They valued their independence and often remained childless, like pianist and singer Jeannie Hoffman.

A Portland native, Hoffman started sitting in at Williams Avenue clubs in the early 1950s, then moved to San Francisco. Her first album was recorded in that city's fabled Jazz Workshop. In 1959, she made another live album (*Jean Hoffman Sings and Swings*), and then a studio recording for Capitol Records with national stars Howard Roberts and Shelly Manne.

Hoffman was the epitome of the hip beatnik chick, and she drew admiring audiences of young people in the Bay Area and on her return trips to Portland. Unfortunately, her mid-'60s album, *The Folk-Type Swinger*, hit at just the moment the Beatles and other new rock groups were topping the charts; Capitol dropped her along with most of its jazz artists. Hoffman returned to Portland in 1973 for a long-term engagement at Ray's Helm, one of the key clubs of the era. There she began playing with bassist David Friesen, and a few years later the two (with guitarist John Stowell) made an album, *Gonna Plant Me Some Seeds*, that reflected the counterculture spirit of the times—and pointed the way toward the jazz renaissance to come.[4]

ADAPTABILITY

One of the reasons for the positive audience response Hoffman and Mayfield received was their adaptability—a persistent theme in most musicians' recollections of the 1960s and early 1970s. "Working in nightclubs, you almost have to be versatile," Mayfield said. "Everybody talks about the pure forms of jazz, but if you're going to eat and sell to an audience that can afford to come and see you, you have to perform a mix. Something old, something new—and most of it borrowed." Hoffman's repertoire included blues, pop, and even a few children's songs in addition to straight-ahead jazz.[5]

Indeed, the most flexible Williams Avenue and Jackson Street stars, such as Warren Bracken in Portland and Floyd Standifer in Seattle, continued to work steadily throughout the 1960s, especially as social norms changed and more downtown jobs became available to African American performers.

"For those of us who knew how to read music," said Standifer, "and how to carry ourselves in certain situations—among white people, let us say—[it] worked out alright. Many of the other black musicians, however, never were able to cross over from music as they had known it in the after hours clubs...and by '61, it was gone."[6]

White instrumentalists also had to adapt, and the careers of Seattle pianist Jerry Gray and bassist Chuck Metcalf reveal contrasting responses to the slowest time ever for jazz in the region. Their choices represent those made by many others whose stories are not as well known.

Gray came to prominence while playing at Pete's Poop Deck, one of several modern jazz nightclubs to spring up in the late 1950s and early 1960s. Reputed to have been "the best pianist to ever play in Seattle," Gray stopped performing in public in 1966. "He quit drinking, smoking, and playing music in public all in the same day," Gray's colleague Metcalf said. "It was like he walked through a door into a different life."

Paul de Barros asked Gray about it, and his answer says as much about jazz in the Pacific Northwest at the time as it does about Gray himself. "I came to the wrong town," he said. "Very few people here thought of themselves as going anywhere or doing anything particularly consequential. There was a kind of 'we're just folks' attitude here. It was disastrous for me." Gray became a busy teacher, and never performed in public again.[7]

Metcalf, however, found the Seattle scene in the early '60s a stimulus to begin performing again after he'd spent most of the previous decade raising a family and pursuing a career in architecture. He worked at the newly opened high-class club The Penthouse in 1960, where he backed touring stars until singer Anita O'Day hired his whole trio for a tour that took Metcalf to Los Angeles. When he returned to Seattle, he worked steadily because he was willing to play commercial jobs as well as jazz gigs. In 1966, the year Gray quit, Metcalf helped start the Seattle Jazz Society.

When the Puget Sound economy collapsed in 1971, Metcalf moved to San Francisco. He worked with top jazz players, toured Europe with bebop star Dexter Gordon, and didn't return to Seattle until 1982. He'd left when he had to, returned when he could, and never stopped performing because he adapted his art to the work that was available.[8]

THE GREAT DIVIDE

And so began what has become a deep divide in the jazz community between musicians willing and able to play more popular styles and those who pursue jazz as art music exclusively. This split between "cocktail jazz" and more freely improvised forms reflected tendencies in the larger society, where divisions over civil rights, the war in Vietnam, sexual freedom, and other social and political issues highlighted the clash between innovation and the status quo. In Seattle, the two diverging paths jazz followed thereafter were neatly illustrated by the contrast between black educator and saxophonist Joe Brazil and white bandleader and clarinetist Chuck Mahaffey.

Brazil came to Seattle from Detroit in 1962 and provided a blast of energy. He built an audience for his all-star sextet that featured Jackson Street veterans, and made a double album with John Coltrane that was recorded the same night a live recording of Coltrane's band was made at The Penthouse. It was a wild scene, and the band played two and a half hours nonstop.[9]

After he finished, Coltrane and his sidemen joined Brazil for a twelve-hour session in a studio in nearby Lynnwood that was released as the album *Om*, on which Brazil played flute. One of Coltrane's most challenging, the twenty-nine-minute recording features Coltrane and tenor saxophonist Pharoah Sanders chanting from the Bhagavad Gita and the Tibetan Book of the Dead. Writer Peter Lavezzoli claims Coltrane was using LSD during the session. "The recording sounds disjointed and hallucinatory," he wrote, "almost as though Coltrane is not in full control of his normal faculties.... The opening chant is followed by some of the most dissonant and paint-peeling shrieks on any Coltrane recording.... The music communicates an intense feeling of unrest."

That unrest reflected the mood of the day, as did the album Coltrane recorded earlier that night, *Live in Seattle*. It also marked a turning point in Coltrane's career, when his music became more innovative and difficult.

Those words might also describe Brazil's career in Seattle. He came west initially to work at Boeing as a toolmaker. Another member of the generation that relocated for jobs, he exhibited that generation's ambition, too, studying math and computer programming on the side to land a better position.

In addition to his day job and playing at night in such clubs as The Penthouse with Jerry Gray, Brazil joined a committee of African American leaders to address social justice issues and began teaching at Garfield High School. In 1967 he founded the Black Music Academy, later called the Brazil Music Academy (BMA), where many Jackson Street veterans taught. One of Brazil's students at the BMA was Ed Lee, who later became a high school music teacher and jazz performer.

"He was the guru! When I got out of the Army in 1964, I went to a little club down on First Avenue, and that's where I met Joe," Lee remembers. "He took me right home with him," says Lee. "We played a little bit and listened to tapes, and from then on I was hangin' with Joe and absorbing all his knowledge.... In Detroit, Coltrane and McCoy Tyner and all those guys hung out at his house."

Indeed, historians have remarked on the legendary jam sessions at "Joe's Basement," where jazz artists could share information free from commercial constraints and out of the public eye. Brazil's impact in Seattle also went beyond music instruction, according to Lee: "Joe saved a whole bunch of guys on dope.... There are a lot of guys playing today because of his influence."

In 1968, the Black Student Union at the University of Washington demanded that the music department hire Brazil, and he remained on the faculty until 1976, a struggling pioneer in both black studies and jazz programs.

"His methods were viewed as very nontraditional, which they were," Lee remembers. "And that was a good thing.... He brought whole bands into his class—he brought Sun Ra into class! I was in Joe's group, and he'd bring us in and have us demonstrate.... It was a tremendous inspiration for young musicians."[10]

University administrators didn't see it that way, and when Brazil was promoted to Assistant Professor in 1972, tension with the School of Music increased over his use of live jazz performance in the classroom. Brazil's employment ended when the School of Music voted to deny him tenure, citing "a travesty of classroom teaching." 350 people marched on the university president's office, chanting "Justice for Joe." All to no avail. After twice suing the university unsuccessfully, Brazil retreated north to Bellingham.[11]

Chuck Mahaffey took another approach, aimed toward grooming the younger generation for success in the business, according to Tamara Burdette, a member of Mahaffey's band in the 1960s. Her father was a jazz bassist, and she played her first professional job on the instrument at age fourteen. Before Burdette left Seattle for a career in Los Angeles, she learned the business from Mahaffey. He also employed young guitarist Larry Coryell, who had come to Seattle from eastern Washington. Mahaffey, from Helena, Montana, studied classical clarinet (he also played drums) at the University of Washington. In contrast to Brazil, the quintessential "outsider" in the Pacific Northwest, Mahaffey was an "insider." He was already well established when Burdette joined him.

"He taught you things like looking good, not showing up drunk, knowing what you're going to play, knowing your tempos, your keys," Burdette recalled. "Respect your audience: establish eye contact, keep the pace going.... We always kept it danceable," she continued, "but we also stretched out and soloed. We were working at the Casa Villa, and Chuck called me: 'You're going to start singing.' I was very righteous about being a bass player, and I told him, 'I don't sing!' He said, 'If you want to keep working, you're singing—tonight.' Okay, that night I sang... [and]

« John Coltrane recorded two albums of his most challenging music in Seattle, marking a turning point in his career.

In the 1960s, Warren Bracken found success by adopting a more commercial style. He was one of the few black members of the predominantly white Musicians Union in Portland.

it wasn't more than a couple of months before you couldn't keep me away from the microphone. The same went for Larry Coryell—he had to sing, too.... Larry called Chuck his main mentor."[12]

In Portland, musicians were facing similar choices. Pianist and bandleader Warren Bracken had to begin singing and playing "more commercial," he said. It paid well, and he was always dressed sharp. Bracken was one of the few African American artists to be a member of Musicians Union Local 99 and work downtown. It wasn't easy.

"When I first joined the union, they didn't want you to play downtown," remembers Bracken. "They were saying, 'Oh, you can't have that job, man, we've got white musicians out here walking the streets that need the work,' and 'What's the matter with the jobs over there?'" But if you stood up and fought, he learned, you got what you wanted.

MENTORS AND STAR PUPILS

Bracken shared his success by offering opportunities to younger musicians, including drummer Ron Steen and American Indian saxophonist Jim Pepper, part of a circle of young admirers who clustered around the pianist in the 1960s. Pepper turned out to be the most famous of them all. Raised in Portland with a knowledge of tribal traditions, he was charismatic and popular in both Native and white worlds, though the tension between them later proved difficult for him, and alcohol and drug abuse dogged his career and personal life. In high school, he played with bassist Glen Moore in The Young Oregonians, a student band sponsored by the state's largest daily newspaper. Pepper was also a member of the Walter Bridges Big Band.

"When Jim Pepper was just learning his horn," Bracken recalled, "he didn't know any melodies, he would just take off. There wasn't nobody going to give him a job. But I'd have him come in and play with me."

Pepper moved to New York in 1964, though he returned to Portland frequently during the late 1960s. Of Kaw and Creek descent, he devised a powerful style

Warren Bracken: "A completely different life up here."

When I met Warren Bracken, he weighed 400 pounds and was unable to work. But in the photos he showed me, you could see it wasn't always like that.

In LA, in 1947, for instance, it looked like he had it all.

Fresh out of the Navy and rail-thin, they made him house pianist at Billy Berg's before he could take the uniform off. He was there when Charlie Parker and Dizzy Gillespie made a West Coast tour, the right place and the right time for a polite young man from Kentucky who'd write arrangements and play the music of the day.

He was riding high on winds of postwar change, when black veterans thought, "Now's the time." But the world was divided by race and full of pain; black and white, junkie and straight.

"Oh, how it broke the hearts of the musicians when Slim Gaillard would bring Frankie Laine up to sing 'Shine' in our jam," he says.

And though he looks quite slim in photos back then, a hunger he'd never contain was building. "It wasn't like I was on a diet or nothing," he says, "I just hadn't had a chance to stop and eat nothing yet." Or to feel enough pain.

First, he lost his wife. "We didn't have any home life," he says, "She was a vocalist, fine looker, beautiful lady. The agent didn't want us on the same job; we were like strangers when we'd meet."

Then he lost his friends. "Surrounded by dope fiends, it's a fight, man." He's crying. "Everybody shooting up, you're staying clean. It's hard. You're not one of them...and everybody telling you, 'Come on, man, you can't fight it.' Oh, what a sad feeling."

Then, in 1950, he saw Portland. By that time, he'd been on the road with Billy Eckstine—good job, big name, but the whole band was using; hard enough just being black in America. So when he met a Portland girl and musicians here said, "Any time you want, come on back," he did, and never left again.

"It was just a completely different life up here, man, like somebody had lifted a load off my shoulders." A new wife, a family, and work on the Avenue, where young boppers gathered around him and the pounds started to mount up. He could still dance, but no place was safe in a world divided by race, and the losses began again.

First, he lost his band. "Oh man," he says. "We were doing good jobs, big dance places, until Dinah Washington came through and took my best men. Wasn't that many black musicians in Portland, see; I couldn't replace 'em, and it got pretty hard for me."

And harder still when most of the clubs on Williams closed and he lost bebop: "I was playing progressive," he says, "until one night the owner says, 'I'd like to keep you, but you gotta sing more, put some melody in, or I'm going to have to let you go.'

"So that's what I did," says Bracken, showing photos of swanky places and white faces. "I started playing more Erroll Garner style, singing more; we got to drawing more people and making more money, and I didn't feel like getting away from that."

And there he was in the 1960s, hand-painted ties, women on his lap, the weight going up; one of the few black musicians working westside jobs. Until finally even those dried up, and the more he lost, the more he ate.

But for a moment in the 1970s, when the Basie Band invited him to sit in after the leader had taken sick, it felt like he had it all again. "And it worked out nice...oh, man," he says, "oh man." Afterwards, people came up, mistaking him for the bandleader: "Oh, Mr. Basie, we loved your music," they said.

Finally, he was too heavy to get out of the house. Music itself was slipping away, and in a wheelchair, he couldn't keep up. But he did play me a tune, voice muffled and fingers thick. "Just an old love song," he says. But it rose almost weightless to the heaven that Portland had once been for him. "Just a completely different life up here, man."

Jim Pepper devised a powerful style that wedded American Indian culture to jazz.

that wedded American Indian culture to jazz. It was so compelling that it won a prominent place on European stages before his death from lymphoma at age fifty in 1992. His best-known tune, "Witchi-Tai-To" (based on a healing chant of the Peyote religion), reached the top ten on jazz charts in 1971. He had also recorded it several years earlier with the groundbreaking band The Free Spirits, which included guitarist Larry Coryell, who'd come straight from Seattle. It was the first recording of the new jazz-rock fusion style.

Even unheralded sidemen such as Portland bassist Omar Yeoman helped bring along the generation coming of age in the 1960s. As a teenager, drummer Ron Steen received a series of lessons from Yeoman. Some were sartorial. "Look at how I look, man," he'd say to Steen, "I've got this suit on, and you look all raggedy." Other lessons were musical: "Make your stuff rhyme," he instructed. "Everything's call and response. You listen to Miles, all those guys, Blakey, Philly Jo, they throw an idea out there and then they resolve it, they answer." Simple lessons, but essential.

"You don't really learn about jazz from schools," Steen says. "It's a cultural thing.... We used to be taught by hanging out in clubs, and learned by hanging

Jim Pepper: A Personal Reminiscence

Tom Grant, October 27, 2002

I thought Jim Pepper was beyond cool. He was so magnetic and powerful with his big resonant speaking voice and huge beautiful tone on the tenor saxophone. Pepper had an incredible presence that was deeply affecting to an audience. His look was exotic, his manner could be fierce, even menacing. But when he wanted to charm, he had a deep reservoir of warmth.

And that warmth was never more apparent than in Jim's playing of a jazz ballad. He could squeeze so much emotion out of tunes as to make listeners weep. He loved to play R&B saxophone in the tradition of King Curtis and Junior Walker, too. And in just about every solo he played, Pepper... would do this upward cascading atonal spiral of notes culminating in a fierce high squawking or bellowing full of nasty overtones.

While in New York, he hooked up with Ornette Coleman, who encouraged Jim to mix into his jazz playing the Native chants that he had learned as a child. This eventually resulted in the pop hit "Witchi-Tai-To," based on a peyote chant of the Plains Indians.... With Comanche and English lyrics, it became a cult classic. Its hypnotic cadence and mystical-sounding lyrics captivated audiences worldwide.

Pepper tried often in his career to hit this magic combination again. In 1970, he took his flute-playing wife Ravie, his father Gilbert, and myself back to New York to record... a whole new batch of tunes based on chants but with contemporary pop chord changes.

That record came out in 1972 and didn't do much business. When I listen to it now, it has a kind of mayhem quality to it, probably owing to our youthful exuberance. But there was a sweetness in the grooves that owed to Pepper's singular ability to coax musicality out of chaos. The album was a critical success and the already burgeoning Pepper cult embraced it with enthusiasm. But it had no hits. Pepper eventually had a row with the producers and pretty much killed the potential for serious promotion.

Jim's personal demons caused a kind of irascibility in him that often led to such stumbles. He struggled with alcohol and drug addiction for much of his adult life. He was troubled and angry. Every musician who knew him had stories about outrageous or astonishing behavior. He would boast (true or not) of sleeping with the wives of friends. He also claimed to have written songs that he didn't.

Pepper had a way of being obnoxious or confrontational without ever being challenged for it. For instance, he was playing a church service where the congregation listened adoringly as he stopped in mid-performance to yell: "You motherfuckers! Don't you know that Custer died for your sins!!?"... He was like a bad boy in a protective bubble.

Jim and I had a major falling out in the '70s.... It concerned money and jealousy and pettiness on both sides. There was a lot of hollering over the phone in the middle of the night, and when the dust cleared, we had a nearly fifteen-year falling out.

I went to see Jim as he was dying at his childhood home on 106th and Fremont.... In the background, a tape of solo Native flute fluttering and floating against the rhythm of drum and shaker was playing.... His arm shot straight up in the air, his hand taking my hand, momentarily interrupting his dying. In that instant, all the slights and fights of the past went quietly away, floating off with the song of the flute.

Years later, a young guitar player from San Francisco organized a concert memorializing Pepper and his music. The group featured various luminaries from Jim's life, including pianist Gordon Lee, who after his long association with Jim referred to him as "the brother I never wanted."

I joined them in Portland for a concert that really captured the Pepper spirit: it was chaos. But without the charisma of the big bear himself standing up there with his shakers and pointing his horn like a death ray at the audience and doing his war whoops and yelps and invoking the tribal names, this assemblage had nothing around which to congeal. We were left only with the chaos.

Left: Portland native Ron Steen remembers running straight to the Memorial Coliseum from a Pony League baseball game, still in his uniform, to see Stan Getz.

Right: "We used to be taught by hanging out in clubs, and learned by hanging around cats who could play," says Ron Steen (center, with Peter Boe, Phil Baker, Thara Memory, and Eddie Harris).

around cats who could play. And if you had that desire, you'd go home and practice all day long."

One of the clubs where Steen hung out was the Upstairs Lounge, near the former Williams Avenue district. In the late 1960s, Steen, Pepper, and Tom Grant performed there while still in their teens. Nationally touring acts also appeared. Just having a venue where those stars could perform was crucial in keeping jazz alive in the Pacific Northwest: Steen and other young players were inspired by hearing the biggest names. He remembers running straight to the Memorial Coliseum from a Pony League baseball game, still in his uniform, to see Stan Getz.

THE NEXT GENERATION COMES OF AGE

The younger generation was also forming bands of their own. Ron Steen performed at Portland's Benson Hotel with Glen Moore and Ralph Tower before they set off for New York. Steen was soon leading a band too, and by 1970 he'd recruited pianist Tom Grant.

Grant had grown up listening to jazz in his father's shop on Williams Avenue, Al Grant's Madrona Records. He attended the University of Oregon, earned a master's degree, and ended up teaching high school in the tiny logging town of Mill City in the Santiam Valley. On weekends, he'd drive to Portland to play with Jim Pepper.

After two years, the dual life broke down. "It was such a nutty thing to go from this conservative logging community to Portland to be around jazz musicians," he said. He began playing with Steen and others, including bassist David Friesen. Together, the three went on the road with trumpet star Woody Shaw as well as Grammy-winning saxophonist Joe Henderson, with whom they toured Europe.

And though Steen, Grant, and Friesen worked—separately and together—with some of the biggest names in jazz of the 1960s and '70s, all three quickly returned to the Pacific Northwest.

It's the people a musician works with every day who have the greatest impact. Most jazz players read music, many have classical training, and all listen to recordings by leaders in the field. But jazz is learned by ear, and the practice room or play-along records can't prepare a musician for the bandstand experience.

That's where David Friesen learned his craft. Primarily a self-taught player who grew up in Seattle, he started on piano and took up bass while he was stationed in Germany with the US Army. Discharged in 1964, Friesen returned to Seattle at the same time as trumpeter Ed Lee. Both men—one black, one white—quickly found what they needed: for Lee it was Joe Brazil; Friesen got together with Jerry Heldman. And around Friesen and Heldman coalesced a loose group of musicians whose explorations would have a powerful impact on the direction of jazz in the region.

RISE OF A PACIFIC NORTHWEST AVANT-GARDE

Jerry Heldman, a bass player and drummer, discovered a kindred spirit in David Friesen. Both were influenced by bassist Scott LaFaro, who had come to national prominence as an independent rather than purely supportive voice in the Bill Evans Trio. Both Friesen and Heldman accompanied each other on piano, and both composed. They drew others into their circle when Heldman opened a coffeehouse near the Eastlake Bridge in Seattle that he called Llahngaelhyn. It quickly turned into a center for local as well as touring musicians who were seeking a jam session. Joe Brazil's quartet, with his notable young associates Rufus Reed on bass and Carlos Ward on saxophone, also joined in. Guitarist Larry Coryell, playing "cocktail jazz" with Chuck Mahaffey downtown at the time, also became a regular. It only lasted two years, but the music that came out of Llahngaelhyn in mid-1960s Seattle set the direction for a distinctly Pacific Northwestern version of the avant-garde.[13]

After the coffeehouse closed, Friesen moved to a farm outside Portland; for a while he and Heldman played together strictly for the joy of it in their homes. When Friesen opened a coffeehouse in Portland called Selah in 1972, they again had a venue for public performance. Like Llahngaelhyn, The Way Out, and other bohemian venues at the time, Friesen's place had no liquor license. It was a new era.

Selah was located on the corner of Northeast Alberta and Williams Avenue, near what had once been the epicenter of the city's African American district, by then run-down and offering cheap rent. Portland musicians still remember the late-night sessions that ended only when morning light streamed through a stained glass window above the piano.

During times of low public visibility, jam sessions are one way the community has kept itself alive artistically: players gather, often for little or no money, in order to refine their skills and share the joy of making music together. Those sessions still go on everywhere, but they are particularly important when public performance opportunities are scarce—as they were in the Pacific Northwest then. No longer sustained by dancers, alcohol or gambling revenue, or by big tips from pimps and

David Friesen: Called to Play

After a concert in the Soviet Union in 1983, David Friesen was surprised when Russian jazz fans presented copies of his albums for autographs. Friesen was in the USSR as a member of the Paul Horn Quartet. His records had never been officially distributed there. He had eleven albums by then, but he was just beginning to make the transition from sideman to leader. What a surprise to find he was known so far from home.

More than thirty years and fifty albums later, with fans in Europe and Japan as well as the US, it's no longer remarkable when they show up for an autograph. He's received five-star reviews and is a member of the Jazz Society of Oregon's Hall of Fame and the Oregon Music Hall of Fame. His recordings have made a number of "best of" lists, and he was named one of ten "New Superstars for the '80s" by Japan's *Swing Journal.*

But he's no superstar. Friesen lives simply in the bungalow in which he and his wife raised four children in a working-class Portland neighborhood. "I don't have delusions of grandeur," he said. "I don't expect a lot; I have a lot of albums, but my audiences aren't vast. . . . I'm just happy surviving and doing what I'm doing."

Friesen remembers a conversation with his sister, the Hollywood actress Dyan Cannon. "She says, 'David, we have to get you better known out there.'" He laughs. "Dyan gave Kenny G the idea for his Christmas album . . . so she says, 'But you'll never play like Kenny G, will you?'" Friesen shakes his head. He measures success a different way.

A man of faith, he feels he's been called to play. And he's approached that calling with energy and persistence.

"David and I met in New York," remembers guitarist John Stowell, who ended up working closely with Friesen for the next eight years. "He had driven all the way across the country, with no work lined up, in January! He had this strong drive to get out there, make some connections, and have his music heard. He did it three times that year."

It was on such connections—and the extensive travel required to make them—that Friesen built his career.

His partnership with Stowell resulted in improvisational music that was melodic and often featured an open, folk-like sound. It expressed the spirit of the times, and their album, *Through the Listening Glass,* was voted one of the top ten albums of the 1970s by the *Los Angeles Times.* In the early 1980s, Friesen broadened his audience even more in a series of recordings and tours with pianist Mal Waldron, a former accompanist for Billie Holiday who became an avant-garde sensation in Europe.

Since the 1990s, he has focused on leading his own groups and developing an improvisational approach to his compositions that produced a series of excellent recordings, starting with the 1993 trio album *1–2-3* with Portlanders Randy Porter and Alan Jones.

"I've always wanted a group like this, where we don't have any preconceived ideas of what or how we're going to play," he says. "There are no arrangements and no rehearsals. We never play a tune the same way twice."

Gradually, Friesen has made that approach work with all of his bands—made up almost exclusively of Portland residents. But the artist who calls himself a "traveling minstrel" is still out on the road. In 2015, at age seventy-two, he and fellow Portland bassist Glen Moore made a fourteen-city US tour, and then they headed for Europe.

"I like traveling," Friesen says. "But I always long to come back home quickly."

David Friesen's experimental yet approachable style had a powerful impact on the direction of jazz in the region.

prostitutes, there was much less money to support jazz, and the decreased musical activity led many in the general public to consider jazz a relic of the past.

Jazz was rarely covered by the mass media in the 1960s, and increasingly it was aimed at jazz fans; coupled with a diminishing audience for straight-ahead styles, that marginalization helped fuel the growth of an emerging avant-garde. Nationally, mostly in the hands of African Americans, the avant-garde became associated with Black Power movements of the late 1960s that rose up against persistent inequality. That urgency was not felt as strongly in the Pacific Northwest, where the avant-garde was whiter and its music less politically charged. Thus the aesthetic of a David Friesen, with its strong emphasis on melody and swing feel, became more prominent than the approach favored by Joe Brazil. Of course the two played together at those Llahngaelhyn sessions, so to focus on their differences is to miss the deeper connection between them—neither was playing the music that had once animated Jackson Street.

THE RIOTS ENDED IT

Although they were experimenting with freely improvised music at the Llahngaelhyn, "the music played there also remained grounded in blues, bebop and the swing tradition," writes Paul de Barros. "No matter how 'far out' musicians in the region seem to go, there is always a strain of healthy conservatism about line, blues and traditional jazz feeling that anchors them, a graceful balance of heaven and earth."[14]

And that tradition remained the foundation for the most prominent jazz styles in the Pacific Northwest into the 1960s and beyond. It was what you'd hear at the Cotton Club on Vancouver Avenue, the last black-owned nightspot for jazz in the Williams Avenue district. Like many that preceded it, the Cotton Club offered a vaudeville-style floor show with comics, dancers, female impersonators, R&B, and jazz. Sometimes, African American celebrities who were passing through town stopped by, including boxer Joe Louis, Sammy Davis Jr., and Big Mama Thornton. Billy Larkin and the Delegates, an organ trio with young drummer Mel Brown, was a popular draw. It was the last vestige of a time when visiting a black club still seemed an exotic walk on the wild side for middle-class whites. But things had changed, and Cotton Club audiences seemed to self-segregate—another sign of the impact that racial conflict was having on the more integrated scene of earlier years.

"Doug Baker of the *Oregon Journal* used to come to the club and write about it in the paper, and the next night the whites would come pouring in," recalled Cotton Club owner and Portland native Paul Knauls, who operated the club from 1963 through 1968. "Whites would come on Tuesday, Wednesday, and Thursday. Blacks would show up on Friday, Saturday, and Sunday. The place was going, I mean really going."

And then the crowds stopped. "There were riots everywhere," Knauls explained, "in Portland, too, after the deaths of Dr. King and RFK [Attorney General Robert Kennedy]. It was a terrible time. Whites stopped coming up here.... The riots ended it."[15]

COMINGS AND GOINGS

Though the Jackson Street and Williams Avenue scenes were gone, only a few of the established Pacific Northwest jazz musicians moved away or quit playing during the 1960s and early 1970s. One of those who moved on, the pianist Elmer Gill, left a powerful impression on the coming generation, including David Friesen, who toured and recorded *Three Sides of Elmer Gill* with him. And Gill didn't leave Seattle because he lacked work—his unhappiness with racial prejudice and discrimination in the US was the primary reason for his move to Canada in the late 1960s.

Gill came to Seattle in 1946, after he was discharged from the Army at Fort Lewis, an accomplished player in the Nat King Cole style—like R. C. Robinson, who came a year later, transformed himself into Ray Charles, and left. But Gill stayed and took a courageous stand for equality. Not only did he lead the first all–African American group to play in a downtown Seattle hotel, Gill also specified in his contract that "anybody, regardless of race, creed, or color, as long as they were acting in accordance with the place, and the policy of the place, and so forth, then they could come into the place while I was playing."[16]

The pianist even bought a half interest in a Jackson Street club, the Ebony Cafe. He intended to run it as a classy restaurant, not just another after-hours joint. That was important, he believed, to elevate the image of jazz.

A number of younger musicians also left the region in the mid-1960s, including Jim Pepper, Larry Coryell, Randy Brecker, Glen Moore, Ralph Towner, and Mel Brown. Vocalist Nancy King (then Whaley), who had worked with Moore and Towner while all three were at the University of Oregon, decamped for San Francisco to work with former Seattle saxophonist Pony Poindexter. Even outside the region, Pacific Northwest natives tended to stick together, as did Moore and Towner when they got to Manhattan in 1967. They also found like-minded peers, and they began forming groundbreaking new ensembles that included Return to Forever, the Mahavishnu Orchestra, Weather Report, and the band Oregon.

Oregon became the first world-music chamber jazz ensemble, and many claim the group's music evokes the landscape and countercultural attitude prevalent in the Pacific Northwest at the time. In part that's a result of the Oregonians' experiences, but original band member and woodwind player Paul McCandless and multi-instrumentalist Colin Walcott (neither from the Pacific Northwest) added classical sensibilities as well as influences from Africa and India, and the yearning of McCandless's double reeds became a definitive element of the group's sound.

When the Portland Trail Blazers won the NBA title in 1977, a documentary about their impact on the community, *Fast Break*, featured the music of Oregon. It included a quintessential Pacific Northwest scene where Blazers star Bill Walton is pumping his bike along the coast to Towner's tune "Waterwheel."

New players were arriving in Portland in the early 1970s, including trumpeter and composer Thara Memory, pianist Janice Scroggins, and Ghanaian drummer Obo Addy—all leaders whose influence would be felt in years to come. Also returning to Portland in 1970 was pianist and Spokane native Eddie Wied, who had first learned his craft on Williams Avenue in the 1950s. In another example of the ways in which regional artists adapted to changing circumstances, Wied had just spent fifteen years in Las Vegas and on tour with pop-jazz vocal group the Modernaires, including a four-month stint on *The Johnny Carson Show*. When he returned, Portland had a new "professor." Over the next thirty years, Wied contributed greatly to the sound and character of jazz in the region.

Though he held a bachelor's degree in music and a master's degree in art, had attended the Juilliard School, and was trained classically, Wied learned to play jazz at "the University of Williams Avenue," he said. Stylistically, he was rooted in the bebop of the 1940s and '50s, reminiscent of such nationally ranked pianists as Hank Jones and Tommy Flanagan. Wied's work as a teacher and mentor to younger players, in addition to his regular nightclub performances, provided a crucial link between Portland's jazz past and the twenty-first century.

JAZZ, BLUES, AND R&B

While jazz audiences declined in the Pacific Northwest in the late 1960s, an active blues scene was building that helped carry on the traditions of Jackson Street and Williams Avenue. Perhaps one band—led by guitarist and singer Tom McFarland and featuring guitarist/keyboard player Isaac Scott—best represents that generation of blues musicians and what they shared with the jazz community.

McFarland, who grew up in the tiny logging town of Sunny Valley outside Grant's Pass, was white; Scott, raised in Portland, was black. They were the same age, came from working-class families, were inspired by B. B. King, and shared a single-minded focus on music. Scott, though, had toured with the Five Blind Boys of Mississippi and other gospel groups, and he played a more aggressive, Jimi Hendrix–inspired guitar than his white partner (the nephew of noted West Coast composer Gary McFarland), who had a jazzier, Chet Atkins–influenced sound. Scott also brought with him the music of the African American church. That's where Portland bluesman Norman Sylvester first encountered him.

"I was awestruck when I first saw him playing guitar at the Faith Tabernacle Church," Sylvester recalled. "Isaac was playing an old Silvertone Sears and Roebuck guitar, in that open tuning style, with that Freddie King kind of sound. . . . He had the whole church jumping up and down with excitement."[17]

Blues had always been a part of the Pacific Northwest jazz scene, and was presented in many clubs in the African American entertainment districts. Jump blues had always been popular in the region too, as it was nationally, and blues singers routinely appeared with jazz bands. It was no stretch for former Williams Avenue regular Art Cheney, for instance, to unpack his tenor saxophone after a shift at a nearby steel mill and join McFarland's band at the White Eagle Tavern.

In the early 1970s, McFarland moved from Portland to Seattle, and began a long tenure at the Boulder Cafe on First Avenue near the Pike Place Market in what was still the city's skid road district. With B-girls and pull-tab gambling devices on the bar, and a bright orange wall just fifteen feet in front of a stage the band shared with strippers, it was a scene reminiscent of the Jackson Street era. Most of the clientele were Filipino seamen or workers from the nearby construction of the King Dome, not the younger crowd McFarland drew at other venues. Scott first played with McFarland at The Boulder—on piano until they decided the two-guitar front line would draw bigger crowds. In the process—both together and, later,

Glen Moore: The Landscape of Improvisation

He arrives at his studio off Grand Avenue on a bicycle, carrying only a small bag. Glen Moore's bass, made in 1715 and topped by a carved griffin's head that towers seven feet above the floor, is waiting for him in Italy. He'll soon embark on a tour there with the chamber jazz group Oregon, which he cofounded in 1971. On this fall morning in Portland, though, a few days before his sixty-fifth birthday, Moore is anxious to get his hands on a piano.

He sits down, begins to play, and we enter "the landscape of improvisation," as Moore calls it. A challenging, playful, and invigorating place. That territory is the source of Moore's lively, complex music. And though he's lived a lot of places since growing up in the small town of Milwaukie—from a farm on the Siletz River to a crack-infested neighborhood in New York City—he is never far from the improvisational territory where his music is born.

His first glimpses of that territory came from the radio during the 1950s, when he was moved "by all the jazz and popular music at that time, and by the pictorial immensity of what came out of the piano. My idea of a good time was a piano in a room with the lights out."

Though radio and records brought the music to Moore, his vision developed at a distance from the world he dreamed of. That contributed to the uncompromising artist he has become. "I couldn't see many musicians live, so I listened to records over and over again and just imagined all those things you do when something is mysterious and makes your spine tingle. That made me stubborn," he adds. "When you feast on a record for a year, hold onto it as an ideal, you don't let go of it easily."

Moore soon learned the wisdom of flexibility, after he left Eugene with a degree in history and landed in New York in 1967 with Ralph Towner and other like-minded peers. All had come to play with Miles Davis and the musicians who played with him. By the time they arrived, it was too late: Davis was on his way to the churning electronics of *Bitches Brew*.

They didn't become the jazz players they had dreamed about, but they found another way to make music that would lead Moore farther into the landscape of improvisation.

And for Moore, improvisation is key. But the process doesn't always yield a uniformly polished result. And though he's worked productively with Towner and McCandless for thirty-five years, a debate among them still goes on about how much of the process an audience should hear.

"You can't just pick the good stuff and edit out the turmoil," Moore insists. "That's what Ralph and Paul want to do when we record a free piece. But free pieces replicate the roller coaster ride that is life, and moments of resolution are hard-won. There should be some turmoil in there, and we have to give the audience credit for being able to work that out on their own."

Don't mistake disagreement for discord, however. The group's music remains remarkably integrated, a model of freedom and cooperation. That's due in part to their ability to change over the years while not losing their trademark sound: light percussion; a classical, acoustic touch despite the electronics; the melody carried by McCandless's wind instruments; and the extended compositions of Towner, which comprise nearly 90 percent of the group's repertoire.

And that sound is remarkably balanced—a quality Moore himself has sought in his personal life as well. Art like his, made equally from meditative solitude and active engagement, requires balance, and he has managed to find it by moving between country and city, home and the road, between his need to enjoy the natural world as well as an urban area that keeps his ears and fingers alive.

Look! There he goes now, on a bicycle through the landscape of improvisation.

Guitarist Tom McFarland's band often featured former Williams Avenue saxophonist Art Cheney, who would join them at the White Eagle after his shift at a nearby steel mill.

singly—McFarland and Scott opened a number of Seattle venues for the blues, including the Central Saloon in Pioneer Square and the Jolly Roger Roadhouse.

Then, in 1976, McFarland moved to Richmond, California. He was a featured performer at the San Francisco Blues Festival and toured with Otis Rush (black) and Charlie Musselwhite (white), further highlighting the mixed-race showcase the blues became for a time in the early 1970s. It wasn't always an easy fit, and McFarland even adopted the stage name "Sonny Black" for a while as an ironic commentary on racial expectations. He later returned to Portland and became a force behind the city's Underground Blues Festival in the 1980s.

Other Pacific Northwest blues players didn't need to leave town to find steady work because the local blues scene was thriving. Paul deLay and Lloyd Jones led two of the bands that were performing regularly for enthusiastic, dancing crowds drawn to the bar-boogie blues popular at the time. In Eugene, Curtis Salgado was just getting his start.

Neither McFarland nor Scott had known the man who'd kept the blues alive in Seattle before they arrived—David "Guitar Shorty" Kearney. He first made a name for himself on Chicago's South Side, where such giants as Muddy Waters and Howlin' Wolf developed the urban blues. He'd also made a couple of records and toured with Ray Charles before he brought his flamboyant act, full of somersaults and behind-the-head picking, to Seattle. He was an influence on the young Jimi Hendrix, too. "Hendrix took a lot of his style right from him," claimed Kearney sideman Gary Hammon—an observation backed by Ed Lee, another Kearney associate. Lee also noted that the fusion of jazz and blues they played with Kearney in the late 1960s was similar to the sound of Miles Davis's groundbreaking 1970 album, *Bitches Brew*.[18] Both Hammon and Lee had been students of Joe Brazil and moved from the avant-garde to the blues with ease.

That fusion of jazz and blues was also taking the form of another rising style called funk that grew out of the work of James Brown, Sly Stone, and other soul stars and became an indisputable part of jazz when Herbie Hancock and the Headhunters released the hit "Watermelon Man" in 1973. As happened in Philadelphia, Dallas, and Los Angeles, funk developed out of jazz/blues fusions in the Pacific Northwest and drew a mixed-race audience. In a few years, one version of that new sound would debut in Portland as the Jeff Lorber Fusion—a group that eventually included Seattle saxophonist Kenny G.

Those fusions were built on the R&B that had been one of the bedrock sounds in the Pacific Northwest since the early 1940s. In addition, musicians who came of age in Seattle in the 1960s had grown up on a mix of jazz, R&B, and gospel music on local radio stations KZAM and KYAC. Funk joined the organ trios that had grown out of soul jazz in the late 1950s and early '60s. Notable among those organ bands was a mixed-race Seattle trio with Billy Tolles, Oscar Holden, Jr., and Tommy Adams. Despite the rhythmic foundation of funk and soul-jazz, however, young listeners were increasingly turning to rock music.

HITTING BOTTOM

"Rock was really starting to push jazz out of the clubs," recalls broadcaster Jim Wilke, "so about 1965...[we] started the Seattle Jazz Society. We wanted to both create gigging opportunities for local musicians and to promote performances by them." And they did. With sponsorship from Rainier Brewing, they produced concerts at Seward Park that paired local musicians with national acts such as Herbie Hancock, Miles Davis, and Cannonball Adderley. In 1970, in partnership with Chuck Metcalf, the Society opened a club called The Jazz Gallery in the space previously occupied by Llahngaelhyn and inaugurated jazz cruises on the Virginia V steamship.[19]

It turned out that rock wasn't the real enemy, however. It was the economy. And those Seattle jazz initiatives sank along with it.

Due to the simultaneous decline in military spending, slowing of the space program, national recession of 1969–70, and Boeing's debt as it built the 747 airliner, the company and the Puget Sound area, home to several military bases, suffered a severe downturn. When Seattle unemployment hit 14 percent and Boeing went from 83,700 employees to 20,750, a billboard appeared near Sea-Tac airport that read: "Will the last person leaving Seattle please turn out the lights."

Urban renewal in Portland continued to favor real estate and banking interests over community needs, and the construction that had taken out the heart of the Williams Avenue entertainment district in 1958 was followed in 1970 by the destruction of nearly three hundred homes and businesses in North Portland when the city and expansion-minded Legacy Emanuel Hospital razed the residential center of the city's African American community. Much of the land was left undeveloped for years.

So it's apt that Mel Brown, who cut his teeth in the Williams Avenue jam sessions and grew up in that neighborhood, should set the local jazz scene on the road back to the popularity of earlier times when he returned to his hometown in 1973. The Puget Sound area would have to wait a few years for a similar revival.

Built for the World's Fair in 1962, Seattle's Space Needle represented a city leaving its past behind. That upward trajectory was interrupted by a devastating economic downturn in the early 1970s that severely reduced jazz activity.

4

The Renaissance: 1973–1982

"When I first moved to town, a friend said, 'Go to the Jazz Quarry every chance you get and hear Eddie Wied. Meet Eddie Wied, watch Eddie Wied.' So there I was, sitting right by Eddie's side, watching his fingers on the keyboard."

Mark Simon

ZERO TO SIXTY IN EIGHT YEARS

"When I first got back to town, there was nothing going on. I couldn't even find a jam session." Mel Brown was shocked by what had happened to the scene he'd left more than a decade ago. He'd toured with the Temptations, the Four Tops, Martha and the Vandellas, and Diana Ross and the Supremes; recorded with George Harrison; and played the Apollo Theater. And he was about to leave town again, when his mother intervened. "Don't run from the problem," she told him. "Do something about it." So Brown decided to jump-start the scene himself. First he brought a trio into Fracasso's Prima Donna, a downtown restaurant. Brown started on a Wednesday; by Friday, there was a line out front. It was 1973, and the jazz renaissance was underway.

Two years later, tired of struggling with club owners over pay and other issues, he opened Mel Brown's Drum Shop and was busy selling equipment and teaching—as well as sweeping the sidewalk, painting, and doing the books. It finally became too much, since he'd also started to tour with Diana Ross again. He closed the shop and returned to performing full-time.

Still, Brown was torn. Sometimes he wanted to leave Portland and go back on the road, or even move to Los Angeles for studio work; other days he'd think about what he'd gained by returning home. "I like being back here, I really dig my family. This is the greatest time of my life right now," he'd say.

When Mel Brown came back to his hometown in 1973, he couldn't even find a jam session. He decided to jump-start the scene himself, and two years later, a jazz renaissance was underway.

He had already lived the jet set dream—he didn't need to do it again. But there were frustrations in Portland that included the ups and downs of the nightclub business and the dearth of well-rehearsed ensembles. The biggest difficulty he faced, however, was the common misperception that he was "just a local musician" unworthy of the same pay and respect that promoters and audiences gave to outsiders. Other artists in the Pacific Northwest faced the same problem, and sometimes even harbored that provincial inferiority complex themselves.

Not Brown. Always striving for excellence, he soon started putting together the Mel Brown Sextet, a hard bop ensemble modeled on Art Blakey's Jazz Messengers. The group played a southeast Portland club called The Hobbit regularly in the 1980s, honing their repertoire and approach. "I base all my other bands on that band," said Sextet trumpet player and Grammy winner Thara Memory. "We started a five-day-a-week, two-and-a-half-hour-a-day thing, and we trained. I mean, these are professionals, [but] we trained like animals."

Eventually, the group produced a critically acclaimed album and won a nationwide competition that landed them an opening slot at the Playboy Jazz Festival

Mel Brown: The Golden Thread

In the sprawling tapestry of jazz in the Pacific Northwest, one thread stands out from the rest, a single strand that pulls them all into a pattern: Mel Brown. The drummer and bandleader has lived the whole story; trace his trajectory through the years, and you'll touch nearly every important moment of jazz in Portland. He embodies the history, carries it forward with him, and has passed it along through exemplary musicianship and teaching—as well as through his son, bandleader and drummer Christopher Brown. Other musicians in the region have been equally influential, but Brown's career is unique.

It began when he was a fifteen-year-old high school freshman and a couple of top neighborhood musicians took an interest.

"Bobby Bradford and Cleve Williams would wait for me after school," Brown remembers, "and I'd go over to Cleve's house and they'd show me how to set up certain figures with the Walter Bridges Big Band."

On Brown's first paying job, with the Marianne Mayfield Trio, he also learned from Julian Henson, the trio's pianist and one of the region's top instrumentalists since the late 1930s. Brown was further schooled by many other players who frequented James Benton's converted garage on Williams Avenue.

"I wanted to play good," Brown said, "and I was always trying to play catch-up, so I worked extra hard. I've always been a hyper kid; I've always just worked."

Indeed. While attending Portland State University and playing with Billy Larkin and the Delegates in the mid-1960s, Brown got a day job at the Social Security Administration; in the 1970s, he ran the Mel Brown Drum Shop while performing full-time; and since the 1980s, he's run Metropolitan Accounting and Tax as well as played five nights a week.

Brown made his first record with Portlander Billy Larkins's trio *(Pigmy)*, went on the road with Earl Grant's organ trio, and then began a long association with Motown when he was hired by Martha Reeves of Martha and the Vandellas. He toured and recorded with the Temptations, the Supremes, and others *(The Temptations Live at London's Talk of the Town; The Temptations Live at the Copa; TCB* with the Temptations and the Supremes; and *The Magnificent 7* with the Supremes and the Four Tops). By the time he was thirty, Brown had hung with the Beatles in London, lived like a jet-setter, and come home again to jump-start the local jazz scene, where he's been a central force ever since.

Though he continued touring occasionally with Diana Ross (taking along his young Portland bandmates George Mitchell and Phil Baker), at home he was building the Mel Brown Sextet, a hard bop group modeled on Art Blakey's Jazz Messengers. They made a record *(Gordon Bleu: The Mel Brown Sextet Plays the Music of Gordon Lee)* and opened the Playboy Jazz Festival in 1989. He also teamed with legendary bassist Leroy Vinnegar for trio and quartet work at the city's top clubs, and then created the Mel Brown B3 Organ Group, whose grooves recalled the organ trios he'd worked with in his youth. That band helped launch the local funk-jazz movement of the mid-1990s.

Today, Brown leads bands three nights a week at Jimmy Mak's, the city's premier nightclub, where he has performed for seventeen years and whose stage bears his name. He helped shape the club's music policy in discussions with owner Jim Makarounis. And Brown's son's band, The Chris Brown Quartet, follows his father's Quartet at Jimmy Mak's every Wednesday.

Brown was named Portland's Jazz Hero for 2015 by the Jazz Journalists Association. He's performed several times with the Oregon Symphony. Brown is a member of the Jazz Society of Oregon's Hall of Fame, has served on the board of the Mt. Hood Jazz Festival, and founded the Mel Brown Summer Jazz Workshop at Western Oregon University, where many student players learn directly from working professionals, including the Grammy-winning Esperanza Spalding.

Trace Mel Brown's trajectory through the years, and you'll touch nearly every important moment of jazz in Portland. Here he's leading his Septet (pianist Gordon Lee not pictured).

in the Hollywood Bowl. At the same time, the band released the album *Gordon Bleu: The Mel Brown Sextet Plays the Music of Gordon Lee*. All the compositions were by pianist Lee, who left the East Coast in 1977 for Portland, which he calls "the most beautiful place in the world."

During those years, Brown started a bookkeeping business that he's maintained even beyond his seventieth birthday. Running a small business offers a measure of independence to musicians in small markets. This was what he'd sought with the Drum Shop, but the one-man operation at Metropolitan Accounting and Tax was a better fit for him personally. Such day jobs integrate musicians directly within their communities. Artists are perceived as part of a neighborhood when they also prepare taxes, teach the kids, sell computer gear, or work in an office.

Not all high-level artists were so practical. Vocalist Nancy King returned to Eugene in 1975 after nearly a decade in San Francisco. She'd been singing at the fabled Jazz Workshop, then spent some years on the road and even performed in Playboy Clubs. She had three children with saxophonist Sonny King, though the relationship didn't last. She often made the 250-mile round-trip drive to Portland for performances, and though she was a single mother living in poverty, King was so dedicated to her art that she passed up several record deals that weren't to her liking. King's choices offer a striking contrast to those made by Marianne Mayfield a decade earlier.

Considered one of the top vocalists in the country by many critics and performers, King set a standard matched at that time by few other singers in the region. Such consummate artists helped reinforce the pride in craftsmanship and technical competence that characterizes the Pacific Northwest approach.

"This town has such a wonderful tradition and such great players. The education I got at Delevan's and some of those clubs, you couldn't buy at Juilliard," says Phil Baker (far left, with Antonio Hart, Jimmy Cobb, Nat Adderley, and Bill Beach).

The abundance of jazz in the late 1970s was especially notable in Portland, where it grew along with the activities of the fledgling Jazz Society of Oregon (JSO) and its more established counterpart in Seattle. Founded by a small band of enthusiasts in 1973, the same year Mel Brown returned to Portland, the JSO drew such large crowds to its events that club owners began to take note and booked more jazz themselves. The group started its annual First Jazz concerts in 1975, sponsored jazz picnics with live performances, produced a monthly newsletter, and promoted tours by national stars. A volunteer organization, it's another example of the region's DIY spirit: a small group of people who wanted to hear more jazz found ways to make it happen. Both jazz fans and musicians benefitted.

By 1981, Portland had more live jazz than any other West Coast city. Out of 150 establishments offering live music, forty-eight were presenting jazz in some form or another, from solo piano to big band, according to *The First Book of Oregon Jazz, Rock, and All Sorts of Music*.[1] By that time, both Jazz Alley and Parnell's had opened in Seattle with nationally touring acts every week, so the renaissance was now well underway in both cities.

Nancy King at Sixty-Seven

It's her sixty-seventh birthday, and Nancy King is singing. High cheekbones, big smile, a wicked laugh. Won Miss News Photographer in 1958. Grew up on a mint farm, knowing jazz had chosen her. She started out playing drums—you can hear it when she scats—but Nancy was called to sing.

She had perfect pitch, see, so she was always right. And she was just as sure about civil rights when asked to leave to leave the University of Oregon for standing with the few black students there. So she headed to San Francisco, sang bebop with Dizzy and Miles, performed with Seattle's Pony Poindexter, and met her future partner, the wild saxophonist Sonny King.

And what a long, strange trip it's been: Playboy Clubs, singing in Vegas, on world stages, but always hand-to-mouth, it seemed. Always insisting on being who she is, whether in struggle or triumph, like the night of her sixty-seventh birthday.

Picture her there, on a stool, surrounded by admirers. Of course the song she's singing is "Four."

"Of the wonderful things you get out of life there are four," she sang, "They may not be many, but nobody needs any more. Truth, honor, and happiness, and truth takes the lead . . .

"And to relax knowing the gist of life, it's truth you need.

"Then the second is honor, and happiness makes number three. Put them all together, you know what that last one must be:

"So to truth, honor, and happiness, add one thing more—meaning wonderful, wonderful love, that'll make it four.

"And there ain't no more," she'd add in a hipster moan. It was her own crazy signature.

At that moment, she had 'em all—truth, honor, happiness, and all the love she'd need, on a stool surrounded by admiring musicians. Hair in a ponytail, she shouted, encouraging her sidemen, and told funny stories with a wicked laugh. She leaped tall buildings in a single breath, scatted speeding bullets, and built momentum like a freight train.

She's one of the world's best, after all; Grammy-nominated, though it had been a long time coming and wasn't enough. Nothing could be—except when she was singing.

It couldn't be enough after the life she'd been leading. Once, behind on rent, she almost lost her house; phone cut off, too, though she'd just recorded with the Metropole Orchestra of the Netherlands and played big festivals in Europe and Israel. And her teeth were still bad. And she'd raised three kids single-handedly, driving from Eugene to Portland just to sing, and then back in the wee hours for a day job that made her sad and sick inside.

And she'll tell you that tale of woe, too, then laugh about it. "Playin' my tiny violin again," she says, because she understands why things worked out the way they did.

"I don't like decisions being made for me," she says.

She's lived the way she wanted, and still believes in justice. "I'm confident the universe is taking care of me 'cause I'm doing what I'm supposed to be. Wouldn't trade my life for security. I'd rather be me than anybody."

But talent alone won't pay the rent, and truth doesn't always bring honor to even the best. She didn't want to be told what to do, nor marketed like candy, so it was uphill all the way for Nancy.

Yet the truth did bring her happiness when she was honored by peers in her hometown. And she'd better be happy with who she is, because it's lonely out there—except when she sings, the world disappears, and Nancy's surrounded by friends and admirers, a reward for following the jazz path, being just who she should be, and staying steadfast.

Like the song says, "Let your voice be heard, spread the word . . . and take a tip from me, the world's everything it ought to be . . . as long as you're sure, there's no more to life than the same old four."

"And there ain't no more," added Nancy on her sixty-seventh birthday.

Grammy-nominated singer Nancy King grew up playing drums on a Willamette Valley mint and wheat farm. She's pictured here with long-time musical partner Glen Moore.

YOUTH MOVEMENT

Another factor driving the growth of jazz in the Pacific Northwest in the 1970s was the emergence of younger players, many the products of fledgling jazz studies programs at colleges and universities. Most jazz artists who came of age in the 1970s and later have college training, and many have earned postgraduate degrees. At that time, however, student musicians often had professional mentors who connected them to the sound and practices of the previous era.

Artists such as Brown and Eddie Wied in Portland and Floyd Standifer, Buddy Catlett, and Don Lanphere in Seattle helped pass Pacific Northwest traditions along, as did dozens of teachers and informal mentors in smaller towns in the region. Those relationships were crucial to the preservation of a Pacific Northwest approach. Mel Brown, for instance, plucked pianist George Mitchell and bassist Phil Baker, both Oregon natives, right out of college to join him on the road with Diana Ross in 1980. They'd already been well prepared.

"Even going to Mt. Hood Community College in its heyday, when there were wonderful teachers, it would have been nothing if I hadn't been able, at the same time, to share the bandstand with Ron [Steen] and Tom [Grant] and some of those Portland people, along with Sonny Stitt and Joe Henderson." Bassist Phil Baker has strong feelings about such on-the-job training: "This town has such a wonderful tradition and such great players.... The education I got at Delevan's and some of those clubs, you couldn't buy at Juilliard—not just the luminaries but local greats like Warren Bracken and Eddie Wied, who just had this grace you can't buy. You had to experience it to assimilate it. Jazz has to be handed down [that way] because there's so much that goes into jazz other than notes.

"And the characters! Jim Pepper... you can't find characters like that anymore." Baker said. "If you're up there on the bandstand with Les McCann... something hits your DNA and you assimilate some of that grace they're putting out there, grace they assimilated from *their* mentors. It's an oral tradition being passed down."

Mt. Hood Community College (MHCC), where Baker and Mitchell studied, was a hotbed of jazz in the late 1970s and early 1980s, and the group of young players who came together there (as did their counterparts at the Cornish Institute of Allied Arts in Seattle) went on to have a big impact on jazz in the Pacific Northwest. Located outside the Portland suburb of Gresham, looking east toward the Sandy River and Mount Hood, MHCC turned out a number of first-call regional musicians. Some passed through on their way to New York, such as bassist and educator Ben Wolfe, who became a member of Harry Connick Jr.'s and Wynton Marsalis's bands and a teacher at the Juilliard School. Trumpet player Chris Botti also attended the college on his road to stardom. Others, including drummer Gary Hobbs, a Pacific Northwest native who left MHCC for the Stan Kenton Band, later returned to the area to become top local performers.

One of the most accomplished of those MHCC alumni is pianist Steve Christofferson, whose resume includes a Grammy-nominated album with Nancy King and the Metropole Orchestra of the Netherlands. Born and raised in Seattle, Christofferson came to Portland in 1974, planning to get a two-year degree and return north. He never did: "After being down here for a couple of months, I got the feeling this was the best place for me," he said. "Love, employment, opportunity to learn and listen to the musicians around Portland—they all kept me here. It's the same water, almost the same climate... and the more I traveled, the more I liked the idea of spending most of my time and raising my family here."

The perception that the Pacific Northwest was a good place to raise a family grew; in a few years' time, that image would attract players with established reputations. Meanwhile, more young players were coming from afar, including Chicago native Mark Simon. He enrolled at MHCC in 1979 and was soon pianist for the college's big band that performed at the first Mt. Hood Festival of Jazz. His real classroom, however, was the Jazz Quarry, a Portland club where "the Professor" Eddie Wied played several times a week. One of the clubs that booked jazz exclusively, the Quarry presented nationally touring stars as well as Wied's Sky Trio, and it was a gathering place for Portland's jazz community. For many young musicians in the late 1970s and '80s, playing the Jazz Quarry was a rite of passage.

A RITE OF PASSAGE

"I spent most of my time on Sunday nights attending the jam session at the Quarry," Mark Simon recalls. "I wanted to soak up knowledge from the old pros along with a great bunch of young players willing to learn. A significant moment in my life was when I met Leroy Vinnegar for the first time at a Jazz Quarry Sunday night jam!"

Promoter Brad Winter, cofounder of the Creative Music Guild, also remembers the Quarry as "a happening place. It had that warm 'lived-in feel' so typical of Portland dens in the '70s and early '80s: no pretensions, cheap highballs, all-you-can-eat pizza buffets. It was up close and personal." At the club's threshold, inlaid tiles spelled out "The Mural Room," its previous name.

"The best hang on a Sunday night," guitarist Matt Schiff remembers. "For me and many others, it was pivotal." Ben Wolfe also got his first real jazz experience there: "I was the underage bass player who was always there—had my own stool at the entrance to the pizza side. I worked at the Quarry every week.... The Jazz Quarry was a huge part of my world; I never missed a Sunday."

Portland was home to several other clubs whose booking of both local and touring acts contributed to the city's jazz renaissance, including Chuck's Steak House, PC&S Tavern, and Ray's Helm. They also gave younger players an opportunity to develop on the bandstand. In Seattle such opportunities were fewer, and Parnell's, the city's main jazz club at the time, primarily booked nationally touring stars who were backed by the house trio. So in the Puget Sound area in the 1970s, the best opportunity for young jazz musicians to play with veterans was in school.

THE GENERATION OF '79 MEETS THE MASTERS

Jazz programs in colleges and universities helped change the image of jazz as an outlaw music, but it took a while. When Portland pianist Pat George was a student at the University of Portland in 1950, he and his colleagues Cleve Williams and Bobby Bradford had to "sneak off to some little room to have a jam session. All of us got thrown out half the time because of it."

And as the controversial tenure and firing of Joe Brazil at the University of Washington showed, that battle was still ongoing. But not everywhere. Nearby, a private arts college was building a jazz program that in time would help to transform Seattle from a bastion of the straight-ahead to a hotbed of the avant-garde.

In 1977, the Cornish School of Allied Arts, Seattle's oldest music school, gained full accreditation, became The Cornish Institute of Allied Arts, and began offering a bachelor's degree in fine arts. Trumpeter and educator Jim Knapp had been

One of Seattle's rising stars in the late 1970s, bassist Chuck Deardorf got his on-the-job training with Jackson Street veterans.

working toward that end since 1971, gathering a group of well-known professional jazz players as faculty. They included bassist Gary Peacock, vocalist Jay Clayton, drummer Jerry Granelli, saxophonist Denney Goodhew, and trombonist Julian Priester. The faculty attracted high-level students, and around the college coalesced what Paul de Barros has called "the Generation of '79." That group also included musicians who had studied elsewhere, such as pianists Randy Halberstadt, Dave Peck, and Marc Seales, and bassist Chuck Deardorf. Not coincidentally, they are among the region's elite players today. But they didn't get there straight from the classroom.

"They'd come up through the schools, through the universities; they were the young bucks. But they didn't have any sense of where they were in terms of the jazz tradition that existed here," de Barros observes. That should be no surprise, since they grew up during the dark ages for jazz in the region.

"Then a few of them hooked up with Don Lanphere. And they connected to Bud Shank and Floyd Standifer. And they started to see, 'Oh, this music wasn't invented twelve years ago by John Coltrane and Joe Zawinul. There's actually people around who played the music.' Marc [Seales] particularly. He'd hang out with Buddy Catlett, who worked with Quincy Jones and Louis Armstrong."

As the years went on, the mentors began to hire their students, and so the tradition that had developed along Jackson Street and in Pioneer Square was passed along by artists such as Lanphere, who offered experience that wasn't available in school.

Lanphere returned to Seattle in 1982, a changed man who had finally beaten his drug addition after twenty years in Wenatchee with a newfound Christian faith. Young musicians were drawn to him because he'd played and recorded with Charlie Parker and Fats Navarro during bebop's heroic age—and because of his kindness and generosity. "The image of Don Lanphere that will remain in my heart," wrote *Earshot Jazz* editor John Gilbreath, "is of him on the bandstand—but not playing.... That look on his face while listening to someone else play...that singular countenance of dignified joy, especially if that person had been his student....[He was] a master at encouraging and appreciating growth in others."[2]

Bud Shank came to the Pacific Northwest to reinvent himself as a jazz saxophonist after abandoning the LA studios in the early 1980s. "I had to prove to myself that I could still do it, and I had to prove to other people that I was capable of it."

Lanphere resumed his career as a high-level performer, too, touring Europe and Asia and making albums with former Seattle guitarist Larry Coryell and saxophonist Bud Shank. At the time, Shank ran the Centrum Jazz Workshop in Port Townsend, on the Olympic Peninsula, and Lanphere taught there for a couple weeks every summer.

Shank took a special interest in the music of "Generation of '79" pianist Dave Peck and recorded an album of the young man's compositions, then performed them in concert at the Jackson Street Theater in what was once the city's African American entertainment district. Shank, who'd already had a long career, had come to the Pacific Northwest to reinvent himself. He intended to become the jazz alto saxophonist he had always wanted to be, not the flute-playing studio musician he'd become.

Before making that move, Shank's life had been a struggle to escape the bounds of one box or another. He felt trapped in the symphonic ponderousness of Stan Kenton's Innovations in Modern Music Orchestra, found the strictures of West Coast jazz too formulaic and restrained, and then moved into artistically limited studio work for fifteen years. Escaping from there, he found himself in the equally restrictive framework of the L.A. Four, a commercially successful chamber jazz group. He was angry and frustrated. He owned classic sports cars and a sailboat, but felt he was dying as an artist.

When the L.A. Four broke up, Shank realized he didn't need to live in Los Angeles anymore and turned his Porsche north. "My whole philosophy about music changed when I came out of the studios and got rid of the flutes," he said. So he started over—at the bottom. "I was almost sixty years old and went back to working one-hundred-dollar jobs in little joints in Bend, Oregon. I had to prove to myself that I could still do it, and I had to prove to other people that I was capable of it."

His interest in helping young players grew when he took a post at the Port Townsend Jazz Festival. Soon the new Bud Shank Jazz Workshop was enrolling

Milt Jackson at Parnell's, also known as "Roy's Living Room," a Pioneer Square jazz club operated by Roy Parnell from 1976 to 1980.

more than two hundred students and employing more than twenty faculty musicians every summer.

"It's our duty to pass on what we have learned," he said. "The art form is so fragile anyway, and if there aren't enough of us holding up the good, important principles of what was established before us, from an artistic standpoint, it really is going to go in the toilet."

With the experience shared by such mentors, the musicians who came of age in the late 1970s and early 1980s formed the base for what would become another golden age in the 1990s. That mentoring was vital, providing bandstand and business experience for the increasing number of young players trained in college programs. Fortunately, when jazz artists find themselves in academic roles, their first thought is to put performance at the heart of the curriculum, as did Joe Brazil. Clarinetist and composer Bill Smith, who was hired to run the Contemporary Group, the university's New Music ensemble in the classical tradition, played a different role at the University of Washington. (On his classical recordings, he was called "William O. Smith"; his jazz albums, including one he made with the Dave Brubeck Octet, billed him as "Bill Smith.") While leading the Contemporary Group, Smith also led a small ensemble playing experimental jazz in Pioneer Square clubs. He kept those worlds separate, whereas Joe Brazil tried to bring the nightclub into the academy. Both, however, contributed to the revitalization of jazz in Seattle, and for a while, Pioneer Square came alive again with jazz venues such as Merchants Café and the Bombay Bicycle Shop.[3]

Parnell's in the Late 1970s

Paul de Barros, *Seattle Times,* February 7, 2015

Roy's living room.

That's how jazz fans still lovingly refer to Parnell's, the Pioneer Square jazz club operated by Roy Parnell from 1976 to 1980.

A restless entrepreneur, Parnell started the club because he was inspired by the success—and design—of the Portland club, Jazz de Opus, owned by his wife's cousin. Seating 125, the club had brick walls, large cushions, and Tiffany-style lamps suspended over the tables. Airbrushed portraits of jazz musicians adorned the walls. The owner created the illusion of a low ceiling by suspending two-by-twelve-foot beams, painted flat black, across the room.

"Roy accidentally made the place sound really great," recalled Jimmy Manolides, a hipster raconteur whose stories behind the bar were often as entertaining as the music. "The sound would go up through those two-by-twelves and rattle around up above there and come back down, so it was like a big radiator of sound. The musicians said, to a man, 'We've never played in a place that sounds this good.'"

"I don't know if there ever was a more comfortable jazz club," recalled Jim Wilke, host of *Jazz After Hours*. "It was always like a party in Roy's living room."

Many name players in the '70s hired local rhythm sections there, a boon for Seattle players, said pianist Dave Peck. "It was really influential in the history of the scene," he said. "It was where we could essentially go to school together. It not only became a really great gig for us all, but it was the driving force for us to get better at playing."

In 1980, wanting to spend more time with his family, Mr. Parnell sold the club to Marv Thomas, a former big-band trumpet player whose son, trumpeter and saxophonist Jay Thomas, is a fixture on the local jazz scene. Thomas in turn sold the venue two years later to a group of four investors that included Seattle singer Ernestine Anderson, who renamed it Ernestine's. In 1983, the club closed, in bankruptcy.

ECOTOPIA

What drew Bill Smith to Seattle was the environment. He'd been living in Rome, Italy, and had no interest in teaching until the dean of music at the University of Washington, William Bergsma, convinced him to give it a shot. "Bill was very persuasive," he recalled, "so I came to have a look at Seattle one sunny day, and I thought, 'Gee, this place is gorgeous!' I also like fishing—the Modern Jazz Quartet used to go out of their way to play in Seattle because they loved the fishing here."[4] The natural beauty and recreational opportunities were becoming an important factor in attracting jazz musicians to the Pacific Northwest.

"I always wanted to live at the end of the road leading downtown," says drummer Larry Whitney. In the mid-1970s, the California native's home was an unfinished house he shared with his wife and two young children. He was building it himself above the north fork of the Washougal River, a long drive into the city, where he was working with jazz and blues bands. Around Portland and Puget Sound in those days, however, you could live in a remote forest setting and still be downtown in an hour. Whitney remained active on the jazz scene until he took a full-time job with the State of Oregon testing water from streams and rivers.

Whitney was also an avid fisherman, and the quality of the water he was testing has played a big part in creating a public perception of the Pacific Northwest as a kind of "ecotopia" (a word first popularized by Ernest Callenbach's 1975 novel of the same name). It was more fantasy than reality.

Whitney's well was polluted due to upstream disturbances caused by his neighbor's construction. In the 1970s, when air quality was at its worst, he'd drive into a blanket of smog as he descended from the foothills on his way to work. Portland's raw sewage flowed into the Willamette River until the 1960s, and paper mills dumped dioxin until even later. For almost one hundred years, ASARCO (the American Smelting and Refining Company) operated a copper smelter in Tacoma. Air pollution from the smelter settled on the surface soil over more than one thousand square miles in the Nisqually basin; arsenic, lead, and other heavy metals are still in the soil. In the 1970s and '80s, logging in the region's national forests proceeded at a record pace, and only environmental lawsuits and civil disobedience were able to slow it in the 1990s. Off-road vehicles and a network of unused logging roads continue to further degrade the streams, and logging remains heavy on private lands, where herbicides are sprayed extensively. Numerous federally implemented "Superfund" environmental cleanup sites lurk in Portland and the cities of Puget Sound.

In Callenbach's novel, the West Coast secedes from the US to form its own country whose citizens have shifted to renewable energy and structured their lives around sustainable living. Seattle University professor David McCloskey started using the term "Cascadia" for the region in the late 1970s, linking "Cascadia, land of falling waters," to what he perceived as an emerging "sociocultural unity"—values shared by a significant number of the region's inhabitants, including many jazz performers. It was an overly optimistic analysis, but that image has shaped public perception of the Pacific Northwest and has attracted a number of leading jazz artists over the years. And despite the damage done to the environment, easy access to the relatively unspoiled natural world remains the region's most attractive quality.

Larry Whitney's fly rod took the place of his drumsticks when he went to work for the state, and he only got back into playing professionally after retiring. Many like him have contributed to the character of the jazz community in the Pacific Northwest, choosing to live in rural areas and commute to the city or pursue other lines of work. Such part-time musicians were able to find performance opportunities because of an abundance of jobs during the jazz revival of the late 1970s and early '80s.

And speaking of fishing, one of the key young players emerging in Portland was bassist Dave Captein, a Portland native who attended Western Washington University in Bellingham before returning to his hometown. A recreational fisherman who did most of his trolling for salmon in Tillamook Bay, Captein keeps a wildlife camera outside his family's cabin on the forested slopes of Mount Hood. He shares the footage of bears and wildcats with bandmates.

Such experiences aren't expressed explicitly in the music of the region's jazz artists; Captein isn't consciously mimicking the bear in his bass lines. But the natural world does draw and hold a certain kind of musician—the kind that values lifestyle over fortune and spends days off fishing.

VOLATILE JAZZ MARKET

One of the reasons Captein skipped Seattle, where work was scarce, was the ready availability of jobs in Portland in the early 1980s. Jazz was more likely to be heard in other Oregon cities as well, at venues like the Eugene Hotel (seven nights a week) and Boon's Treasury in Salem. Even smaller towns got in on the action, including Bend, where a three-day jazz festival was staged annually for three years, and Jacksonville, home of the annual Britt Music Festival which included jazz. At the Oregon Zoo in Portland, the Your Zoo and All That Jazz summer concert series began in 1979—Mel Brown led an all-star band in its debut concert—and the first annual Cathedral Park Jazz Festival was held in 1981.

Boosters were calling Portland "Kansas City on the Willamette" in those years: a medium-sized city in an economically depressed time with more jazz per capita than anywhere outside New York. At least that was the claim. Accurate or not, it was a sign of the positive, hopeful attitude that was developing in the region. The abundant jazz activity would continue for several more years. But the ups and downs of the food and beverage industry, to which most live jazz was tied, guaranteed instability as one club closed while another opened, and one cancelled its music while another decided to give jazz a try.

Nevertheless, in the early 1980s, as guitarist Dan Balmer observed, "Portland was a place where even jazz musicians could afford to buy a house." Perhaps it was the national recession, felt acutely in the Pacific Northwest, where more than half of the timber industry jobs disappeared between 1950 and 1980. But government assistance was available, and prices were low enough to make home ownership possible for musicians. Affordable housing has often been cited as a factor in determining where artists congregate and arts activity is most prolific.

Although the community retained the spirit of cooperation and mutual assistance that had developed in previous generations, the competition that is always part of music was increasing—especially with the young players coming out of jazz studies programs, as Seattle bassist and bandleader Pete Leinonen learned.

Leinonen was an established bandleader by 1980. He'd come of age in the early 1960s in what was left of the Jackson Street scene, passed through the Llahngaelhyn jam sessions, and was at the forefront of the jazz renaissance centered around Pioneer Place with Bill Smith in the 1970s. A versatile musician, Leinonen has played a variety of styles, from trad jazz to funk, and he always paid careful attention to the business side. Consequently, he was able to keep his groups, including the New Seattle Three, working steadily.

"I worked a year at The Smuggler with that trio," Leinonen recalled. And it was an excellent group. Drummer Candy Finch, for instance, had been in the house band at Blue Note Records in New York and worked five years with Dizzy Gillespie before settling in Seattle. Leinonen filled the club with nontraditional jazz listeners by putting fliers in hotels and restaurants to draw tourists. "It was a dream job," Leinonen said, "and we were on our third contract when the Cornish kids caught on and begged the owner to hire them for less money... and so one Cornish band followed another, each time the crowds getting smaller and smaller, until the owner begged me to come back... but I had moved on to other gigs by then."

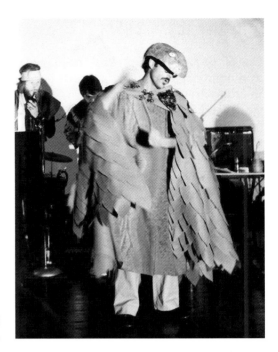

Rich Halley led the growing Portland avant-garde community in the 1980s.

And he did quite well, too, working bands in what he called the society and corporate markets. "We made it a point to learn every request, [and] booked as many as three hundred dates some years," he recalls.[5] His view of "the Cornish bands" indicates an older ethos and musical approach.

After more than fifty years on the scene, Leinonen has concluded that there is a distinct sound that's characteristic of Pacific Northwest jazz. "I have always heard a subtle Northwest quality in our most innovative recording artists," he says. "And I've noticed that the best Seattle arrangers, though influenced by bebop, used a less dissonant approach."[6] That seemed to be the rule in the region during those years, anyway: the more dissonant the music, the smaller the audience.

And yet, both the Cornish Institute and the University of Washington favored that more dissonant approach. And a smaller avant-garde community was growing in Portland, too, led by saxophonist Rich Halley, who went on to make a series of critically acclaimed recordings. He started performing with drummer Dave Storrs and other area improvisers, and they had some success at attracting a younger, open-minded audience.

True to the region's DIY approach, Storrs started a record company and began producing albums that captured some of the experimental energy of the day. Portland's Creative Music Guild—an important presenter of internationally known avant-garde artists—was founded during those years, and the Portland Center for the Visual Arts, founded in 1971, also presented some cutting-edge concerts. By 1982, straight-ahead and avant-garde styles, funk, and blues could all find audiences interested in what they were doing. It had taken a while, but jazz appeared to have more than just its head above water—it was leaping in the sunlight like a killer whale.

Dave Storrs started a record company and began producing albums that captured some of the experimental energy of the day.

JAZZ FUSIONS

Jazz fusion gathered momentum in the Pacific Northwest in 1976, when Jeff Lorber moved to Portland and developed a beat-heavy, funky-but-sweet sound that later morphed into smooth jazz. His bandmate Lester McFarland first introduced thumb-slapping electric bass to the city, and Lorber also gave saxophonist Kenny G his start. It was an exciting time.

Lorber's sound was based on the soul-jazz and organ-trio traditions and the Latin-based boogaloo, styles he'd been exposed to in his native Philadelphia. In Portland, the R&B popular in the region since the 1940s also touched him. Those roots didn't seem to be what attracted younger listeners, however; most were simply drawn to the new sound of the day. The clubs where it was presented, including Ray's Helm in Portland, also booked the more progressive sounds of David Friesen and John Stowell, the singer-pianist Jeannie Hoffman, and the straight-ahead band Freebop. At the time, that kind of variety at a single venue was not uncommon.

In fact, by the early 1980s, a number of Portland clubs were presenting multiple genres, reprising the kind of mix one might have heard on Williams Avenue or Jackson Street in the early 1950s. Young people often chose a club itself as a destination, secure in knowing the vibe would be consistent, whether it presented Latin, fusion, straight-ahead jazz, or blues played by emerging stars like Curtis Salgado. They knew their friends would be there too.

Versatile musicians played in multiple styles, including the likes of drummer William Thomas, who recorded with avant-gardist Rich Halley while also working with the straight-ahead Tom Grant Band. Seattle musicians such as Dave Lewis and Billy Tolles had moved easily between jazz and related styles, including early rock 'n' roll. And so the generation of jazz artists that came of age in the 1970s moved as easily between straight-ahead and fusion styles. Portland saxophonist Dennis Springer, for instance, released a straight-ahead jazz album right after the breakup of the funk band Pleasure, of which he'd been a key member since 1972.

Pleasure was one of the strongest of the singing R&B groups to follow the path laid out nationally by Sly and the Family Stone. They fused funk, soul, and jazz in albums that, for nearly half of the group's ten-year career, were produced by Wayne Henderson of the Crusaders, the band's mentor. On the first of those albums, 1975's *Dust Yourself Off*, the band is augmented by Crusaders keyboardist Joe Sample. The second, *Accept No Substitutes*, features "Ghettos of the Mind," a jazzy, mostly instrumental tune that was the first of the group's nine R&B chart hits. All the members of Pleasure, friends since childhood, were born and raised in Portland.

Pleasure became the definitive Pacific Northwest funk band of the era, and through the later activities of its members, that approach spread. Three of them—drummer Bruce Carter, bassist Nate Phillips, and guitarist Doug Lewis—formed the band Cool'r. Rock historian S. P. Clarke calls it the greatest funk band ever to play the region. But such fusion bands were merely branches on the Pacific Northwest jazz tree.

A PACIFIC NORTHWEST PIANO TRADITION

Despite their shared roots, the music of Pleasure was quite distant from the jazz trios that young Pacific Northwest pianists had been listening to at the Jazz Quarry.

"When I first moved to town, a friend said, 'Go to the Quarry every chance you get and hear Eddie Wied, meet Eddie Wied, watch Eddie Wied,'" Mark Simon recalls. "So there I was, sitting right by Eddie's side, watching his fingers on the keyboard."

"Eddie was an institution, a great musician and human being!" says guitarist Matt Schiff, who began listening to Wied in the early 1980s. Indeed, Wied was an iconic figure who contributed to the region's reputation as a place where nice guys finish first. "He never said anything negative about anyone" is high praise in the Pacific Northwest, and it was often applied to Wied.

The approach he practiced so compellingly came out of a long tradition in the Pacific Northwest. His primary teacher was Gene Confer, who had also been a mentor to many in Portland's earlier generation of modernists. Confer's influence was profound.

"Confer was my biggest influence," Wied said. "How could you not help sounding like Gene if you took lessons from him? The arrangements were irresistible.... Such lovely voicings. He inspired you. All of us that studied with him... sound a little bit like him."

Jean Ronne, who played at the Benson Hotel for thirty years, was another Confer student. "Without his guidance, I wouldn't be playing today," she said. Harry Gillgam agreed: "Gene was the major influence on my career.... He loaded me up on drills and those great chord forms and turnarounds, which I in turn teach my students."

Confer is another example of a typical Pacific Northwest jazz player. Among Portland's first resident modernists, he started performing in 1938 and made his reputation downtown at the Clover Club, where he led an all-white trio that often backed black stars such as Duke Ellington's former singer Ivie Anderson and tenor saxophone giant Ben Webster. Younger pianists, including Pat George, gathered to observe. "All he wanted was to get a beautiful sound out of the piano,"

When Eddie Wied returned to town in the 1970s, Portland had a new "professor." An iconic figure, he contributed to the region's reputation as a place where nice guys finish first.

said George. "He didn't really care if anyone knew how great he was. He could have been a big-time studio player in Hollywood... but he was happy teaching."[7]

Sounds a lot like Seattle's Jerry Gray, who left performing for a teaching career in the mid-1960s. Gray published a series of piano method books, and his influence persisted through the 1990s.

Confer's disciples were almost all white, but the Pacific Northwest piano sound was also influenced by black pianist Julian Henson, who worked in both Seattle and Portland. Called "the closest thing to Art Tatum" in the region by fellow musicians, he was another unsung local who appeared content to work outside the limelight. The sound of straight-ahead jazz piano in the Pacific Northwest developed under the influence of Jerry Gray, Gene Confer, and Julian Henson.

With so many Portland pianists under the Confer spell, it should be no surprise that Mel Brown put together his first trio at The Prima Donna with Harry Gillgam on piano, or that Brown played for several years at the Tuck Lung Restaurant in a trio with Pat George. And in 1986, when bassist Leroy Vinnegar moved to Portland and he and Brown formed a trio, it seemed natural that Wied disciple Mark Simon was with them on piano.

When the legendary Vinnegar arrived, it was only the beginning of the influx of established artists that, among other big changes, was about to affect jazz in the region by further enlarging the scope and depth of its tradition without altering its essence.

But first, jazz moved outdoors for a party.

The Mt. Hood Festival of Jazz began in 1982, hard on the heels of other outdoor summer festivals and jazz concert series. Building on the increasing activity in the region's nightclubs and restaurants, those events would help jazz in the Pacific Northwest's rapidly changing cities to come of age over the next ten years.

5

Coming of Age: 1983–1993

"In 1989, Seattle was becoming trendy.... In a few years, Newsweek *would put then-*Slate-*magazine-editor Michael Kinsley on its cover...clad in a yellow raincoat next to an open-mouthed salmon, with the headline: 'Swimming to Seattle: Everybody else is moving there. Should you?'"*

Ellis E. Conklin

"We had this generation of kids who went to Cornish...all avant-gardists. They'd play anything! They were inspired by Nirvana; they were inspired by anarchists. It was part of that flowering of musical culture that happened when all those guys were here. They were just playing whatever they wanted."

Paul de Barros

THE RISE OF SUMMER JAZZ FESTIVALS

"Now listen! This is a party, a chance for us to get together and tell each other something good about ourselves." Les McCann was preaching to a crowd of more than eight thousand from the stage at the second annual Mt. Hood Festival of Jazz in August 1983. "Can I get an 'Amen'?"

The "Amens" rang out that afternoon and through the years that followed, as the Pacific Northwest jazz community began to feel better than ever about the quantity and quality of music in the region. Jazz was indeed growing along with the population and economic base, despite the ups and downs for musicians, whose earnings were often dependent upon food and drink sales. And the big outdoor festivals were just the tip of the iceberg.

When the festival suddenly lost power during McCann's set, he needed no more than a drum kit, handclaps, and his unamplified voice to keep the crowd engaged until power was restored. It was the festival's best year, according to Wayne Thompson, a festival board member and editor of *Jazzscene*.

"They had VSOP with Herbie Hancock, Ron Carter, Wayne Shorter, Wynton and Branford Marsalis; Ahmad Jamal, Gerry Mulligan, Diane Schuur, Stan Getz, Mel Lewis Big Band, Joe Williams, Dexter Gordon, The Crusaders, Bobby Hutcherson, Sonny Rollins, Betty Carter..." He can recall every name—almost the whole history of jazz on stage during two days in August.

« The Waterfront Blues Festival helped bring attention to Portland as a music city. Its origins show how one city official can have a powerful effect on local culture.

The summer jazz series at the Oregon Zoo and the Woodland Park Zoo inspired a growing number of outdoor concerts at Willamette Valley and Puget Sound wineries. Over the years, jazz acts faded from programs that had once featured the music exclusively.

That lineup set high expectations, both for talent and for the money required to present such artists. It wasn't sustainable. "The reason those stars were there," Thompson says, was "a piece of good luck: the Kool Jazz Festival was in Seattle at the same time. So they were able to bring those artists down for just the performance fee."

Managers weren't so lucky in later years, and the festival ran in the red from then on. That was due in part to the board disbursing all proceeds to its producers, MHCC and the Gresham Chamber of Commerce, and relying on sponsor money and advance ticket sales to cover the next year's event. The strategy proved disastrous in 2002, when the festival lost three name sponsors and declared bankruptcy. With a new board, it became the Mt. Hood Jazz Festival and continued sporadically as a single-day event in downtown Gresham.

"Yes, they spent way too much money," observed Thompson. "On the other hand, in doing so, they created an event that was the equal if not superior to the Monterey Jazz Festival. No other festival in the country had the talent."

The Kool Jazz Festival didn't return to Seattle every year, but along with Jazz Alley, which scheduled top-selling artists every week, and other concerts in a variety of venues, it gave Seattle audiences the opportunity to hear touring headliners on a regular basis beginning in the early 1980s. And more festivals were on the way.

In addition to jazz, the Kool Jazz Festival also featured pop and soul stars of the day, such as Patti La Belle and Bobby Womack. It was a national trend, and by the 1990s the Mt. Hood festival was booking pop fusion acts like Spyro Gyra and Lee Ritenour. Their presence polarized the audience, but accounted in part for the large crowds during the years when the MHCC stadium resembled a beach party more than a concert setting. That was in fact a big part of the attraction.

"First, it was the experience of going out on a summer day, taking my blanket, getting in line way early, literally racing toward the coveted spot," said Thompson. He and his wife also got to know the people seated near them, since season ticket holders tended to return year after year. "So part of the attraction was just sitting there in the sun, the water pistols and beach balls and games of cards. But we did listen to the music. Then, if we got tired of it, or an act we didn't care about, we'd go back to the food. The food was the second thing. They had great restaurants. The third thing was big name talent."

Indeed, down on the grass with picnics spread, the music could sound like distant surf. Waves lapped the shore and invited some swimmers, but the real action was back among the blankets, where jazz was but a distant thunder.

The Mt. Hood festival was modeled on the Monterey Jazz Festival and meant to enhance Gresham's cultural identity and raise money for both the city's Chamber of Commerce and Mt. Hood Community College. Organizers selected jazz because they felt they'd have no problem with crowd control. They were right: despite the party atmosphere, the beach balls lofted above the crowd never seemed to disturb the gourmet picnics, and spray bottle fights never seemed to escalate. In addition, the festival generated a weeklong workshop for student musicians and an ancillary weekend of concerts in Gresham restaurants.

Like other jazz festivals, it was subsidized by donated facilities, and nearly six hundred volunteers performed an enormous amount of unpaid labor. The Mt. Hood festival was often described in those days as "a community event." Marriages took place on its stages, friends enjoyed annual reunions on multi-blanket encampments, and it became a summer destination for many fans.

The jazz festival format was an excellent model for music retailing: its forty-five-minute sets on several stages in a variety of styles offered something for everyone, all in one location, with food and beverages available. There seemed to be no better way to see so many headlining acts in one place at one time.

But there was—for *local* jazz. Portland's Cathedral Park Jazz Festival lacked the big names and ancillary attractions, but it had large leafy trees, views of the Willamette River, and a beautiful band shell in a grassy amphitheater. More importantly, admission was free. The volunteer-led event was held annually in a park created when neighborhood activists reclaimed wasteland under the soaring arches of the St. John's Bridge. Thousands came and went during those July weekends. Between sets, organizers passed the hat. Although the Cathedral Park Jazz Festival was like a neighborhood grocer compared to the one-stop megastore of Mt. Hood, both helped raise the music's profile, attract a wider range of listeners, and bring the jazz community together.

Jazz in the out-of-doors was not new, but in the 1980s and '90s, outdoor concerts and festivals gained great popularity, and many of those events became part of life in the Pacific Northwest. But to musicians like celebrated saxophonist Phil Woods, who learned his craft from the giants of a previous generation, the festivals weren't entirely good for jazz.

"European festivals are usually held indoors, in nice concert halls. They have outdoor things, with the same circus atmosphere, but they usually put groups like mine where they belong—they don't make us compete with Santana outdoors," Woods says. "After all, jazz was born in a brothel, and it is an intimate art form. Once you get too much bigger than life, you lose something in jazz."

The first outdoor jazz festival in the Pacific Northwest was the Bellevue Jazz Festival, which began in 1978 at Bellevue Community College under artistic director Jim Wilke. An annual event that featured acts on three stages concurrently, it stayed at the college until 1987, when it moved to a downtown city park. After three years, it moved back to the college again. It was sponsored by the City of Bellevue through its Parks Department at both locations, and it continued until 1993.

Many festivals during those years involved partnerships between nonprofits, city or county governments, and private businesses, including the first concert series of its kind in the region, Your Zoo and All That Jazz.

It debuted in 1979 at the Oregon Zoo and became the longest continuously running series of its type in the region. Seattle's Zoo Tunes at the Woodland Park Zoo followed in 1984. Today, neither features the straight-ahead jazz they opened with: five of Woodland Park's concerts in 2014 presented jazz-related music like blues and funk, while Portland's Zoo series presented only one jazz-related show that year. But for two decades the Oregon Zoo was a highly successful venue for outdoor summer jazz: on the path to the amphitheater were chimpanzees, polar bears, and river otters; elephants swayed to the music; and during intermission, hawks and falcons swooped over crowds that reclined on the lawn.

It seemed like a can't-miss formula: place jazz in an attractive setting and it will be viewed positively, receive more press, and draw larger audiences at all types of venues.

Indeed, the series at the Oregon Zoo inspired a growing number of outdoor concerts at Willamette Valley and Puget Sound wineries. They drew on the funding strategy worked out by promoter Steve Reischman, who booked both the Oregon Zoo and the Woodland Park Zoo concerts.

These were also the years when Pacific Northwest wines achieved international recognition, and new local connoisseurs were another target audience for those outdoor concerts. Such was the reputation of jazz among young urban professionals, and so attractive the jazz/picnic model, that promoters could sell out the cutting-edge fusion of Pat Matheny as well as the earthy R&B of Ray Charles.

At Sokol-Blosser Winery in the rolling hills of the western Willamette Valley, the sloping concert area faced the coastal mountains and setting sun that filtered through tall white oaks. The grapes in nearby vineyards hung in green bunches, and bottles of wine stood in buckets of ice on folding tables. But the food and beverage industry is notoriously fickle, and eventually those audiences moved on. While the two Zoo series, with settings far more enticing than open fields and expansive views, continued to draw full houses, jazz gradually became a smaller and smaller part of the programs.

In Seattle, however, a more sustainable, membership-based arts organization dedicated exclusively to jazz was about to be born.

Otter Crest Jazz Weekend became an annual event that attracted nationally recognized musicians and demonstrated that an audience for jazz existed outside urban nightclub venues.

Otter Crest Jazz Weekend

In 1978, the Jazz Society of Oregon sponsored its first Otter Crest Jazz Weekend at the Inn at Otter Crest on the Oregon Coast. Promoters Jim and Mary Brown produced the three-day event in a format now known as a "jazz party," where a number of well-known musicians perform together in different configurations for several hundred dedicated fans in a resort setting. The jazz weekends at Otter Crest became an annual event that brought many musicians with national reputations to the area and demonstrated that an audience for jazz existed outside urban nightclub venues.

The jazz parties drew a different audience than you'd typically find in a nightclub—or at an outdoor festival, either—a trend observed by Wayne Thompson, a former *Jazzscene* editor who attended many of these events. "They were far more serious about the music. They didn't want any talking, they didn't want any noise."

Jazz party patrons, Thompson observed, often attended more than one a year. "Like a jet-set group," he said, "they'd fly to Denver, Florida, or California." And the promoters tailored the experience to the patrons' preferences: "Jim and Mary Brown had a real good sense of what jazz listeners wanted to see and hear," said Thompson. "They did a lot of [audience] surveys. That [later] caught on in California. I went to several of the West Coast Jazz Parties in Irvine. They'd ask you to write down the musicians you wanted to hear, and they'd actually follow those suggestions. So you could see you were having an impact. And you could put criticisms down and see that changes were made.

"And Jim also had an even better sense of what musicians wanted. Scott Hamilton and Ken Peplowski both told me they didn't like to go to a place where they play twice and then sit in the audience the rest of the time. At the Jim Brown event, they got to play all the time."

The Otter Crest Jazz Weekends ended in 1995 after a seventeen-year run. In 2003, the Oregon Coast Council for the Arts brought jazz back to the area in a jazz party format with its annual Jazz at Newport festival.

BIRTH OF AN ARTS POWERHOUSE

"We need to do something about this jazz scene." They'd been saying it for years. And it was true—jazz in Seattle had seemed so promising just a few years before, but now, all they heard were pickup groups playing standards. So in 1984, Seattle writers Gary Bannister and Paul de Barros got tired of complaining and decided to do something about it. They began with a monthly newsletter, formed a nonprofit called Earshot Jazz, staged a few concert series that featured original music, and proved they could be a success. By 1989, what had started with a handful of friends had become a legitimate arts organization with grants from city, state, and county, and a paid executive director.

The first Earshot Jazz Festival took place that year, and the series continues annually today along with the organization's eponymous magazine and its educational programs. Like the Jazz Society of Oregon and the Seattle Jazz Society, Earshot Jazz is another example of the region's DIY spirit. Its focus, however, is on original, progressive work. "That's why we started out," says de Barros. "Our idea was to promote a creative scene." Over the years, the evolution of the Earshot Jazz Festival would parallel the changes in jazz around the Sound as it moved in a more avant-garde direction.

HEARTS OF GOLD: THE CITY COUNCILLOR AND THE PROMOTER

In Portland, the Waterfront Blues Festival, which kicked off in 1987, helped bring attention to Portland as a music city, boosted blues in the region, and incidentally raised the profile of some of its jazz players. But it is most important to this story as an example of how a city government, or even one city official, can affect local music and shape a regional culture.

It began as the Rose City Blues Festival and featured a lineup of top regional musicians as well as blues legend John Lee Hooker. The following year, the Oregon Food Bank started producing the festival. By 2014, it had grown to a five-day extravaganza that had raised a total of ten million dollars and eight hundred tons of food. But it might not have gotten off the ground without the support of then city commissioner Mike Lindberg.

A longtime devotee of the blues—he was often seen on the dance floors of local clubs—Lindberg wanted to reverse the policy of a former mayor who considered music in the parks a bad idea. So Lindberg worked closely with the first Blues Festival organizers, smoothing the way through the complex process of securing the necessary permits. It was an easy sell once the event got rolling, and the city continues to recognize it as an event that fosters a sense of community and togetherness.[1]

The success of the Blues Festival spurred other city and county parks to institute concert series that often presented jazz. One of those, at Multnomah County's Blue Lake Park—where Al Pierre's band had played in the 1930s—was also booked by Steve Reischman, promoter of the Zoo series. Because of the scope of his programming and promotional work, Reischman had a major impact on the sound of jazz in the region during the '80s and '90s.

Jazz in the Pacific Northwest was reaching one of its high points just as projects like the renewal of Pike Place Market and Pioneer Square were transforming the region's cities. The revitalized area soon became home to The New Orleans Restaurant, which continued as a top Seattle jazz venue for thirty years.

Again, in a small market, a single individual can make a big difference. And Reischman—a musician himself and a California native who moved to Portland in the early 1970s—reflected the region's countercultural bent. He was a smart businessman who embodied the target demographic, and his ability to match artist to audience was key to his success. Reischman was even the subject of an *Oregonian* feature titled "The Promoter with the Heart of Gold," a portrait of Reischman as a businessman who put artist and audience ahead of maximizing profit.

The abundance of festivals and other summer events boosted the amount of work available to resident musicians and contributed to another peak in the popularity and visibility of jazz in the region in the 1990s. The festivals also reflected social and economic changes, and the tastes of a growing niche market composed of musically sophisticated baby boomers. Together with physical changes in the major cities, those forces would soon make the region a magnet for jazz immigrants.

CHANGING CITIES

While jazz in the Pacific Northwest was reaching one of its high points, the region's cities were also being transformed. Most significant for the jazz community was the renewal of Pike Place Market—one of the Seattle's primary tourist attractions—and Pioneer Square, which had been home to jazz in Seattle since the music's earliest days. In the 1980s, its skid road origins still provided the atmosphere that made going to a jazz club feel like a walk on the wild side.

And then the tech money started rolling in. Bill Gates and Paul Allen, founders of Microsoft, moved their small company from New Mexico to the suburbs of their native city of Seattle in 1979. Annual sales topped $140 million by 1985; by 1990, $1.18 billion. Seattle was beginning to lose its image as a blue-collar town.

"In 1989," according to the *Seattle Weekly*, "Seattle was becoming trendy. "In a few years, *Newsweek* would put then-*Slate*-magazine-editor Michael Kinsley on its cover...clad in a yellow raincoat next to an open-mouthed salmon, with the headline: 'Swimming to Seattle: Everybody else is moving there. Should you?'"

Left: "I guess I'm just a hometown boy," says Tom Grant. "I feel safe and comfortable here. I'm not a very competitive person, so I've never had a burning desire to go mix it up in New York or LA. I like it here."

Right: The Tom Grant Band of the 1980s filtered the fire of Grant's former employer, drummer Tony Williams, through the sensibilities of a schoolteacher who was raised at his dad's record shop. Left to right: Jeff Leonard, Carlton Jackson, Tom Grant, Dan Balmer.

Indeed, it looked like a good place. The city's first African American mayor, elected in 1990, was called "Mayor Nice." Affordable rents helped make the city attractive to artists looking for a cleaner environment and like-minded peers. But everybody *was* moving to Seattle—almost a half-million new people poured into the Puget Sound in the following ten years.[2]

As the city and its reputation grew, so did the number of Puget Sound jazz venues, from just a handful to nearly thirty in Seattle alone, with another half dozen scattered around the Sound. The influx of top-level jazz artists also contributed to the increase. And those artists helped change the direction of jazz in the region. The physical alterations taking place at the same time in the cities contributed to the environment that drew them.

In Portland, a downtown freeway was removed and the city's relationship to the Willamette River revived with the building of Waterfront Park—part of the infrastructure necessary to support the concerts that soon filled the mile-long greensward with music almost every summer weekend. The idyllic setting also helped make the Waterfront Blues Festival one of the world's most successful events of its kind in terms of fundraising and artistic excellence.

Downtown malls or enclosed shopping areas were opening during those years, too, including Portland's Yamhill Marketplace, where the Jazz Society of Oregon held its 1983 First Jazz concert on New Year's Day, when it was closed to the public. The JSO employed forty-seven musicians, and more than one thousand listeners were able to move about the mall to hear and see the performers from a variety of vantage points, giving it a festival atmosphere. A city administration committed to modernization also completed a full-block-sized public space, Pioneer Courthouse Square (1984), and a light rail line (1986). At the same time, several office towers were built, including the U.S. Bancorp Tower, the city's second tallest, where jazz trios entertained diners in its thirty-seventh-floor restaurant. The

Tom Grant: Hometown Boy

On a rainy April evening, at the grand opening of Yoshida's Fine Art Gallery in the Pearl district, Tom Grant is playing "Hometown Boy" from his new album *Solo Piano*. Few of the three hundred guests hear him. They're carrying small plates of food and talking. The gallery opening is also a release party for his nineteenth album. With cover art by nature photographer Steve Terrill, the disc looks right at home in the gallery, as does Grant. Wearing a dark suit sans tie and a green shirt that sets off his black hair, the Portland native plays his role gracefully.

And if you listen to the music from that production—its sweet optimism, its touch of bluesy regret, its familiar, American rhythms—you'd say that Grant is indeed the hometown boy of the song. He could be a Norman Rockwell character, subtle and skilled yet cheerfully accessible. That persona has made him one of the city's most popular performers.

There's more to this hometown boy than the pleasant entertainer. Of course the good looks and listenable sound, as well as his professionalism and social ease, have contributed to his appeal. And they also helped Grant achieve national success as a smooth jazz pioneer with recordings on the charts for a decade while he led a polished touring band.

But behind the pop singer stands a man who has worked for years to become a skilled interpreter of the Great American Songbook. Behind the keyboard stands his command of the acoustic piano and the straight-ahead jazz that has always been his foundation. When smooth jazz moved too far from those roots, Grant stopped touring and continued the quest that animates all serious musicians—the development of his own voice. Eventually, he found it right in his own backyard.

Born in 1946, his father owned Al Grant's Record Store in the city's African American entertainment district. His older brother Mike, a beatnik jazz pianist, and his father, a self-taught pianist and tap dancer, inspired him. His primary teacher was Gene Confer, mentor to many of Portland's modern jazz pianists.

His path to jazz didn't run straight, however. All through college, he only performed occasionally, and after earning a masters degree he took a teaching job in Mill City, a logging town in the Santiam Valley. On the weekends, he began driving to Portland to play with American Indian saxophonist Jim Pepper and finally moved to the city. There he worked with drummer Ron Steen and bassist David Friesen for five years; they toured with trumpet great Woody Shaw as well as Grammy-winning Joe Henderson.

Then he spent three years with drummer Tony Williams, the prodigy who transformed Miles Davis's sound and then helped pioneer jazz-rock fusion. Grant joined him in 1979; leaving that band remains his greatest regret.

"I was going out on my own before I had taken full measure of the precious apprenticeship under such a huge musical spirit," he says. "The record I made was called *You Hardly Know Me*, [but] it could just as easily have been called 'I Hardly Know Myself.'"

"It took me a long time to really tap into my inner core and have my playing be an expression of myself," he says. "I didn't have my own voice until long after."

Not until long after he'd made a series of albums that had long runs on new adult contemporary and smooth jazz charts during the 1980s and early '90s. By then he'd had enough of smooth jazz radio, and Grant returned to Portland's straight-ahead scene, leading jam sessions and working with old friends. Eventually, he did find his own voice. It retains the sunny charms of his best smooth jazz and incorporates the rhythmic variety and harmonic depth of the straight-ahead jazz he learned as a kid.

It's his own sound at last. The sound of his hometown.

internationally celebrated ad agency Wieden+Kennedy also opened its doors in 1982, a harbinger of the creative culture to come.

And the beginnings of what would be known as Oregon's "Silicon Forest" was being built in suburban Washington County. Tektronics became the largest private employer in Oregon, and the arrival of Intel, the world's leader in developing memory chips and integrated microcomputer systems, gave the area national visibility. Between 1984 and 1986, the Japanese companies NEC, Epson, and Fujitsu each bought large sites in Portland suburbs.

THE MUSIC OF URBAN SOPHISTICATION

The transformation of Portland and Seattle fit well with the public perception of jazz as the music of urban sophistication, a soundtrack for a revitalized Pacific Northwest. It was part of a national trend in the late 1980s, spurred by a cadre of neotraditionalists led by New Orleans native Wynton Marsalis. They played in a style developed in the early 1960s by such artists as Miles Davis. Their focus on the past and the seriousness of the art form was in part a reaction against the rise of smooth jazz, funk, and other party-down, R&B-related styles as much as it was a gesture of respect for past masters. This group of young stars received media attention and record contracts while middle-aged artists were passed over.

In the late 1970s, the Tom Grant Band was still playing in that straight-ahead style. But something different began to emerge after Grant spent three years touring with former Miles Davis superstar drummer Tony Williams, whose music was as loud and fiery as rock but retained the improvisation and rhythmic freedom of jazz.

That experience inspired Grant's greatest success when his version of jazz-rock fusion turned out to be a precursor to smooth jazz. Oddly enough, he developed that approach attempting to recreate the music he had played with Williams, although it may not have been apparent to his listeners. The Tom Grant Band of the 1980s filtered the fire of Tony Williams through the sensibilities of a former schoolteacher who was raised at his dad's record shop. For some years, that was exactly what listeners wanted to hear.

His recordings had long runs on new adult contemporary and smooth jazz charts; several, including *Mango Tango*, *Night Charade*, and *In My Wildest Dreams*, enjoyed lengthy stays at number one. Those albums, like his first national hit in 1983, mixed pop and jazz in a way that was different from Chick Corea's jazz-rock fusion, the funk of Herbie Hancock, or the instrumental R&B of David Sanborn. When the Tom Grant Band toured the country, the song he had learned from Jim Pepper, "Witchi-Tai-To," was his anthemic closer.

A key member of the Grant Band was guitarist Dan Balmer. He was only twenty-four when he joined, but he played an important part in its success. The Portland native wrote several of Grant's hit songs, and his guitar became a key component of the band's sound. By that time, Balmer had moved away from the burning pyrotechnics that were his calling card when he was a student at Lewis & Clark College, where his father was a political science professor. And though smooth jazz was rejected by many purists, Balmer feels they were failing to hear the "real jazz" in it because of the rock beats and catchy vocal hooks. "On a lot of

The career of Tacoma native Diane Schuur hit a peak in the late 1980s, when she won two Grammy awards. Both Dan Balmer and Patrick Lamb have toured internationally with her band.

our tunes, I will play things that are the very essence of contemporary jazz guitar," Balmer said at the height of the Grant Band's popularity. "They just don't hear it because Tom's music is so nice."

And it paid well, too, compared to what musicians earned in local nightclubs. Balmer took pride in having his work validated by fair compensation. But the pay wasn't reward enough to keep him on the road. At heart he is, like Grant, a dyed-in-the-wool Pacific Northwesterner who can't wait to get back to Portland after a few days in New York. "I always thought that I'd be dead by the time I was thirty," Balmer says, recalling his youth, "like the jazz musician who's kind of crazy, has no control over his life, and lives that way to create this art form. But now I realize I'd rather live here in Portland, rake the leaves, play the best I can, and spend my one hundred dollars [performance fee] on a downspout for the house instead of on drugs. This is a different time."

In the end, Grant too decided he'd had enough of the road and the music that had brought him success. "Smooth jazz was becoming so syndicated that by '94 I couldn't even buy airplay. I was trying to fit into a format I helped create, but then I was copying other people who had developed it."

Grant had another reason for leaving the road behind, one he shares with many leading artists in the region: "I guess I'm just a hometown boy," he says. "I feel safe and comfortable here. I'm not a very competitive person, so I've never had a burning desire to go mix it up in New York or LA. I like it here."

And so he stayed, still working in the smooth jazz style, but gradually, over the next decade, transitioning back to the straight-ahead acoustic piano he'd grown up with, and in the process deepening and relaxing his singing voice. Before he did, Grant hired saxophonist Patrick Lamb. Today Lamb is the region's leading R&B-flavored jazz star. He also tours frequently with Canadian singer Gino Vanelli, who for a time lived in the Columbia Gorge and hired many regional players. Both Balmer and Lamb have also traveled to Latin America and Europe with vocalist and Tacoma native Diane Schuur.

Schuur is a straight-ahead singer who also plays piano. Her career hit a peak in the late 1980s, when she won two Grammy awards in a row, including one

No group better represented what success looked like in the late 1980s jazz scene than Portland's Tall Jazz Trio. Left to right: Mike Horsfall, Dave Averre, Dan Presley.

with the Count Basie Band. Her work fit well with the New Traditionalism that by this time had become the dominant jazz style and reflected the conservative mood in the country during the Reagan administration. When Portland restaurant Delevan's changed hands and became Remo's in 1984, owners decided to keep the jazz policy because of the music's "sophisticated" image—and that meant "upscale." Only a certain kind of jazz was appropriate. So musicians adapted again, and none better represented what success looked like at the time than Portland's Tall Jazz Trio.

Following the model of the Modern Jazz Quartet and other tuxedoed groups, Tall Jazz became one of the region's most popular attractions and released a number of recordings through their own label. Vibraphonist and piano player Mike Horsfall, a Tall Jazz member who grew up in Bellevue (his mother had played in the Garfield High School band with Quincy Jones), also maintained a busy schedule as a freelancer—a necessity where musicians must perform in a variety of configurations and styles to earn a living. That trend echoed what had happened in the 1960s, when musicians likewise had to adapt to the evolving tastes of their audience.

For some artists, those changes were disturbing and restrictive: "One of my prime motivations for coming here was that I felt Portland's jazz audience was very hip," said saxophonist and Chicago native Michael Bard in 1986. "But the audiences have gotten more conservative, and things are continuing to get more closed."[3]

He was right; opportunities for experimentation declined overall in Portland, and most well-paying jobs were in restaurants where the music was often treated as background. The same dispirited scene in Seattle had moved activists to create the Earshot Jazz organization. By 1985 the number of eating and drinking establishments presenting live jazz in Portland was nearly half what it had been four years earlier—and shrinking fast. Cousin's, a major nightclub, closed in 1986, the Jazz Quarry followed in 1987, and Parchman Farm closed in 1988. Geneva's, the last in the Williams Avenue district, had closed several years before. The number of jazz musicians, however, continued to grow, and a *Willamette Week* article claimed almost 120 active jazz players in Portland alone in 1984. If it had not become a "Kansas City on the Willamette," it still supported a scene that was dynamic and an important part of the growing arts culture. The city even began sponsoring the annual Artquake, a festival that prominently featured jazz. Outside of those special events, however, jazz listeners were more likely to hear a duo or trio than the quintets and larger groups that had been more widely employed in previous years.

Into that environment came the jazz giants whose active involvement with the community would help kindle a golden age in the 1990s.

Jazz in the 1980s: The Age of the Duo

In contrast to the big floor shows, shake dancers, and table singers featured along Williams Avenue in the '40s and '50s, the Portland jazz renaissance of the 1980s often created opportunities for duos and trios. And they played in bars and restaurants where the music was a sideshow rather than the headline event.

That was the case on a gray Thursday evening in June at Digger O'Dell's in Portland. It's a long, narrow room with a curving wooden bar and, in a corner with high windows behind them, David Friesen and John Stowell play Friesen's flowing, unfamiliar originals. There is a murmur of low voices, the clack of empty plates, an occasional burst of laughter. Tasteful prints hang on walls with brass valances, stained glass, and burgundy wallpaper.

The musicians draw into their own space, as if huddling around the music. Plants hang near their shoulders. They turn toward the window. Friesen's hair fans around his face like a screen, head bent over the bass; his hands on the fingerboard seem large, as if the energy of his entire body were in them. His shoulders roll, he rocks on his stool. Beside him, Stowell is still, the neck of his guitar pointing straight up, close to his face. Only hands, wrists, and forearms move. His eyes are closed. He looks thin in a collarless shirt.

A group of officers from the Rose Festival fleet are having dinner and drinks at the back of the dark-paneled room. They clap. Friesen and Stowell turn toward them, then quickly back to the windows. The sky darkens and it begins to rain. When the front door opens, the sound of tires on wet pavement comes in.

They've been playing for over an hour when a guy lurches away from the bar and weaves across the room toward them, waving a dollar bill in one hand and a cigarette in the other. He demands a dedication. The smoldering cigarette moves dangerously close to Stowell's face. The guitarist reaches up, gently takes the man's sleeve, restrains his hand, and then lets go. The guy continues his monologue, waving the cigarette ever closer; Stowell again catches the sleeve, gently pushes the hand away, and again, until Friesen, who's been sitting with head down, strikes a ferocious booming chord and motions for the barman, who escorts the drunk to the door.

The incident is unusual. More often than not, the musicians are ignored; there's no microphone to announce the tunes or otherwise engage the audience, who've often come only to socialize anyway. Not a lot is expected of listeners here—or of musicians. The dress is casual, as is the presentation. The Navy men tip on their way out. A young fan at the bar remains, a couple tables, a single in the back. Friesen and Stowell turn toward the window.

JAZZ IMMIGRANTS:
THEY CAME FOR THE LIFESTYLE AND CHANGED THE MUSIC

From New York, Stockholm, San Francisco, and Los Angeles they came, carrying instrument cases and resumes full of international acclaim. And though they followed other jazz players who had relocated to the Pacific Northwest, these new immigrants weren't looking for teaching jobs or other work outside music. They came for a better quality of life.

In the Pacific Northwest, they could take their kids to the mountains or out sailing, ride bikes along the water to a farmers market, and afford to live on leafy

Leroy Vinnegar, "Father of the Walking Bass," is featured on more than six hundred albums. When he came to Portland in 1986, he made himself part of the community, working closely with locals and serving as a model of high-level musicianship.

streets. Although the pay was considerably less than what they earned on the road or in New York, they were happy to be in a cleaner, safer place. Drummer Dick Berk, a former Californian who'd played with Billie Holiday and many other jazz legends, came from Las Vegas looking for better schools for his daughter. Portland also became home to singer, pianist, and songwriter Dave Frishberg, a four-time Grammy nominee, and to legendary bassist Leroy Vinnegar. Guitarist Jerry Hahn moved to Portland during this time as well, and pianist Larry Fuller came to Seattle in 1988 to work with singer Ernestine Anderson, who had again returned to her hometown.

Pianist and composer Wayne Horvitz relocated to Seattle in 1989 to raise his family in an environment more congenial than New York's Lower East Side. So did guitarist Bill Frisell, one of the leading jazz artists in the world. He arrived right after Horvitz, and for many of the same reasons.

"A doctor couldn't have come up with a better prescription for health," bassist Red Mitchell said about his move to Salem, Oregon. "I've really been made to feel at home here."

The welcome Mitchell received was accorded other jazz immigrants as well. Pianist Jessica Williams lived in Portland in the early 1990s. "It's so refreshing

Leroy's Shoes

When Leroy Vinnegar died in 1999, his partner gave his suits to fellow musicians; only the tall ones, though, because Leroy was a big man. One night, years later, saxophonist Rob Scheps pointed to his leg. "These are Leroy's pants," he said. "This is where he spilled candle wax; I'm never washing it out."

They're playing his tunes, even wearing his suits, but nobody'll ever fill Leroy's shoes.

Revered and honored in Portland, his adopted home, "Father of the Walking Bass," they called him. His accomplishments were huge: on more than six hundred albums, he always worked for the top people, and was right at the heart of jazz on the West Coast until the LA smog choked him out and Leroy headed north. But it wasn't just his music that made him a Portland hero.

Big smile, rumbling voice, generous with his time; Leroy showed folks how to play right with stories and gentle chiding.

"You're not swinging," he'd say, but always nice, though he'd never suffer a bad musician.

Because Leroy knew time, had nothing left to prove. In fact he'd almost died, but the doctors brought him back. "Saved my life," Leroy laughed.

He wore a beautiful topcoat, wheeled oxygen on a cart fifteen hours a day for his failing heart.

"At least I can come out and play," said Leroy, who never complained. "With this condition, you never know, man," he'd say.

Leroy knew time.

"I know you're good, Leroy," I said, "but with so many great bassists, why'd all the leaders choose you?"

"Because I'm a nice guy, I disciplined myself," said Leroy. "Didn't talk back, did what I was asked—gave 'em what they wanted."

And when it came time to solo, Leroy just stayed right with a steady four-to-the-bar, just kept on with the walk, developed it into his own voice, made the walk his talk.

Because Leroy knew time.

"All musicians love a strong bass player," he said. "You're not going to be up there if you're not strong. Like 'Trane said, 'You would beat a person right into the ground with that time you got, Leroy!' Right into the ground!'

"Well, that's how I was raised," said Leroy. "Raised with Art Tatum, you can't escape the time."

So guys would ask, "What was it like playing with Bird, with 'Trane, with Tatum?" And often he told them, but not always direct.

"I wanted this classic Mercedes, see," he said. "But my credit wasn't strong enough—fifteen hundred dollars it cost then. But I wanted that car.

"Then I signed with Michel Legrand. So I go back to the car lot, and I say, 'I just signed a contract with Michel Legrand.' So they knew the money was good, and the man says, '*Mister* Vinnegar, come get your car.'"

And Leroy laughed, but with the sadness of a man whose wife had died in a car crash, the sadness of a man who knew time.

One night we shook hands. Mine disappeared between his smooth palms; Leroy held on.

"I'm not seventy-six," he said.

"No," I answered.

"But you said I was seventy-six in that story you wrote."

"Oh, Leroy, I'm sorry. I must've reversed the numbers."

"That's alright man," Leroy laughed. "I just found out I've been spelling my own name wrong my whole life." And Leroy—who spelled it "V-i-n-n-e-g-a-r" with two Ns, not the usual way with one—laughed again, reassuring me. "It's gonna be alright, man, it's gonna be alright."

Because Leroy knew time.

to be greeted here with smiles and have all these great musicians to play with, and not meet all that misogyny I've found elsewhere," she said. Mel Brown, Leroy Vinnegar, and Dave Captein are on several of her albums.

The guitarist Ralph Towner, a Bend native and cofounder of the band Oregon, also returned to the region in the early '90s. He taught at Cornish and recorded with several Seattle players, including a duo with Frisell, before relocating to Italy. His imaginative improvisations and harmonic intricacies fit the scene around Cornish well.

As the years went by, the impact of those new high-level artists on the local scene became evident—as did Cascadia's impact upon them. On arrival, many thought all they'd need from the region was its beautiful landscape and an airport; they expected nothing from the local scene. But after a while, most of them found that it was in fact just what they needed. Dave Frishberg, for instance, was Portland's most famous resident vocalist, but he rarely performed his clever lyrics in town. Though he traveled to London, Los Angeles, and New York for solo shows, in Portland he chose to work primarily as a pianist.

"One of the songs on my last CD was called 'I Want to Be a Sideman,'" he said shortly after he arrived. "I really like to play in an ensemble; it's one of the things I like best about being a musician." So he started a duo with old-timey cornetist Jim Goodwin, an Ellington scholar. They'd play in a loft some twelve feet above the tables at Portland Brewing Company. It was what he'd been missing: "I knew I had to make up my mind not to sing on gigs in Portland," he explained. "In Portland, I get to be a piano player."

By the end of the decade, Frishberg was accompanying vocalist Rebecca Kilgore in the swanky Heathman Hotel. The albums they recorded together boosted Kilgore to national status and satisfied another musical joy Frishberg had been missing. "What I really enjoy now is playing for singers," he said. "I love being an accompanist." The man who wanted to be a sideman again, as he'd been for the first fifteen years of his career in New York, got his wish in Portland.

Leroy Vinnegar also found what he needed in the Pacific Northwest: another chance at life and a productive extended career. Vinnegar was known for his warm, rounded tone and as a master of the walking bass, the four-beats-to-the-bar technique he perfected in the 1950s. He appeared on more than six hundred albums, and recorded with Stan Getz and Sonny Rollins as well as Van Morrison and the Doors. In 1986, when he arrived in Portland, Vinnegar thought he was moving to a quiet place where the air was cleaner and he could work on his autobiography and play a little on the side. Suddenly, a heart condition put him in the hospital. "Good Samaritan Hospital has the best doctors and nurses in the world!" he asserted two years later. "They brought me back to life."

Vinnegar made the most of the years he had left before his death in 1999. He and Mel Brown formed a trio and, following the trend at the time, began regular weekly performances at the upscale Atwater's Restaurant in the U.S. Bancorp Tower. The group's pianists included Mark Simon and later Jof Lee, who had relocated to the Pacific Northwest in the early 1980s. Lee first worked as music director and pianist for Portland icon Marianne Mayfield, and he played on two of Vinnegar's Portland albums, including *Walkin' the Basses*.

The jazz immigrants of the late '80s and early '90s who had the greatest impact

Before settling in the tiny Columbia River town of Cathlamet, Washington, Hadley Caliman not only worked with jazz greats of the 1950s and '60s, but also toured with Santana in the 1970s.

were those who made themselves part of the community—like Vinnegar. He worked closely with local musicians and served as a model of high-level musicianship and the straight-ahead jazz that had been dominant in the region since the 1940s.

A tall man with full head of white hair, the affable Vinnegar was a compelling figure on stage, and his reputation commanded respect. His quartet (guitarist Dan Faehnle, who later worked with Diana Krall and the band Pink Martini; drummer Mel Brown; and saxophonist Gary Harris) played to packed houses of listeners in their thirties at a venerable nightclub called the Jazz de Opus.

Vinnegar made his mark in Portland in other ways, too. He sponsored a series of Monday-night shows for the Jackson-Mills Big Band when they had trouble finding gigs. The Pander Brothers, young graphic novelists and filmmakers, created a Leroy Vinnegar story for the pioneering Dark Horse Comics. In 1995, the Oregon legislature proclaimed May 1 "Leroy Vinnegar Day." He was the first inductee into the Jazz Society of Oregon Hall of Fame, and drummer Alan Jones released *The Leroy Vinnegar Suite*, an album dedicated to and with compositions inspired by Vinnegar.

Making that album showed Jones just how powerful his inspiration's impact had been. "As I was writing it, everyone was saying, 'Yeah, Leroy, Leroy, Leroy,' and it became clear that he is an archetypal figure; all the stuff I learned from him, other

"We had this generation of kids who went to Cornish... all avant-gardists: they'd play anything. They were inspired by Nirvana; they were inspired by anarchists. They were a part of that flowering of musical culture," says Paul de Barros. Saxophonist Briggan Krauss later worked with Wayne Horvitz.

people have learned from him, too. He was a magnet for anyone who cared about real jazz. Anywhere I went, if Portland came up, Leroy's name came up with it."

In addition to his inspirational example, Vinnegar provided a link to the previous era, as did Dick Berk, who shared stories about his days playing with jazz legends. And saxophonist Hadley Caliman offered that same living connection to the jazz past when he arrived in the lower Columbia River town of Cathlamet in 1980.

For the first few years he lived quietly. "If you want to lose momentum as a jazz player," he said, "move to a little country town and teach."[4] Surprisingly, he liked it. Removed from the influences that had enabled his drug addiction, he was also comfortable with the rural area's affection for people of color when, as was the case for Caliman, there is only one in town. Nevertheless, after a few years he was commuting to Seattle to teach at the Cornish Institute. He continued that long-distance relationship until shortly before his retirement, when he moved to Poulsbo, a small town on the Olympic Peninsula just a ferry ride from Seattle.[5]

In California, not only had Caliman worked with many jazz greats of the 1950s and '60s, he had also toured with Santana in the 1970s, as did fellow immigrant Michael Shrieve, a drummer who arrived in Seattle in 1989 after making eight albums with Santana as well as having written for, produced, and played on several other million-selling discs. He quickly found kindred spirits and added quality and inspiration to the scene.

Another musician with a heavy resume who settled in the region in the 1980s was saxophonist Charlie Rouse. He had performed with Thelonious Monk for eleven years, and originally came to the Pacific Northwest on tour with pianist Mal Waldron. Rouse fell in love with a local woman and decided to settle down outside the little town of Canby, some forty miles south of Portland. A city dweller from birth, he started growing green beans and tomatoes, set up a bird feeder, and once, while he sat on a boulder in a mountain stream playing the flute, a monarch butterfly danced around his head and landed on his hair, flew up, and landed again, its black-and-orange wings beating to his breath. "I wish I'd known about this thirty years ago," he said.

But Rouse still spent a lot of his time on the road, traveling the West in a big Pontiac wagon with his new wife at the wheel. He bought cowboy boots and a black Stetson hat. He didn't perform frequently in the Pacific Northwest, nor put together bands with area players. His presence, however, helped raise standards and inspire others, as did all of the master musicians who came at the time. His last concert, in Seattle, was a tribute to his former mentor, employer, and father figure, Thelonious Monk. That show was recorded and released as *Epistrophy: The Last Concert*. Rouse left the hospital where he was being treated for lung cancer to perform. Almost no one in the audience knew, and he died shortly thereafter.

Another jazz immigrant who didn't take a prominent role in the local jazz community was Blue Note recording artist Andrew Hill. He came to Portland in 1992 to take a faculty position at Portland State University. Like Jessica Williams, Hill didn't stay long; after four years, the African American pianist moved back to New York. And though he never felt like he fit in the Pacific Northwest, he did find what he needed at the time.

"I needed to come to some place to regain my love of living," said Hill, who was devastated by the death of his wife the year before. Walking became his therapy, and his daily strolls along the Willamette River took him past the Japanese American Historical Plaza in Waterfront Park. Inspired, he began writing a symphony to capture in sound the experience of the Japanese in Portland during World War II. And then he met the dancer Joanne Robinson, who was also from the East Coast and teaching at PSU. They married and returned east together.

Had Hill found a position in Seattle instead of in Portland, he might have remained in the region. Up north, the scene was moving away from the pastel hues of Towner and Goodhew and toward a more dissonant approach better suited to the likes of Hill.

PUNK JAZZ AND "SEATTLE'S LAST GREAT GENERATION"

By the late 1980s, in booming Seattle the number of jazz players had reached what Paul de Barros called "a tipping point...a critical mass of talent that suddenly manifested itself. We had this generation of kids who went to Cornish, like ten of them: Brad Shepik, Briggan Krauss, Aaron Alexander, John Silverman.... They were all nineteen, twenty, twenty-one years old, all avant-gardists: they'd play anything. They were inspired by Nirvana; they were inspired by anarchists. They were a part of that flowering of musical culture. They were just playing whatever they wanted."

Most of that group—what de Barros calls "the last great generation" of Seattle jazz players—eventually moved to New York, where they found success in the downtown scene of the 1990s that included such hotbeds of avant-garde jazz at the time as the Knitting Factory. Bellevue-raised trumpeter Cuong Vu also joined that scene after college in the east; unlike the others, he returned to the

A punk-jazz iconoclast, Seattle saxophonist Skerik cofounded the jazz prankster band Critters Buggin in the 1990s and toured with rock groups Pearl Jam and Ween as well as The Meters and the Headhunters.

Pacific Northwest fifteen years later to teach at the University of Washington. In addition to the job, Vu returned for the environment: "I really miss it there," he said in the years before he came home. "It always feels much more relaxed, and the clean air is revitalizing, not to mention the beautiful waters and mountains. Living is certainly easier there. I feel I've aged twice as fast being in New York."[6]

Another Seattle-based musician who came of age in the late 1980s took the city's penchant for innovation in a different direction. The saxophonist Eric Walton, who goes by the name Skerik, stayed in the Puget Sound area, but not for school.

He came up through the wealthy Mercer Island school district's jazz programs, but the straight-ahead tradition quickly lost its appeal for him. That was in part a reaction against the mood of the times: "You start getting older, you start seeing the 'jazz arms race,' is what we called it, where there's more of a priority on the accumulation of jazz knowledge than actual pursuing of yourself and the spirituality of the music and the greater message that it has. I got really turned off by that, so I went into rock music."[7]

Skerik toured with Pearl Jam and Ween. He was also a key member of the funk-rock band Garage A Trois that has included such nationally known jazz artists as guitarist Charlie Hunter. He cofounded the wild "free rock" (or jazz prankster) band Critters Buggin. He is versatile, however, and also toured with old-school funk bands such as the Headhunters and the Meters. In 2011, the *Los Angeles Times* called him "one of the most significant West Coast saxophonists of the past fifteen years."

A punk-jazz iconoclast, Skerik represents the flip side of the neotraditionalists. In practice, his quartet's loose grooves, ambient sounds, and pure noise build from funk rhythms to chaotic cacophony. The band has performed in Mexican wrestling

When writer and part-time percussionist Rick Mitchell (third from right) founded Portland's punk-funk band Le Bon, he intended to play rock clubs, not jazz venues.

outfits and shiny suits, and the shows don't encourage passive listening. Skerik's goal is to subvert: "Charlie Parker, Jimi Hendrix, and John Coltrane were all very revolutionary, just as some of the political music from the punk movement of the '80s was very revolutionary. To me there's no difference between Charlie Parker, Jaco Pastorius, John Coltrane, or Jello Biafra. They're all just freethinkers."[8]

That freethinking streak has always been strong in the Pacific Northwest, but in jazz it's taken on a variety of guises: the Coltrane-inspired music of Joe Brazil in the late 1960s; the hippie jazz developed by the likes of David Friesen at the Llahngaelhyn jam sessions in the early 1970s; the robust, Chicago-influenced free jazz of Rich Halley; and the rock-infused mayhem of Skerik-led bands. That spirit also inspired Portland punk-funk band Le Bon.

Jazz radio host and music critic Rick Mitchell put that group together in 1983, after losing his job when the *Oregon Journal* was absorbed by the city's other daily. He was in the mood to see some bridges burn, and he had ideas about the direction jazz should go. But he needed a band to test his theories, so he brought together guitarist Dan Balmer, bassist Dave Captein, drummer Carlton Jackson, and two horn players. A part-time percussionist, Mitchell wanted something like free jazz pioneer Ornette Coleman's electric group, but with more rock and roll—he intended to play rock clubs, not jazz venues. They needed a singer.

Billy Kennedy was perfect. He declaimed in falsetto, howled fractured lines of poetry, and invented many of his lyrics spontaneously in performance. "I'm much more interested in the rhythmic meter of the words and the way they come out as a horn than I am in the actual message they manifest," Kennedy said. And he added visual interest, giving Le Bon the performance art style of other cutting-edge groups at the time. "If we were an instrumental band," Balmer said,

"we'd just be standing up there playing weird music. But when Billy comes up, all hell breaks loose."

"My style is built around playing in the street and catching people by surprise," explains Kennedy, who accompanies himself on guitar when busking. "A lot of the antics I use come from being a mediocre Willie Nelson/Bob Dylan singer, and out on the street everybody would pass me by. So I just started screaming at people, 'Hey, gimme a quarter! Ooohooohoowow!!'"

Whether it was a Miles Davis or a Jimi Hendrix tune they covered, Le Bon kept the melody and groove but usually took it elsewhere, sometimes honking and barking in cacophonous rut, sometimes simply riffing over the rhythms; there was always a growling dissonance at the edge. And the audience danced to it. The band stayed together for several years and captured a counterculture spirit that has always been strong in the region.

Such bands remained on the margins, however, unable to draw the large audiences rock commanded and unsuited to straight-ahead jazz clubs that were becoming more conservative as they tailored their ambiance to attract young urbanites with disposable income. Perhaps the Oregon Symphony and its conductor, James DePreist, had that in mind when they featured the elegant vocalist Shirley Nanette singing with the orchestra. The gulf between those orchestral jazz nights and Le Bon was unbridgeable—unless you were Le Bon drummer Carlton Jackson.

BLACK AND WHITE

A Portland native, Jackson began working as a professional at age fifteen, and by the 1990s he'd been a first-call drummer in just about every possible jazz-related setting, from driving a big band to laying down backbeats for the Piano Throwers or "jam grass" (progressive bluegrass) rhythms for Darol Anger's Strings for Industry. He spent thirteen years with the Tom Grant Band; he played jazz fusion and the blues. In most of those bands, Jackson was the only African American. It was nothing new—he'd been one of the students bused from an inner city neighborhood to a suburban junior high school in the early 1970s. It was another gulf he learned to bridge.

Top: Elegant singer Shirley Nanette performed with the Oregon Symphony under the direction of former jazz drummer James DePreist.

Bottom: John Stowell worked for eight years with bassist David Friesen. He spends much of his time on the road, teaching and performing.

Journalist Don Uhl conducted an informal survey of six hundred Pacific Northwest jazz listeners he encountered at nightclubs, festivals, and concerts between 1977 and 1982. It revealed the average jazz fan to be a homeowner with a college degree and middle-class income. Forty-two percent were married, 65 percent could read music, 86 percent said they enjoyed classical music, and 90 percent expressed an interest in the visual arts.[9] The majority were white—no surprise in a region where less than 10 percent of the population is African American. But the typical racial makeup of the bands on stage was also changing.

From its beginnings through the 1950s, jazz was thought of as "black music" by many Americans. And it was, considering the culture from which it emerged and its chief innovators. "I always thought of jazz as something black people had that white people could get," said flautist Paul Horn. Horn grew up in New York City in the 1930s and later became a pioneer of new age jazz while he was living on Vancouver Island. He led a quartet that included David Friesen and John

Paul Horn, a resident of Vancouver Island in Canada, led a quartet including David Friesen and John Stowell on a tour of the Soviet Union in 1983. They were the first North American jazz band to perform for the public in Leningrad since 1927.

Stowell on a tour of the Soviet Union in 1983. They were the first American jazz band to perform for the public in Leningrad since African American jazz pioneer Sidney Bechet in 1927. They were all white. By the mid-1980s, the face of jazz in the Pacific Northwest had become much whiter.

ENTERING THE NEW AGE

That trend toward a whiter jazz scene was most evident in the artists who played what came to be called new age jazz. It wafted up to the Pacific Northwest from its California birthplace on the diaphanous wings of Windham Hill Records. Its trademark acoustic, chamber-like folk jazz appealed to baby boomers who had reached their thirties, not ready for easy listening but no longer eager to boogie the night away. The sonorous resolutions of the label's remarkably homogeneous sound reached the mainstream when, in 1984, pianist George Winston's seasonally themed solo piano albums generated sales in excess of twenty million dollars for a company that had begun with its founder selling albums out of the back of a station wagon. By the late 1980s, Winston's albums were outselling prominent jazz pianist Keith Jarrett's by a ratio of ten to one.

Despite the variety of performers under the Windham Hill umbrella—from solo acoustic guitar and piano to soft jazz-rock fusion and ambient electronic soundscapes—a common thread of pastoral sensibilities united them. But most of the region's jazz artists who also shared that impressionistic sound, such as David Friesen, were too unpredictable and dissonant for many new age listeners.

The bassist Patrick O'Hearn, a Pacific Northwest native, did find a comfortable fit within the new age style. Raised in Portland, where he began playing jazz in the early 1970s, he also studied at the Cornish Institute before moving to San Francisco, where he performed with top jazz masters and joined progressive rock star Frank Zappa's Mothers of Invention. O'Hearn began working with Mark Isham, a Windham Hill artist who has gone on to write music for film and TV. His influence can be heard on O'Hearn's album *Between Two Worlds*, which was nominated for a Grammy award.

Other Pacific Northwest residents who recorded new age jazz during the 1980s came mostly from the folk scene, like the onetime-Irish-music band Nightnoise with former gypsy jazz violinist Billy Oskay and flutist Brian Dunning. The band's

Thanks to Ron Steen (right), Portland has not been without a regular weekly jam session since 1983. Pictured here with Bill Beach, Bobby Hutcherson and Phil Baker.

Ron Steen: Some Honest, True Music

At the center of the jazz tradition is the jam session. It serves as classroom and rite of passage, laboratory and social event. Jazz players seek out jam sessions to polish their skills and to hang with their peers, networking and talking shop. It's a collaborative art, and without jam sessions, there is no jazz scene. Thanks to Ron Steen, Portland has not been without at least one every week since 1983.

A Portland native, he was brought up by supportive family and community members in a culture he has helped sustain. In the music he plays as well as the sessions he runs, Steen represents some of the important qualities of jazz in the region.

He spent time in New York when he was younger, and he traveled with Ted Curson and Woody Shaw, among others, before touring with Joe Henderson for more than three years. But his major work is grounded right in the city where he grew up. He's proud of his accomplishments, but Steen is adamantly self-effacing.

"The only goal I really have is to play some honest, true music. If you take care of that, then you're doing all you can.... I feel extremely privileged to have the ability to play jazz," he said in 1983, when he led the house band at Delevan's, the top supper club in town. "There's no greater honor than being able to carry on [this music].... That's payment enough.

"At this point, I just love what I'm doing. I can't wait to go to work. I could work every night of the week! I just love doing it. I can't wait to work tonight," he says, and then repeats it three more times.

"What you need is a major hang," Steen says about the qualities that make a great jam session. "In my day, we'd wait for hours just to get to sit in. That's the way it should be. Because everyone is not equal.... Now these young guys come up to me and say, 'Ron, I've got to go to work tomorrow,' or 'Ron, I've got an early class.'

"That's what I like about Dick Berk," he says. "Dick's old-school all the way, one of the greatest drummers in the country. Dick loves to hang. This is as important as the music. And that's part of the lesson, too, man. It's not just music school, it's the whole shebang."

Steen almost secured the ideal situation when his name was up on Martin Luther King, Jr. Boulevard, where he booked a variety of local players at Steen's Coffeehouse.

"Families would come every week to the coffeehouse in the afternoons," he says. "There wasn't much money, and they had to pass the tip jar, but there was room to play, and we have so much talent here that people kept asking if they could bring a band in.

"I loved it, it was like a family," he says, and for a moment pain crosses his face as he recalls the business partner who brought the enterprise down.

The conditions have varied over Steen's years on the bandstand, but he has always managed to create a satisfying musical experience by performing with quality, compatible players right from the beginning.

"I feel blessed," he says. "My whole life has been fortunate.... I just love doing what I'm doing."

Windham Hill releases feature simple melodies carried by pennywhistle or flute over elaborate textures from harmonium, guitar, acoustic piano, and synthesizer; the restrained violin provided counterpoint.

It was a sound designed not for dancing but for contemplation, a concert experience that audiences treated much like chamber music. The excellent musicianship appealed to the region's listeners, who often filled mid-sized concert halls for new age artists in the 1980s and early 1990s. It became a significant alternative for those who enjoyed instrumental music but found new age more accessible—much like smooth jazz, whose rise paralleled the emergence of new age music but drew a more racially diverse audience. Both cut into the market for the straight-ahead style.

The new age formula didn't sit easily with some who recorded for the label, however, including Nightnoise guitarist Mícheál Ó Domhnaill, an Irish immigrant who earlier had revolutionized traditional folk guitar. "Now people want their music to be a washing, cleansing, spiritual experience," he said. "Music historically didn't serve that purpose at all. Music was a social thing, where people got together to dance and visit with each other. And I'm wondering, is it right? Is this the way man should be going with music?"

Ó Domhnaill was one of many notable musical immigrants from outside the US. Two others made contributions to the region's jazz scene that were different but equal in magnitude to those of other masters: drummer Obo Addy from Ghana and Brazilian pianist Jovino Santos Neto.

THE WORLD COMES TO CASCADIA

"Jovino has had a tremendous impact," says de Barros. "His knowledge of Brazilian rhythms has really been disseminated into the community." It's common to hear such praise for the former music director for legendary Brazilian composer and multi-instrumentalist Hermeto Pascoal. In fact, it was Pascoal who first brought Santos Neto to the Pacific Northwest. In 1991, they played the Backstage in the Ballard neighborhood. The next day, on a ferry to Victoria, BC, Santos Neto saw a pod of orcas surface just off the bow. A year later, he moved to Seattle with his wife and two children.

He enrolled as a student of composition at the Cornish Institute but, when the faculty discovered who they had in class, they urged Santos Neto to apply for the first teaching position to open up. It wasn't long before he'd been hired. While in Seattle he was awarded a Chamber Music America commission that allowed him to produce the Grammy-nominated album *Canto do Rio*.

"I'm blessed to be in his company," said drummer Mark Ivester, a member of Santos Neto's Quinteto. "Jovino is a force, an extremely positive one. I often think of [him] as a fountain . . . no, make that a *geyser* of music."[10] During its early years, the Quinteto also included saxophonist Hans Teuber. Another jazz immigrant who came to Seattle in the 1980s, Teuber became an integral part of the local straight-ahead scene; he's on nineteen albums from Seattle's Origin Records alone. He was also a member of Skerik's Syncopated Taint Septet.

By comparison, Obo Addy's influence has perhaps been even wider. He arrived in 1978, and within ten years he'd put together two distinct bands: a traditional

Ghanaian ensemble called Okropong and the Afrobeat band Kukrudu. Both were built around the drum, but Kukrudu featured trap set, horns, electric guitar, and bass as well as West African hand drums. Many Portland jazz artists passed through Addy's bands, including Thara Memory, Janice Scroggins, and saxophonist Gary Harris.

Born and raised in Portland, Harris joined Kukrudu in 1984. Soon he was playing concurrently in Leroy Vinnegar's quartet as well. Within ten years, he had appeared on Addy's album *Let Me Play My Drum* and Vinnegar's album *Integrity*. Though the personal and musical styles of the two masters were different, Harris found that their message was the same: "Focus on the rhythm. Leroy and Obo both teach me that you have to get inside the rhythm, to understand it and play off it." Neither leader had much tolerance for error, either. "All those guys are like that," says Harris. "They really have to hear it the way it's supposed to be."

It took a determined man to bring African music to the Pacific Northwest in the 1980s; the region's population included few people from West Africa, and its music was only heard in occasional concerts by touring Afrobeat superstars. Addy was one of fifty-five children of a Wonche priest in the Ga culture who healed the sick in dance-and-drumming ceremonies. From his father, Addy learned traditional drum techniques; then he started his career as a James Brown–styled R&B singer. After Ghana gained its independence in the early 1960s, Addy returned to the traditional music of his youth in government-sponsored programs to spread indigenous arts. It became his life's work; Addy's Homowo Foundation booked hundreds of workshops and demonstrations in schools around the US. He also brought family members to Portland from Ghana to dance and drum in Okropong, and several made their homes permanently in the area.

The new perspectives and techniques that Santos Neto and Addy brought were the first direct, person-to-person links between jazz in the Pacific Northwest and world music. Had either settled in a larger city, as did several of Addy's brothers in Washington, DC, their influence would likely have been less. But in Portland and Seattle, a significant number of musicians played with them, and their work was highly visible. They helped pave the way for a broader opening of the local scene to world music that accelerated in the 1990s.

ON THE RADIO

Jazz on the radio also contributed to the healthy regional scene in the 1980s and early '90s, and there was plenty available on the airwaves. KBOO, in Portland, had been airing jazz since the late 1960s. KPLU, located at Pacific Lutheran University in Tacoma and home to the widely syndicated "Jazz After Hours" program hosted by Jim Wilke, switched its music from classical to jazz in 1983. And KMHD, then located at Mt. Hood Community College, began broadcasting in 1984. Other listener-supported radio stations in the Puget Sound and Portland area also broadcast jazz during the 1980s and early '90s.

At the time, jazz was also on commercial stations KKJZ in the Puget Sound, which played smooth jazz, and KCNR in Portland, which maintained a straight-ahead format. KCNR was born of a whim of owner Bill Failing, DJ Rita Rega remembers. "He was selling the signal, so he said to Ray Horn, 'Ray, you've always

Obo Addy learned traditional drum techniques from his father, started his career as a James Brown–styled R&B singer, and then returned to the Ghanaian music of his youth. He settled in Portland in 1978 and, along with Jovino Santos Neto in Seattle, helped bring world music to the region.

wanted a jazz station. Here's the signal, I'm giving it to you.'" Horn, a Portland DJ since the 1940s, jumped at the chance. New owners changed the station's call letters to KKUL after Horn's brief tenure, although its jazz format persisted for two more years.

So, in 1986, a total of 270 hours of jazz was available each week on Portland radio alone. And though those hours decreased over the years, and today there is no commercial jazz radio in the region, the strong public stations became part of the foundation necessary to sustain an active scene. As of 2015, KMHD and KPLU are among the top jazz stations in the nation; together, they reach nearly three hundred thousand listeners a week. Keeping both classic and contemporary jazz available to a large number of listeners is a necessary part of an active jazz scene.

ALWAYS A STRUGGLE

In addition to that infrastructure, an active jazz scene is sustained by unheralded locals who support themselves by cobbling together performance, teaching, and studio work—or combine them with jobs outside the music industry. "A lot of the older heroes struggled, too," Phil Baker noted. "It's always been a struggle with this music." As Mike Horsfall points out, "Being a professional musician is like saying 'yes' to everything. It's very much a patchwork quilt, real hardscrabble. Unless you're super great in one thing you do, you kinda have to be a little of a chameleon."

That kind of flexibility has always been required of all but the most famous jazz artists in the Pacific Northwest. It's what kept Seattle pianist Bob Nixon working. He arrived after discharge from the Army in the early 1960s and immediately began playing with some of the city's top musicians, many of whom had been stars on Jackson Street. The experience he'd gained with legendary bassist Charles Mingus had prepared him well. Nixon was house pianist at the Penthouse, accompanying many touring stars there as well as at Parnell's and Jazz Alley. He accompanied Ernestine Anderson for five years and played for vocalist Dee Daniels. Then, in the 1980s, when jobs became scarce, he began teaching at area community colleges.

Teaching positions in growing jazz studies programs were opening all the time and offered credentialed artists a way to come in out of the cold. Marc Seales, one of Seattle's biggest names and a definitive regional voice as a composer and pianist, also turned to teaching after his heyday with the New Stories Trio in the late '80s and early '90s. And Seales could provide his students with a direct connection to the region's straight-ahead past, since he had worked with bebop master Don Lanphere for eighteen years. Seales credits Lanphere (along with Floyd Standifer) with shaping his sound. And that sound has been heard on recordings by many artists in the Pacific Northwest, including Portland drummer Gary Hobbs, who also appears on a number of Seales's albums.

Hobbs, who started his career on the road with the Stan Kenton Orchestra in the 1970s, returned in the 1980s to Vancouver, Washington, to live just a block from the house where he grew up. One of the few Portland musicians to work regularly with Seattle players, Hobbs also began teaching at the University of Oregon in Eugene. That kind of commute is just one example of the accommodations jazz players have made in order to stay in the region.

The Pacific Northwest may not always have offered the amount of work that transplants to the region wanted, but it did provide a refuge of sorts, where it was possible to practice their art in the company of other high-level performers seeking something similar in terms of both community and environment. And their arrival, along with a higher public profile, was a signal that jazz in the Pacific Northwest had come of age. By 1992, Seattle and Portland had become attractive destinations for musicians, the economic boom of the Clinton years was underway, the quality and quantity of resident jazz was at its highest point since the 1940s, and the stage was set for even bigger things. Between 1994 and the end of the century, jazz in the Pacific Northwest would reach its zenith.

6

A Rising Tide: 1994–1999

"People want to live here. They choose to. So there's a certain defiance: 'I'm not going to move to New York, not going to one of those places; I live here.'"

John Bishop

SEEKING REFUGE, THEY FOUND EACH OTHER

Strange music spilled into homes around the country on Halloween of 1994, when Gary Larson's animated cartoon *Tales from the Far Side* was broadcast on network television. The soundtrack was by Bill Frisell, a friend of Larson and a fellow Seattle resident. Symbolically, it represented the integration of Frisell's generation of jazz immigrants into the scene—and the changes that produced in both newcomers and residents. It was also a sign that jazz in the Pacific Northwest was entering another golden age. And by the end of the century, the region's cities wouldn't be seen as just incubators or way stations on the road to more happening scenes but as desirable jazz destinations in their own right.

At first, Frisell had seen Seattle as a good place to raise a family, greener and safer than Manhattan. New Yorkers called his move west in 1989 a "retirement," and at first, he kind of agreed: "I guess I came here to hide out a little," he said. "New York was this place of constant input, but you were bombarded with stuff. It was hard to sort out."[1]

But he hadn't retired, just taken refuge. Gradually, Frisell discovered more local musicians he wanted to play with and a scene he wanted to explore. And as he began to work more often with fellow jazz immigrants like Eyvind Kang, Wayne Horvitz, and Michael Shrieve, Frisell encountered instrumentalists who also shared his values. "My thing about playing music with people is as much about my personal relationship with them as it is about the

Thara Memory came to Portland on tour with R&B star Joe Tex in 1970, worked with Obo Addy as well as Leroy Vinnegar, and later became one of the most important jazz educators in the region.

instrument they play. I'm happy that Eyvind plays the violin, but it's more about him as a person."[2]

In addition to finding compatible colleagues, Frisell discovered that many of the musicians who chose the region shared his thinking about music, too; especially the rapidly expanding group of New Music improvisers in Seattle, several of whom were in his *Far Side* band. He still traveled, but at home on the Upper Left Coast, Frisell felt he was among his people—and that didn't mean musicians only.

Cartoonist Larson is just one of the nonmusicians in Seattle who have influenced Frisell. Jim Woodring is another. His whimsical, cinematic art hangs in the guitarist's home, and Woodring created the cover for Frisell's 1998 album *Gone, Just Like a Train*. In the handwritten album notes, Frisell says he has "more in common with Woodring than with most musicians because we are both trying to scratch beyond the conscious veneer."

They also found that artists in the territory of Cascadia could be world-renowned figures and just folks, too. That suited Frisell perfectly.

He first met Larson, who grew up near the Tacoma wetlands, at Jazz Alley, and the two began jamming at each other's homes. The accommodating Frisell focused on blending in with Larson, an amateur guitarist. "I think there is something in Bill's personality where he'd rather play with lesser players who make a lot of mistakes but play from the heart than with great players who aren't showing any emotion," Larson says.[3]

IN THIS BRIGHT FUTURE, YOU CAN'T FORGET YOUR PAST

The extroverted young violinist Eyvind Kang was in Frisell's band for the *Far Side* soundtrack. But when he first came to Seattle from the prairies of Canada to study at the Cornish Institute, Kang had a lot to learn: "For instance, I thought bebop was in the past," he said. "Then I met Hadley Caliman and Julian Priester at Cornish.... Here were living spirits, not just some unidentified person on a recording. Just the way Hadley taught jazz history: he would talk about his life, tell stories, then throw on some Coltrane and start dancing!"[4]

Such experiences were vital. On the one side, jazz was opening up to international influences as well as absorbing more from rock and newly emergent hip-hop; on the other, contemporary classical music was also entering the field. Without a connection to its core traditions, jazz was in danger of losing its identity, even when it seemed to be riding high. And that connection had to be personal.

That's what pianist Darrell Grant acquired on the bandstand with such older generation stars as Roy Haynes and Betty Carter. "Actually being around Roy Haynes and seeing him off the job: how he talks, how he walks, how he carries himself ... that's all part of the music," Grant said.

Opportunities for such mentoring of younger musicians were few in Portland in the mid-1990s. So Grant organized "A Tribute to the Old Cats" at Portland State University, where he's now an associate professor, soon after he arrived in Portland. The concert program featured veterans of the Williams Avenue scene playing together and with a student ensemble. He hoped the symbolic torch-passing would inspire more direct contact between the generations.

Bill Frisell: Walking in Seattle

Bill Frisell is walking.

"Hear those crows?" he asks. He's looking toward Puget Sound from his Seattle neighborhood. It's too foggy to see the water.

He's just returned from another tour.

"Yesterday, I walked for six hours," he says. "When I get home, I just start walking, and I can't stop."

The walks are part of clearing away the clutter, he says, so he can play his guitar.

It might seem like that would be simple for Frisell, who's recorded more than twenty albums and been widely hailed as a master of the instrument.

But playing the guitar is "a constant struggle," he says.

"My whole life in music, I'm hearing this sound that's just beyond my grasp," he explains. "Sometimes it's very clear...but you can never get it right—it's this constant grasping at something you can never get.

"I used to think, years and years ago, that there was a point you'd get to—if you practiced really hard and did all the right things—where you'd feel music flowing out of you, it'd be this constant ecstasy. But it feels the same today as when I first picked up the instrument. You have to find a way to be comfortable with that, you have to embrace it."

Maybe that's what has made him such a productive artist. His *Unspeakable* won a Grammy Award for Best Contemporary Jazz Album in 2005; two other releases of his have received Grammy nominations. His songs have been featured on the soundtracks of such movies as *Finding Forrester*. He has performed works by all sorts of American composers, from Aaron Copland to Muddy Waters, and has written soundtracks for three Buster Keaton films.

It started when he first studied with revered guitarist Jim Hall.

"When I met him...I saw how he was getting his ideas from other instruments. That was the beginning of taking my attention away from the guitar and just thinking about music in general, and putting my attention toward the band.

"That's where my philosophy comes from. And that's where I get the most enjoyment: playing with other people. When everyone's focused on everyone else in the band, then the music just takes off, you just go into this amazing world."

The crows again rise with woody cries, almost like the sound of a clarinet—Frisell's first instrument.

"That also had an effect on what I play on guitar," he says, "just the feeling of the breath. And I did experience playing in bands and orchestras and woodwind quintets, playing with acoustic instruments and having to blend and balance—that affected me a lot."

His latest album, *All We Are Saying...*, sets a bigger challenge: to evoke the voice of John Lennon without using his words. It's another round in the constant struggle. He'll never reach the end of it, as he learned one night from Bill Evans.

"He was one of my biggest heroes, and he played in this little bar in Denver around 1971," Frisell recalls. "I went every night with my friends, and we couldn't believe how glorious this music was. One night, two in the morning, there's Bill Evans standing in the street, completely lost and alone, and he said, 'Hey, can you give me a ride to my hotel?' And on the way, we tell him how amazing the music was, and he's moping around and saying, 'Man, this whole week I haven't been able to get anything happening, I can't get it to work.'

"I was stunned. 'How can that be after what I've just heard?' And then a light went on, and I went, 'Oh, this is it; I guess I'm gonna feel this way my whole life.'"

Not coincidentally, the men who had taught Mel Brown about jazz thirty years earlier were some of the same musicians Grant recruited: Bobby Bradford, Cleve Williams, Sam Schlichting, Art Cheney, "Sweet Baby" James Benton and Eddie Wied. The six of them went on to a weekly gig; Brown played drums in the band.

Meanwhile, in Seattle, the "old cats" in the Legacy Quartet (with former Jackson Street star Floyd Standifer) kept on breaking records for the longevity of their tenure at the New Orleans Restaurant in Pioneer Square, a historic Seattle location in the old State Hotel Building. One of the first structures built after the great fire of 1889, the place felt cluttered, like husks of old tunes were caught among the cobwebs, and the wood floor was dark. It opened in 1985 and presented jazz and blues and New Orleans food until it closed nearly thirty years later. The Legacy Quartet took the stage every Wednesday night for all but five of those years. Toward the end, the club hosted numerous memorials for the generation that was passing, and the Legacy Quartet was gradually staffed with players in their forties who had learned directly from the Jackson Street veterans.

That changing of the guard at the New Orleans reflected other developments, too, as musicians moved out of the nightclubs and into new roles in their communities.

Bill Frisell left New York for Seattle, where he found a community of like-minded collaborators, including cartoonist Gary Larson.

A PLACE IN THE COMMUNITY

By the end of the century, jazz was being made under conditions quite different from those that had existed before. And jazz players were supplementing their income from music in different ways, too. Instead of day jobs as pipe fitters, secretaries, and barbers, jazz artists in the 1990s were working as college professors, high school band teachers, or private instructors. Some took day jobs in other fields. Some joined the growing numbers of stay-at-home dads. Once seen as folk poets who played a dangerous music and lived an outsider life, now they'd become middle class.

It was a change for the better for those who found sanctuary in academia, if only part-time; those jobs allowed resident players to survive the inevitable ups and down of nightclub, pit band, and studio work. Jazz programs were becoming more common in colleges and universities, and even middle schools had jazz bands. And those teaching jobs, especially at institutions of higher education, brought more high-level players to the region than ever before, including Darrell Grant, who came for a position at Portland State University in 1996. Like Frisell, he had come to make things happen.

In addition to continuing his recording and performing career, Grant helped establish a degree program in jazz. He launched and managed the university's jazz club, LV's Uptown, which was designed to connect students with a living jazz culture. After all, what had most inspired Grant about Leroy Vinnegar was the way the big-hearted bassist made himself part of the community.

"A while back I was offered the job as piano chair at Berklee [College of Music in Boston]. When I turned that down, I started thinking about why I really wanted to stay here and what I wanted to do. So I decided I wanted to try to connect the music more with the community."

Grant's more public role led to something else he'd come looking for: "a place where you walk down the street and people know who you are." The twenty-four-page booklet accompanying his 1999 album *Smokin' Java* tells the tale, in fictionalized form, of how he found that recognition in Portland. The story follows a jazz pianist whose day-long odyssey is capped by a coffeehouse performance where he not only finds the coffee and acceptance he's been looking for, but also realizes that his adopted city is a pretty good place to be.

The booklet included photos of prominent Portland personalities posed to represent its characters. It was an attempt to package a jazz album in a way that would bring listeners to the music with a welcoming attitude, encouraging them to think of it as an expression of shared experiences. He launched the album with performances in coffee shops.

"It's another way to build a bridge," he said, echoing his fictional pianist, who had come looking for community and discovered that it wasn't quite so simple. "Community was not something you found, it was something you opened yourself to, and that opened you in return."

And it freed him to be more fully himself.

"When I made *Black Art*," he said, remembering the 1994 album that made the *New York Times*'s list of the year's top ten jazz recordings, "I only channeled those parts of me that would be accepted by the national jazz community. And it was hugely accepted. But since then, every record has been opening more of myself." None of those records made the *Times*'s list, but that wasn't the point anymore. Grant had learned to define success in a different way. "Musicians have been conditioned to feel that success means . . . a big contract and your picture on all the magazines. We've lost sight of the fact that we do something that needs no intermediary."

Drummer Alan Jones would agree.

UNSAFE

Alan Jones was raised in the Pacific Northwest. He built his own drum kit and plays it barefoot. He likes to jump from high places—cliffs above the ocean, for instance, timing the waves to make sure he survives the plunge. He might even throw in a flip to give it some style.

Well-timed leaps with risk and style—projected through the music of the Alan Jones Sextet—drew young listeners to the Jazz de Opus in the late 1990s. They shoved into booths in the historic Old Town club, ordering beers and yelling to their friends. Soon the scene attracted others who wondered what the excitement was all about. Wasn't it just jazz?

Yes, but presented by a drummer of their generation, doing what young people have always enjoyed—taking risky leaps. The group's first album, released in 1998, was titled *Unsafe*, and came in a sealed bag with "Hazardous Material" warning signs and a photo of the band dressed in biohazard suits and gas masks.

"Our pianist, Randy Porter, first called us the 'unsafe sextet,'" Jones recalled. "It's a play on 'safe sex,' but it's really an attempt to describe the spirit of the band."

At the heart of that spirit is simply the adventure of modern jazz—six individuals improvising their way through a score they spontaneously reconstruct at every moment. Like jumping off a cliff. If all goes right, it's an exhilarating

» The adventurous music of Alan Jones's Sextet drew young audiences not necessarily familiar with jazz. The band conveyed the romance of risk-taking without disorienting listeners.

and courageous performance. By presenting the act of playing jazz as something inherently "unsafe," Jones was introducing a new generation to the jazz attitude as well as the music—and doing it with style.

His bandmates weren't all in their thirties. Saxophonist John Gross was in his fifties during the Sextet's heyday; alto saxophonist Warren Rand and trumpet player Paul Mazzio were in their forties. Gross had moved to Portland from Los Angeles in 1990 after a career in big bands, including four notable years with the Akiyoshi-Tabackin ensemble. In Portland, Gross unleashed his more "out" side, and his keening tenor later became a perfect complement to the improvisational excursions of David Friesen.

The sextet reflected the region's stylistic diversity, too, even within the straight-ahead tradition. Pianist Randy Porter had played in a trio with Friesen and Jones and toured with fiery New York saxophonist Charles McPherson. Warren Rand played on bluesman Robert Cray's Grammy-winning *Bad Influence* as well as with Seattle avant-gardists like Denney Goodhew. And Paul Mazzio was out of the big band and bebop tradition. With versatile bassist Dan Schulte, their tight and uninhibited music had much in common with the jazz coming from Seattle's straight-ahead players at the time.

Jones didn't hatch his project out of thin air. Since returning to his hometown after several years in Europe, he'd connected directly to local history as a member of David Friesen's trio. But it was Mel Brown who provided the foundation.

Nola Bogle: A Voice Borne on Long Memories

Nola Bogle has just released her first album, a fine example of the classic vocal style of the '40s and '50s. Her story opens a window on the diverse cultural heritage that shaped jazz in the Pacific Northwest.

The story begins in 1958, when the young singer (then Nola Sugai) took a bold step into her future.

With a father of Japanese and mother of Chinese ancestry, she had endured a lonely childhood in the eastern Oregon town of Ontario, where the family settled after their release from the Minidoka internment camp at the end of World War II. But that isolation steered her to music.

"There were no other Japanese people living in town, so there wasn't much for us to do as children except go to movies; that's where I really picked up on music," Bogle recalled.

From her father, a pro wrestler and amateur guitarist, she acquired a taste for the spotlight. Opportunities to sing were limited, however, so the underage Bogle had to find a pianist in nearby Payette, Idaho, who would let her sit in. Eventually she graduated to Boise, where her nearly unprecedented career really began.

Her desire to sing eventually carried her to Portland in 1964, where she soon had a job—and shortly thereafter a marriage to the city's handsome club-owning pianist, Sid Porter.

At Porter's club, a focal point for the jazz scene after the demise of the scene on Williams Avenue, Bogle sang six nights a week. It wasn't glamorous: "You were doing everything," she remembers, "sometimes waiting tables, sometimes bartending, sometimes cooking; a lot of cleaning up. Sid never took a break from the piano from the time he sat down."

After Porter died in 1970, Bogle continued performing for three years, but the needs of her children finally drove her into a secretarial job, from which she emerged only for rare performances. But she was preparing to sing again.

"In the years when I wasn't doing music, I was storing up a lot inside that I wanted to give out," she says. "So today I have a greater feel for what I put into the music."

What she puts into the jazz standards and show tunes on her album *Something Cool* is understated emotion and assured ease. With her alto voice out front in the gorgeous but spare arrangements by Darrell Grant (the album's producer and pianist), Bogle's leisurely interpretations of such challenging material as "Lush Life" and "'Round Midnight" turn the songs into dramatic vignettes.

Those interpretations grow out of the camp at Minidoka, the isolation of Ontario, the nightclubs of Payette, Boise, and Portland. And they include emotions stored as a mother and a secretary. It's a story she tells in every song—an Oregon story.

"I started at age fourteen, when Mel had his drum shop. It was an institution!" Jones remembers his first real instruction. "The most important thing I got from Mel was a sense of grace in playing. He was so beautiful. There was technique behind that. He gave me an understanding of the connection between technique and beauty."

Part of a young musician's development includes rejecting the past, and Jones had to separate from such a powerful influence in order to find himself. Since Brown's music made a listener feel safe and on familiar ground, Jones had to make his sound like a cliff dance—and dress the part, too.

"Mel always carried himself so well. For most of my career I rebelled against that. Mel had a very calculated style. And that, I recognized, was a real benefit, an important part of the presentation of the music. But I didn't want to copy Mel's style. I wanted to use the ideas in my own way."

With his sextet, Jones finally did build the vehicle he needed to express those ideas, and he wrote music in which the unpredictable improvisations of his bandmates were framed by melodic structures. Thus he conveyed the romance of risk-taking without completely disorienting his listeners. At the same time—again, to be expected, considering the intergenerational connections in the Pacific Northwest—Jones was also playing with Vinnegar, to whom he dedicated his sextet's second album. That music was adventurous, too, and dissonant at times, but accessible and tied closely to the straight-ahead tradition.

By contrast, keyboard player and composer Wayne Horvitz came to Seattle from a New York scene where "unsafe" was just the starting point. And when he arrived in 1988, Horvitz took improvisational music in the Pacific Northwest in a new and challenging direction.

"He sacrificed being on the cutting edge in New York," observes Paul de Barros, "and he became more involved in the Seattle music scene: teaching,... being in touch with people who run jazz programs in the schools, and mounting programs that use local musicians. I think of him sort of like a modern Charles Ives for our town," de Barros adds, comparing Horvitz to the iconoclastic classical composer of New England. "He uses local people, isn't necessarily worried about fame and success... just contributing to the community."

His energy captured the spirit of the '90s, when anything seemed possible and optimism was in the moist Puget Sound air. Horvitz began working himself into the fabric of the region's experimental music community, moving toward the major role he'd play in the new century. By then, the imagination that had fed off the discordant grit of Manhattan would be altered by his new diet of soft-edged greenery.

That didn't make him any more mainstream, however, and the fact that an activist from the country's leading experimental music scene could flourish in Seattle made it clear: the flag of the avant-garde had been raised over a city where the straight-ahead banner had once flown. Under it sheltered a diverse community of artists. Many were products of jazz studies programs and, by the 1990s, there were a number of graduates in the area—and a burgeoning audience interested in something new.

Daughter of a Chinese mother and Japanese father, Nola Bogle started her career in small eastern Oregon and Idaho towns before she moved to Portland and married pianist Sid Porter. At his club, she sang six nights a week.

SEATTLE'S AVANT-GARDE IN THE '90s

The new was busting out all over, as *5/4 Magazine* proclaimed: "Nineteen ninety-four brought forth a sense of freedom in jazz in the Seattle area. Many small cafés began to sponsor jazz and jazz poetry on a regular basis, while clubs devoted to rock have given over at least one night a week to jazz. An enormous field of experimentation has opened, and cross-pollination of musical talent has taken hold in the community like never before."[5]

It even had the momentum to carry iconoclastic saxophonist Bert Wilson into the Tacoma Art Museum for a program of readings, exhibits, and live music. One of the region's most respected avant-gardists, Wilson had been confined to a wheelchair since the age of four by polio. The disease affected his lungs, and he

Top: Living in Portland has given Darrell Grant the freedom to explore his musical vision. Since recording the acclaimed *Black Art*, which contained only music that Grant felt the national jazz community would accept, he says that "every record has been opening more of myself."

Bottom: Avant-garde bassist Michael Bisio gained international acclaim with his album *In Seattle*. "He's like a beatnik, a white guy into militant black music. He's stayed true to his vision: he's an avant-garde player, has developed his own style, plays what he wants to play, and has never compromised," says Paul de Barros.

credited saxophone playing with their recovery. With the lung capacity he'd built up, Wilson developed techniques for playing two and sometimes three notes at a time, called "multiphonics," and extended the range of the tenor saxophone several octaves. His chest was big, appearing all the larger in contrast to his wasted legs. His head seemed large, too, his face framed by long hair and a bushy beard. He was an inspirational figure.

Early in his career, Wilson lived alone on the sixth floor of a New York building with no elevator. "They would carry him up two flights," said his long-time partner, flutist Nancy Curtis, "then take him over the precipice to the roof of the next building, where they'd go up the elevator."

Life got easier when two members of the band Obrador threw a benefit to raise money to move Wilson from New York to Olympia in 1979. He became a powerful influence through his teaching and uncompromising performances, though his music was always on the margins. He did perform frequently at the Earshot Jazz Festival and other major events, however, and for a time he played weekly with saxophonist Chuck Stentz at an Olympia cafe. And Wilson was just one of the fearless adventurers working the outer fringes of the jazz tradition.[6]

Bassist Michael Bisio's 1987 album *In Seattle* put him on the international avant-garde map. He'd relocated from upstate New York in 1976 to study at the University of Washington, and it turned out to be a good fit. Like Bill Smith, who was on the faculty at the time, Bisio had a background in both jazz and classical music. But the bassist put his tools to very different use. He arrived at the university just as African American studies pioneer Joe Brazil was being let go for using live jazz performances in the classroom instead of traditional instructional methods. There were marches on campus. It was the run-up to the rambunctious "Generation of '79." In that unsettled and exciting atmosphere, Bisio found a home.

"Bisio is one of those wild and wooly guys on the edge, who also has big-time classical chops," writes Paul de Barros. Bisio didn't like to emphasize that background. "It might give people the wrong idea," said the man de Barros described as "a ferociously free improviser who often attacks the bass with anything but European decorum."[7]

"He's like a beatnik, a white guy into militant black music. He's stayed true to his vision: he's an avant-garde player, has developed his own style, plays what he wants to play, and has never compromised," says de Barros. Ultimately, however, Bisio had to move to New York City, where the audience was larger and collaborators fiercer.

But Bisio and Wilson represent only one approach in the Puget Sound's diverse avant-garde scene. Among its most accessible variations was a pastoral approach that is perhaps more typical of the region. Even before that sensibility was widely expressed in jazz, the group of Seattle visual artists called "Northwest Mystics" was bringing the landscape and its history into their paintings. In an era when abstract expressionism ruled New York art circles, those regional artists were producing works with a connection to the environment that was later echoed by some influential Pacific Northwest jazz players.

The dreamy sound of Frisell's guitar has become more spare and hallucinatory over his years in Seattle. Bassist David Friesen, a Puget Sound native and pioneer of open, folk-like harmonies in jazz, also took up shakuhachi flute in the 1990s,

Darrell Grant Finds a Community

Darrell Grant was moving fast. So fast that, at age forty-five, he had already achieved many of his musical goals. So fast that he needed a sabbatical. At mid-career, it was time for renewal and a new beginning.

In his twenties, Grant had something to prove, so he settled in New York. He had a bachelor's degree in classical piano from the Eastman School of Music and a graduate degree in jazz studies from the University of Miami. In bands led by Roy Haynes and Betty Carter, Grant showed he could play and deserved his place.

In his thirties, he made his mark with the 1994 album *Black Art*, which critics received with great enthusiasm. But that wasn't enough.

"I didn't feel my music was having the kind of impact I wanted," he recalls. "I was looking for a sense of community, a place where I could make a contribution and serve."

So in 1996, when a position in Portland State University's music department opened up, Grant was ready. In the eventful ten years since, the Denver native has indeed made a contribution and established a vital place for himself in the area.

Besides advancing his national reputation with the three albums he's made since coming to Portland (*Smokin' Java, Spirit,* and *Truth and Reconciliation*—the first two of which reached jazz radio's top ten charts), Grant achieved local recognition with a performing schedule that found him on Portland stages nearly every week.

To accomplish all that, the adept cultural entrepreneur borrowed the collaborative techniques of nonprofit arts groups, creating partnerships with businesses and government agencies to help build jazz in Portland.

And then it was time for a change.

Grant's new direction probably began to take shape with the album *Spirit*, the first on which he released originals that were not in the straight-ahead tradition. And "Spirit" was the first recording on which he sang.

"I said, 'OK, this is the music I care about, and I'm just going to play it in the most meaningful way I know how.'" And then came the 2007 double album *Truth and Reconciliation*: "The record I always dreamed of making," he says. "I was never bold enough to put out this music before because it wasn't jazz enough.

"Every record has been opening more of wedge into myself, and when I was trying to do this one, I made this commitment to myself that I was only going to listen to my inner voice. For me," he concludes, "that was a real challenge, because I was so hyperaware of the externals."

Living in Portland has helped. "Being here, I've been encouraged to explore my own personal vision, and I've had the opportunity to do it," he says. "This musical environment has been supportive of me growing as a musician."

Another factor that helped set him free were changes in the music business. "When I graduated from college," he says, "Wynton was on Columbia and winning Grammys, so that was my goal. But now there's no money in it. All the major labels have gotten out of jazz. So we're not bothering with that anymore, and that's created a lot of freedom."

And the birth of his son, Malcolm, more than two years ago, also spurred his change of course.

"'So what do I want him to know about me?' I asked myself. I want him to know his father was someone who went after his deepest dreams."

echoing the Northwest Mystics' interest in Asian cultures. His former partner, guitarist John Stowell, built his approach on spare voicings and single lines. And in the '90s, saxophonist Denney Goodhew also developed an improvisational approach more pastoral than hard-edged.

A long-time Seattle resident whose career was rocketing upward during this period, Goodhew started teaching at the Cornish Institute in 1974 when he was only twenty-two. He recorded and performed in multiple styles, from avant-garde to blues, soul, and rock, on albums with such diverse fellow Cascadians as Don Lanphere and Wayne Horvitz. He also recorded with his Cornish colleagues Julian Priester and Jerry Granelli.

In the early '90s, when guitarist Ralph Towner lived in Seattle, he and Goodhew had a regular duo act. Their ECM album *Lost and Found* is brimming with a cool, quietly questing Pacific Northwest approach to harmonic explorations. But Goodhew's teeth were giving him trouble, and it became more and more difficult to play his horn. Fellow musicians threw a benefit to help him pay for dental work but, even so, he had to restrict his sax playing. Goodhew decided to concentrate on percussion and painting instead.

It was a typically Cascadian response. Music, like many other art forms, is a personal practice, Goodhew decided; public performances are not its primary purpose. It's the process, not the product that's important. Music expresses an individual's way of life, he reasoned; it is inseparable from the way one lives and breathes. "Becoming a better musician is about the person becoming who they are." That doesn't mean making music is easy—art only results from discipline and rigorous practice, he believed.

He began to put that philosophy into action.

Goodhew moved to Germany and taught at Berlin University of the Arts for five years, at the same time earning a Reiki Master/teaching degree and mounting an exhibit of his paintings in Amsterdam. In 1998, he returned to his teaching job at Cornish, demonstrating the music on hand drum rather than saxophone.

Goodhew believes that growing up in the high desert town of Walla Walla on the Columbia River in eastern Washington led him to be a musician. His grandfather, an asparagus farmer who intended to pull a prank on the boy, told Goodhew that if he listened carefully, he could hear the plants growing. So he spent hours down on his hands and knees, listening in vain. But it turned out to be the perfect ear training for an improvising musician. In his teaching today, Goodhew encourages students to unplug and expose themselves to "that combination of space and silence" he first heard in the asparagus fields above the Columbia.[8]

Though a couple members of the Seattle band Bebop & Destruction did study with Goodhew's colleagues at Cornish, there was little space and silence in their music. They too fed off the kind of madcap energy that animated Skerik's Critters Buggin, but they applied that freedom through the language of bebop. From 1994 to 1996, they played Monday nights at Seattle's Brick Street Bar and Grill, honing a high-spirited and often exhilarating live act that harked back to the Jackson Street era.

"We tried to take some of the highbrow attitude out of jazz," said John Wicks, the band's drummer. "When the founding fathers started this music, it was about dancing." Bebop & Destruction made use of performance art, as well; the band's bassist Geoff Harper frequently sported a crazy quilt wardrobe for his stage antics.

Two of the moon's craters are named after compositions by Ralph Towner, whose recordings with the band Oregon were sent to space on Apollo 15. He lived in Seattle in the early 1990s.

    The young band also included guitarist Dan Heck, a transplant from Long Island. "This resurgence of young players is definitely what's making things happen right now," he told de Barros, who praised the band's visceral connection with their audience: "The young and convivial crowd may not know 'Green Dolphin Street' from 'Freedom Jazz Dance,'" de Barros wrote, "but they follow the music with their feet and their eyes, whether it's sizzling bop, a Louis Armstrong two-beat, or a '60s-style groove tune."[9]

    Alto sax player Marc Fendel, son of a jazz DJ and music critic, completed the band. Trained in Portland's public school jazz programs of the 1980s, at sixteen Fendel sat in at the Otter Crest Jazz Party with venerable bassist Milt Hinton. Add to that his father's record collection, and you've got the future coming right out of the tradition. Maybe that's why, when Fendel was looking for something different from Bebop & Destruction, he moved toward funk rather than the avant-garde. He was also responding to a funk revival that caught fire nationwide in the '90s. Fendel and his colleagues called their new co-op band Swampdweller. It included B3 player Joe Doria, who went on to lead the popular organ trio McTuff.

    The Pacific Northwest supported a lot of stylistic diversity during those years. It was the beginning of the fragmentation of the Seattle jazz community into the separate scenes that exist today. But it was an exciting moment, as if a thousand

"In this bright future, you can't forget your past." Mel Brown, center, with Eddie Wied, Red Holloway, Leroy Vinegar and Jack Sheldon.

flowers had bloomed at once. The avant-garde certainly was sending fresh tendrils in every direction, while funk and soul-jazz were making a comeback; smooth jazz was on the rise, and straight-ahead still had a considerable audience. The Jazz Society of Oregon, supported primarily by straight-ahead fans, reached a historic high of nearly one thousand members in 1998. Nearly every style found a home in the region's nightclubs, cafés, and restaurants that offered jazz for listening or dancing—including a new club called Jimmy Mak's in a Portland neighborhood that was rapidly gentrifying. Riding the funk revival as well as the city's deep support for straight-ahead jazz, the club prospered in the new golden age. Its growth, and the music that made it popular, paralleled the economic and social changes of those years.

And there was Mel Brown, at the heart of it all once again.

LOCATION, LOCATION, LOCATION

Like the neighborhood where it's located, Jimmy Mak's started out old-school. The original clientele was a mix of workers from neighborhood businesses as well as jazz fans from the rest of the city. The business prospered along with the neighborhood's progressive gentrification, and Jimmy Mak's eventually became the city's top jazz club. The music that owner Jimmy Makarounis wanted, he recalled, was the soul-jazz he'd heard on a rare vinyl album by Billy Larkin and the Delegates called *Pigmy*. He was talking to Brown one day and mentioned it; Brown laughed. It was the first record he'd ever made.

Music alone won't make a happening scene, as Louis Pain understood from the years he'd spent in the Paul deLay Blues Band. Pain was playing the organ in Brown's B3 Group when they started at Jimmy Mak's in 1997. That's where Pain met his future duo partner, Williams Avenue veteran "Sweet Baby" James Benton. At the time, Benton wasn't performing, but he showed up regularly to hear Brown's band—after all, he'd given the drummer a start at his jam sessions on Williams Avenue in the 1950s.

"James and a couple of other older black guys were our 'Amen Corner,'" Pain recalls. "They were at this one table all the time, shouting encouragement. They were just so supportive and vocal, and I really think they helped make the Mel Brown Thursday nights at Jimmy Mak's so popular."

By 2015, Brown's B3 Organ Group had completed seventeen years of Thursday nights at Jimmy Mak's, a record of longevity matched only by that of the Legacy Quartet at the New Orleans Restaurant, and several solo pianists like Portland's Jean Ronne, who played the Benson Hotel's Lobby Lounge for more than thirty years. But a nightclub is a more volatile enterprise, and few last long as jazz venues.

In 2006, Makarounis bought a larger space across the street and turned it into a fine dining establishment seating more than one hundred people with an elevated stage and quality sound system. To the left of the stage was a brass plaque reading "Mel's Place."

The evolution of Jimmy Mak's from neighborhood bar to upscale nightclub signaled the changes coming to all of Portland—changes of the sort that had already transformed Seattle from a magnet for artists to a haven for high-salaried tech workers and others in the employ of corporations like Microsoft and Starbucks.

Louis Pain attributes the success of Mel Brown's B3 Organ Group at Jimmy Mak's to the enthusiastic support of "the Amen Corner"—a group of older black men led by former Williams Aveune singer Sweet Baby James.

ORIGIN RECORDS

Starbucks was not yet the multinational giant it would become, but by the mid-1990s, the coffee company was expanding and had opened its first stores in New York City. Prominently on display there were Kenny G CDs (his 1992 album, *Breathless*, had just sold twelve million copies). Since then, the specialty retailer has stocked selected jazz, indie rock, and singer-songwriter CDs that are played over the in-house sound system and sold at the counter.

Starbucks also hired young jazz musicians from Seattle who were living in New York to play live for the stores' opening season. By day, the musicians were employed as baristas. One of them was drummer John Bishop. Soon after, he returned to Seattle and became one of the most important actors in the unfolding story of jazz in the region when he founded Origin Records in 1997.

Oregon-reared Bishop's original plan wasn't to be big-time; on the label's first three albums, he played drums and did all the production. But then it took off. Soon sublabels were added as well as a partner, drummer Matt Jorgensen, who began handling design and production. By 2015, the catalog had swelled to nearly four hundred albums. That number reflects a growing cadre of highly skilled players anxious to share their work.

Bishop calls the company a cooperative: selected artists bring their recordings to the label and pay the company for design, duplication, and packaging. The label handles distribution and the revenue is split, with the artist getting the lion's share.

The spirit of the jazz that makes up the bulk of the Origin catalog, says Bishop, is pure Pacific Northwest: "People want to live here. They choose to. So there's a certain defiance: 'I'm not going to move to New York, not going to one of those

Rebecca Kilgore: Lucky

A year ago, Portland-based singer Rebecca Kilgore was performing at Carnegie Hall with Michael Feinstein. She's just released her thirty-fifth album, *Why Fight the Feeling? Songs by Frank Loesser*, with Dave Frishberg. Kilgore has been a frequent guest on NPR program *Fresh Air* and has performed twice at the Cabaret Convention in New York. At jazz parties, she's worked with musicians she once idolized, including Scott Hamilton.

Surprisingly, though, Kilgore finds her greatest musical satisfaction at home.

"I don't need those big names," she says. "They're kind of nerve-racking, in a way. Just give me a bunch of good musicians, or one Dave Frishberg, and I'm just as happy as being at Carnegie Hall."

Living in Portland, in fact, has been a boon for the singer's musical development.

"I've been very fortunate because there are such superb musicians in Portland," she says. "I can't imagine anywhere else I would have the good fortune of working with these great musicians."

And yet she's done pretty well in New York, performing frequently in top cabaret and nightclub settings including Birdland and Feinstein's. And she's doing what she loves best: "preserving and interpreting the great vocal jazz of the '20s, '30s, and '40s."

"I'm kind of a song geek," says Kilgore. "I'm an archeologist, an archivist, and I really like finding "new" old songs. It's amazing how many songs from that era I've never heard of, and they're good."

So what makes an old song worth preserving and performing?

"High-quality songwriting and heartfelt lyrics," says Kilgore. "We know it because it lasts. It's deep and beautifully crafted and evokes some emotions. I'm looking for something unusual, clever, [and] a beautiful melody is very important to me. I might gravitate more toward a beautiful melody than the lyrics. But of course the lyrics have to be intelligent and subtle—you don't talk about love by talking about love."

And since so many of the old songs are overdone, she needs to always be out prospecting for songs new to her and her listeners. And she's played for some big audiences, especially during festival performances with the group BED (Becky Kilgore, Eddie Erickson, and Dan Barrett), one of her most important associations since the mid-'90s.

They play music not far removed from the western swing that Kilgore once performed with the Portland group Wholly Cats, or from her work with fiddle player James Mason on their duo album *Cactus Setup*.

She doesn't play that style anymore, but as a western swing artist Kilgore played guitar. She recently returned to the instrument on an album with jazz ukulele master Lyle Ritz titled *I Wish You Love*. Most of her western swing experience was in the 1980s, when she quit her day job as a secretary at Reed College to become a full-time musician.

"It was like jumping off a cliff," she says. "It was scary, but I'm still doing it. I love working," she adds. "And I'm lucky to have the opportunity."

» Drummer John Bishop became one of the most important figures in the region's jazz scene when he founded Origin Records in 1997.

places; I live here.' Here you're afforded time to work through things. I think you can get away with being yourself more."[10]

It's a consistent refrain: the freedom to be yourself, made possible by distance from power, fortune, and fame. You're not likely to make the big time, but like Bishop, you'll earn enough to keep doing it. That's the goal of most jazz players in the region.

THE QUINTESSENTIAL LOCAL MUSICIAN

In a *Wall Street Journal* article about Seattle musician Jay Thomas, critic Nat Hentoff reminds readers of a fact that most Pacific Northwest fans already know: "There are indeed formidable, largely hometown players around the country who never have broken through to the big time."[11] Jay Thomas, Hentoff wrote, is one of them. "The quintessential local musician," Paul de Barros calls him.

Born in 1950, Thomas is a bridge between the Jackson Street era and the twenty-first century. He appears on more than sixty albums that run the gamut from hip-hop to big band. A versatile multi-instrumentalist, he plays trumpet, flugelhorn, and flutes as well as alto, tenor, and soprano sax. He also made his mark in the region as a teacher, was inducted into the Seattle Jazz Hall of Fame, and was named 2012's Northwest Instrumentalist of the Year by Earshot Jazz.

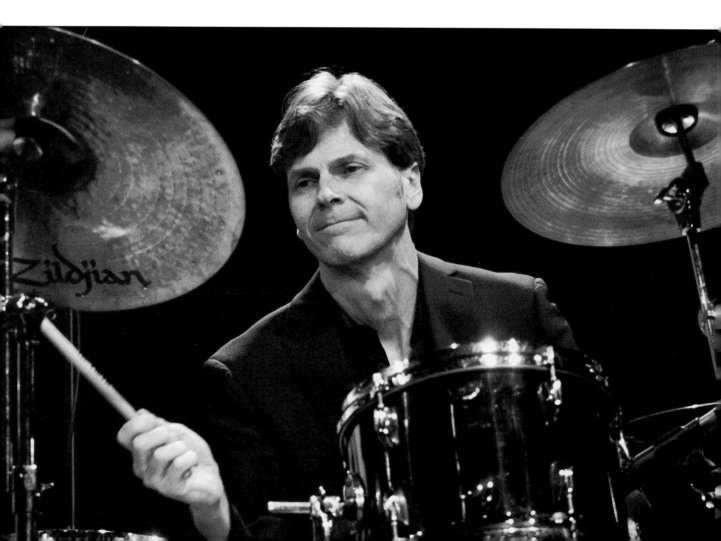

It's a title he won in 1996 and 1998, too. At the time, he'd been back home in Seattle nearly fifteen years after an odyssey that took him from Berklee College of Music in Boston to New York and San Francisco. His father, a former-jazz-player-turned-pharmacist, was co-owner of Parnell's, the city's second-largest jazz club. When Thomas returned to Seattle, he became a member of the house band. Once he'd put drug addiction behind him—it took a while—he began recording and playing with a wide circle of Seattle musicians.[12]

So there he was in 1996, the city's most popular straight-ahead jazz artist. Ready for the next step, Thomas didn't look to New York, though. He turned toward Asia. By then, he'd established himself and understood how the business worked: when you haven't "made it in New York," you tour alone, on a grassroots level. He built a list of friends and contacts in Japan, allied himself with a Japanese big band, and traveled there for six consecutive years.

"I lucked into my situation by meeting Japanese musicians, going over there, and just playing with them," Thomas says. He has played Japan's biggest jazz club, Blues Alley, but more often finds himself in small rooms like Solaka, a restaurant where he was taken one dark night. "It may be one of the smallest clubs in the world," he says. "There's seating for twelve people. Fans pay forty bucks apiece, and I think the club is run by one person. Musicians really love to play there."[13]

Especially musicians like Thomas—and fellow touring jazz artists David Friesen and John Stowell, with whom Thomas has recorded. The Pacific Northwest offered them the freedom to develop highly individual voices, a pursuit held in the highest esteem by jazz devotees. And they found ways to share their unique vision with the world—sometimes only twelve people at a time.

What does the quintessential local musician do when he's reached the top in Seattle? In the 1990s, he took his music global. It was a period of looking outward, of expansive optimism in the Pacific Northwest. "You can have a good life as a musician," Thomas said then. And in those years, many did.

A PEAK MOMENT

"There's a lot of young players who sound awfully good to me," says Thomas, who was a mentor to many in the generation of Puget Sound jazz players coming of age in the 1990s. "One of the things I think is different is that there's a social framework; it's not something out of a classroom. You see them out there in the clubs, and they're actually glad to see each other."[14]

"I think we had a real heyday in the '90s," says de Barros. "We had a lot of young players, well schooled but unstuffy, technically astounding but not show-offs, serious as hell about their music but fun on stage." Some of them were products of the region's excellent high school jazz programs, like the brothers Thomas Marriott and David Marriott, Jr. "Seattle's a really good place to learn," said Thomas, a 1994 graduate of Garfield High School. "There are all these really good, older musicians who are totally accessible—Buddy Catlett, Floyd Standifer, Marc Seales. They'll tell you what you want to know, and they won't dog you out."[15]

Many of those young musicians, like the Marriotts, played in the straight-ahead tradition in which they'd been schooled. That group also included the Davis/Taylor

Project, led by tenor saxophonist Rob Davis, from the suburb of Silverlake, and alto player Mark Taylor, who came up through Seattle high schools; both studied at the University of Washington. Davis later moved to Portland, where he worked with both John Stowell and David Friesen.

Other young players were moving away from jazz, including violinist Eyvind Kang. He may have discovered the living tradition in his teachers at Cornish, but he studied with avant-garde violinist Michael White, too. One year, Kang debuted his 10th NADE composition at the Bumbershoot Music Festival on roller skates, wearing a skirt. Like Kang, guitarist Tim Young, who came to Seattle in the late 1980s, also worked with the experimentalist Wayne Horvitz. Young, however, gravitated toward a fusion of avant-garde jazz with the dissonance, noise, and theatrical presentations of rock.

That youth movement seemed to be another sign that the scene had returned to the vibrancy of the golden age, and de Barros was optimistic: "It felt like everything was in place. We had jazz education, we had Earshot Jazz, we had a street scene, a lot of clubs. Origin Records had started. It just seemed like there was kind of a peak, like everything was in place for a very exciting jazz scene."

Press coverage had never been so complete. The dailies in Portland and Seattle routinely reported on most major jazz artists who played the area, there were profiles of local players, and the festivals received extensive coverage. The Ballard Jazz Festival joined the list of regional jazz events, and smooth jazz had developed a large audience of its own.

Mayor Vera Katz issued a proclamation in January 1998 declaring Portland the "jazz capital of the West Coast." Pretty bold, but jazz in Portland and all over the Pacific Northwest was indeed at a high point.

That peak was built on a well-developed infrastructure: a sufficiently large group of skilled jazz players; support organizations; strong, visible jazz-education programs; record labels and jazz radio stations; presenting organizations and promoters; festivals and other high-visibility events; press coverage; performance venues; music-related employment; a favorable cost of living; the opportunity for a lifestyle attractive to artists; and an audience willing and able to support them.

All that optimism, and the jazz activity that engendered it, stemmed from the economic prosperity of the decade. In 1993, the median US household income was $48,884. Six years later, it was $56,080, and the Dow Jones Index had risen from 2,753 to 11,497.

Even in the best of times, however, the life of a jazz musician was precarious without the security of an academic position or an accommodating day job. Pay for nightclub work was about the same as it had been a decade before, and the cost of living was going up. By 1999, Paul Allen and Bill Gates were billionaires, and literally thousands of their former employees were millionaires. Microsoft spawned a host of other companies in the Seattle area, and Allen went on to build a new football stadium and the Experience Music Project, a world-renowned museum of contemporary musical culture. The corporatization that would transform Seattle into a "San Francisco on the Sound" over the next ten years was underway.

Nevertheless, the Pacific Northwest was still an attractive place to play jazz and pursue a lifestyle that emphasized personal and artistic goals over financial success. So the musicians kept coming, some expecting to find a jazz mecca, others just a nice place to raise a family. No matter what brought them, they eventually found each other. As a result of those collaborations, the sound of the music changed. But the region's core values remained: nice guys still finished first, promising young players were nurtured, jam sessions flourished, and the landscape remained a powerful influence.

It seemed then as if this new golden age would continue indefinitely alongside the region's growing economy. In retrospect, however, it's evident that the economy—much like the cartoon character whose mad dash has carried him over a precipice he hasn't yet seen—kept its legs churning for another seven years until it realized it was running on nothing but thin air, and plummeted. But those were seven pretty good years for jazz in the Pacific Northwest. Despite the hegemony of the new traditionalism during the early 2000s, great variety flourished in the region, and the golden age of the late 1990s extended until the global financial crisis of 2007.

In 2000, Paul Allen of Microsoft built the Experience Music Project, a world-renowned museum of contemporary musical culture that tied the economic prosperity of the day directly to the growth of Seattle as a music city.

7

Riding the Wave: 1999–2007

"I believe boldness is the most important quality in jazz. The more headstrong and bold you are to jump into things, the better."

Dusty York

"We cultivate musicians here. They get to develop, and because of the scene, they can continue developing.

Rita Rega

SUITS/NO SUITS

Now this is where things get interesting—or really complicated. And polarized too. Even though the jazz scene in the Pacific Northwest was drawing more quality players and raising its local profile, it wasn't all smooth sailing. At the dawn of the new century, America was changing, but jazz seemed to be digging in its heels, at least as it was played by the neotraditionalists. So dominant was their definition of jazz, it became something of a straightjacket. And it was about to get tighter.

Wynton Marsalis rose to prominence in the late 1980s as a defender of the jazz tradition. The son of a long-standing New Orleans jazz family, his mission was a return to the hard bop style purveyed by the likes of Miles Davis in the early 1960s, before jazz rock, funk, smooth, and free had come along to muddy what had once been swinging and pure. At least that was the story, and Marsalis had the skills and cultural capital to advance his vision. In 1990, he was on the cover of *Time* magazine. He won Grammy awards in both classical and jazz categories, and his signature project, Jazz at Lincoln Center, involved construction of three halls at the center of the iconic Manhattan landmark at a cost of $131 million. In 2001, the Marsalis view of jazz was canonized in the ten-part Ken Burns documentary *Jazz*. Marsalis was the senior creative consultant and appeared extensively in the $13 million film, offering historical information, demonstrations, and commentary.

Wynton Marsalis rose to prominence in the late 1980s as a defender of tradition. Serving as senior creative consultant of the ten-part PBS series, Ken Burns's *Jazz*, solidified his neotraditionalist view as the dominant image of the genre.

The national broadcast of *Jazz* on public television was a momentous event. With its polished production and compelling story line, the image of jazz that the series presented became widely accepted, especially in the absence of alternative visions able to reach a general audience. Nine of its ten episodes covered the years between 1917 and 1960; only one was devoted to the forty years that followed. Critics claimed that this narrow focus, and the definition of jazz it enshrined, presented the music as a museum piece and oversimplified its complex development.

That image of jazz as a cultural artifact of the 1940s and '50s may well have contributed to the continuing reduction in jazz audiences, especially among listeners raised on hip-hop and rock. The diverse scene in the Pacific Northwest didn't fit neatly into the Ken Burns definition of jazz either. Artists in the region whose music was changing with the times had to counter that restrictive definition if they hoped to develop an audience beyond its aging fan base. Between the turn of the century and the financial crisis of 2007, many jazz musicians found ways to do just that.

AGAINST THE TIDE

One young Portland jazz player tried to buck the tide with the aggressive production and sale of jazz albums. And for a couple years before the financial crash of 2007, it looked like it might work. Saxophonist Dusty York's Diatic Records was devoted to straight-ahead jazz with an edge. His priority was original compositions and unique ensembles from Portland, including young musicians like keyboard player Ben Darwish, age twenty-two at the time. But the Diatic catalog also featured an equal number of veterans. York is the son of the late saxophonist Michael York, and the younger York also released albums by his father's peers, including pianist Gordon Lee and saxophonist Renato Caranto. One Diatic release featured a trio representing three generations: pianist/songwriter Dave

Frishberg, in his seventies; saxophonist John Gross, in his fifties; and drummer Charlie Doggett, in his thirties. York also released an album featuring him and his father playing together.

York had a more hard-edged, dissonant approach than his father, but the young activist was pushing more than musical boundaries. He was hoping to bring a different attitude to what he saw as a moribund jazz scene: "I believe boldness is the most important quality in jazz," he said. "The more headstrong and bold you are to jump into things, the better."

York attempted to increase the audience by combining jazz with visual arts and presenting both in designers' studios and other nontraditional venues. He had a good run, and for eight years Diatic was Portland's most active jazz label. A key component of the scene was lost when York closed up shop. "I want to make music that people want to hear," he said. So he picked up a guitar, started writing songs, and emerged an indie rocker.

THE POWER OF THE PRESS

Fortunately, both of the region's major daily newspapers had knowledgeable and committed music critics reporting on the diverse local scene. Paul de Barros at the *Seattle Times* and Marty Hughley at the *Oregonian* presented jazz as a serious and lively art form. Their extensive coverage raised its visibility and reputation.

A Portland native, Hughley's attention to local music of all genres—and his skill in capturing what was important about it for readers—prompted the music community in Portland to induct him into the Oregon Music Hall of Fame. Major touring jazz stars were reviewed and previewed; even local artists had album releases and other major events featured in the arts section. But Hughley had to report on all the popular music in town, leaving him without the time or column inches to push the coverage of jazz farther. It was hard to justify anyway, given the music's relatively small audience.

Hughley's predecessor at the *Oregonian* faced some of the same problems. John Wendeborn had been a part-time trombone player on Williams Avenue in the '50s, and he made sure there was some coverage of jazz in the 1960s and '70s. But he too was obliged to direct the majority of his reporting elsewhere. Had less knowledgeable or committed journalists been in that position, however, the audience for and chronicle of jazz in the region would have been greatly diminished. In a small city such as Portland, the work of a single individual can have a major impact on the perception of an art form.

As a family-owned newspaper, the *Seattle Times* was able to give de Barros the space and license to report and comment on music he deemed important to readers, and he used that freedom to shape the perception of jazz. One striking instance was his reporting in the 1990s and early 2000s on the award-winning high school jazz bands from Roosevelt and Garfield high schools. Both were historic programs—Quincy Jones and Ernestine Anderson got their start at Garfield. And both schools were perennial winners at student jazz competitions.

"I wrote to sell what they were doing like a sports competition," de Barros says, "because I knew that would please readers and parents and please the kids." The

increased public awareness of their ability and national reputation inspired more students to participate and helped raise funds for travel.

Then, in 1999, the Essentially Ellington competition in New York City opened to schools west of the Mississippi. The Garfield and Roosevelt programs had been winning regularly at the Monterey Jazz Festival's NextGen competitions, and at the Lionel Hampton Jazz Festival in Idaho. But this would pit them against the whole country in the jazz capital of the world. And de Barros was there; his presence, paid for by the newspaper, made the message clear—this is important. Even Starbucks, then a growing corporate giant, took notice: it began sponsoring an annual concert at the Paramount Theater that presented the five Seattle-area high school jazz bands that would be competing in the year's Essentially Ellington competition.

The 1993 book, *Jackson Street After Hours: The Roots of Jazz in Seattle*, is another example of the power of the pen. De Barros's meticulously documented history opened the city's eyes to a neglected and vital part of its past. And that book, coupled with historical reclamation projects during the 1990s, provided momentum for the city's eventual recognition of the Jackson Street entertainment district.

Jazz was riding high in the Pacific Northwest at the turn of the century. The jazz subculture had once again surged to the surface, and the music appeared to be connecting with the larger community more than it had in years.

SMALL IS BEAUTIFUL

Those connections happened primarily on a grassroots level, especially in Portland, where the "small is beautiful" ethic was evident in many local efforts, perhaps by necessity. Drummer Akbar DePriest, for instance, one of the jazz immigrants of the late 1980s who relocated from Los Angeles, created the DePriest Project Family Jazz Concerts to bring the music to his North Portland neighborhood, especially to young people who were receiving no exposure to jazz in the media. DePriest insisted that admission be free for those under sixteen. "We want to get the youngsters in. We've got to let them know what jazz is, and they've got to be taught that jazz belongs to them. Especially African American kids. They're not aware that this is theirs and they should be proud of it."

DePriest's version of jazz was formed by the bebop, blues, and R&B he heard as a kid, all presented together on Central Avenue in Los Angeles, where he used to see Duke Ellington and T-Bone Walker on the same bill. So it was only natural for him to start his career with blues star Big Maybelle, then work with jazz stars Rahsaan Roland Kirk and Eddie Harris. When DePriest brought in nationally known artists for his quarterly events, he deliberately built the show around the connection between jazz and the blues. Often, Janice Scroggins, whose approach to jazz was rooted in blues and gospel, would be in the piano chair.

DePriest staged the concerts at the University of Portland, which was looking for ways to connect its mostly white student body with what remained of the historically African American neighborhood not far away. The series ran for twelve years.

Many similar efforts kept musicians active and small audiences engaged. And they contributed to Portland's reputation for creative culture and a craft ethic based on locally brewed beer, coffee roasting, trend-setting restaurants, graphic

« Saxophonist Dusty York's Diatic Records was devoted to straight-ahead jazz with an edge and featured original compositions by Portland ensembles.

Clarence Acox started teaching in the Garfield High School jazz program, whose ensembles later performed at the North Sea and Montreux jazz festivals in Europe. He was also the drummer in Seattle's long-running Legacy Quartet.

novels, and a small film industry given national visibility by resident director Gus Van Sant and pioneering animator Will Vinton. National publications began repeating the claim that the city had developed a thriving culture of free-spirited individualists. From such rhetoric a reputation was made, despite the difficult realities that local artists like Dave Storrs faced in realizing their vision and finding an audience for it.

Drummer, bandleader, and composer Storrs was the epitome of the "small is beautiful" ethic and a proponent of unfettered creativity. Son of a Portland architect, he was a leader of the city's avant-garde when he released his first album, *Ross Island*. Using long-form compositions, the album evokes the environment, especially an atmospheric tune called "Clouds." Then, in 1989, Storrs decided to leave Portland, let go of his expectations about success, and find the freedom he'd been seeking. He settled in the Willamette Valley college town of Corvallis and, after ten years, remained committed to the vision that brought him there.

Jazz in the Schools

Among the many master teachers who have contributed to making the Pacific Northwest a nurturing place for jazz students, two stand out: Clarence Acox in Seattle and Thara Memory in Portland.

Acox started teaching in the fabled Garfield High School jazz program in 1971. Quincy Jones and Ernestine Anderson had played in Garfield bands in the 1940s, and the school's ensembles later performed at the North Sea and Montreux jazz festivals in Europe. But the early '70s were a hard time for jazz in Seattle, and Acox faced an uphill battle to rebuild a program in shambles.

He wrote arrangements, grabbed kids in the hallways who he thought might be able to play, took them to regional competitions, and soon the program was back to its earlier glory.

Since 1999, when the Essentially Ellington Competition (held at Jazz at Lincoln Center in New York City) opened to schools west of the Mississippi, Garfield High School has won first place four times, neighboring Roosevelt three times, and both bands usually turn up in the top three. In fact, seven Seattle-area high schools have been Essentially Ellington finalists.[1]

Perhaps more important than the wins was the fact that those Seattle schools provided quality education for students of color and equal opportunity to excel in extra-curricular activities beyond sports.

Journalist and broadcaster Rita Rega has observed the Portland jazz scene up close since she moved to the city in 1985. Ten years later, she started writing a Musician of the Month feature for *Jazzscene*.

"We cultivate musicians here," she says. "They get to develop, and because of the scene, they can continue developing. It's the education, the availability of resources.

"Andrew Oliver," Rega continued, "at age fourteen, his mom calls up the Jazz Society to find out who can teach her son. Boom! He's studying with Randy Porter. Why do we have so many great piano players here? It's because of Randy and Darrell Grant, all those guys."

Private camps also figure prominently in the educational landscape of the region. Young drummer Tyson Stubelek and ASCAP Young Composer award winner Andrew Oliver met as kids at a summer music camp. Esperanza Spalding was there too. Her album *Chamber Music Society* was named for the camp. Oliver and many others from the Puget Sound area have attended the summer jazz program at Centrum in Port Townsend, Washington, as well.

Few teachers have seen their work validated at such a high level as Thara Memory, whose student band, The Pacific Crest Jazz Orchestra, won a first at the 2015 Charles Mingus competition in New York City and another at the Essentially Ellington competition. The ensemble also played on Esperanza Spalding's Grammy-winning album, *Radio Music Society*. Memory shared a Grammy with her for an arrangement on the album. And in 2014, Berklee College of Music in Boston bestowed on him an honorary doctorate.

How does he get such high-level performances from his teen-aged musicians? "Just treat them like professionals," he says.

Dave Storrs's goal was not so much to build an audience as to win "a psychic battle for an individual's potential to be creative."

"Corvallis allowed me the freedom of my dream," he said. "It's all about letting go. I'm not worrying about what's happening in the music industry. I'm not trying to keep up with the Joneses or even identify who they are." It's a common refrain, but mavericks must be willing to live with the isolation—his label's releases reached only a handful of listeners. It didn't faze him. "The CDs only set up the possibility that we can play some more. I want to be in the now as much as possible. The only real now is when you're playing." With few performance opportunities, Storrs turned to teaching the town's more adventurous teenaged musicians.

He was dedicated to remaining small. His goal was not so much to build an audience as to win "a psychic battle for an individual's potential to be creative," he said. "People want to be creative, but the notions of big corporations are not healthy for their creativity. I'm on the front line fighting for our souls."

His vision was echoed in the region's DIY zine culture and various other jazz activities, including the Salon de Refuses, Portland's miniature version of the larger and more diverse multidisciplinary scene in Seattle. Besides Scheps, the group included ten artists: a poet, a painter, and a dancer, as well as two drummers, two bassists, and two guitarists drawn from Portland's jazz, funk, and rock scenes. Salon organizer Rob Scheps had moved to Portland in 1997, and his improvised performances with this group created an atmosphere of chaotic action similar to the impact of the Portland band Le Bon twenty years earlier or a Critters Buggin show today. The action on stage wasn't just for fun; there was a message amid the mayhem.

The Salon was only a part of Scheps's varied performance schedule while in the region. He played in several Oregon Symphony productions, led a sixteen-piece big band, and worked with Akbar DePriest in an organ trio with Williams Avenue veteran Jimmy Saunders. An outspoken and knowledgeable leader, Scheps also organized concerts with nationally known elders he brought from out of town, and he performed and recorded with Julian Priester and Hadley Caliman in Seattle. Scheps was serious about jazz as art music, and believed the general public would embrace it if it were promoted correctly. And performed correctly, too; his demanding approach sometimes put Scheps at odds with the nonconfrontational mores of the region.

Larger arts organizations also helped increase the visibility of jazz in Portland, such as the annual "Jazz with Jimmy" concerts produced by the Oregon Symphony and featuring its conductor James DePreist, a former jazz drummer. Over the years, they included a number of blues artists and local jazz stars such as Dave Frishberg, Nancy King, Steve Christofferson, and the Jackson-Mills Big Band.

All those small pieces added up, but the biggest boost to the general public's awareness of jazz in the city in the first years of the new century came from the Portland Jazz Festival. Since 2004, it has demonstrated to the local jazz community that even in Portland, big could also be beautiful.

Rob Scheps was serious about jazz as art music, and believed the general public would embrace it if it were promoted correctly.

PUTTING PORTLAND ON THE NATIONAL JAZZ MAP

With a record of success in the arts management and jazz festival business, Bill Royston came from Pennsylvania in 1999 to be the artistic director of the Mt. Hood Festival of Jazz. At first, his return to straight-ahead performers appeared to work: ticket sales, in decline since 1997, leveled off. But the financial model wasn't sustainable, especially with the loss of several title sponsors after 2001, and in the spring of 2002, the board declared bankruptcy.

A new event, renamed the Mt. Hood Jazz Festival, rose from the ashes that summer. But Royston had already started planning something different—a multiday winter festival that would be staged in downtown Portland. It took two years of planning, but the Portland Jazz Festival finally brought the city's jazz reputation into the national spotlight.

Royston sought out partnerships with the Portland Oregon Visitors Association, nonprofits, airlines, and hotels. He'd had success filling hotel rooms with a jazz weekend in Philadelphia. He did it again at the Berks Jazz Festival, and that approach became the model for his new event in Portland. He also took advantage of tie-ins with Black History Month by scheduling it in February, and partnered with the Jazz Society of Oregon. There were workshops and educational outreach—supported in part by public arts agencies—an Oregon Symphony jazz-themed event, and performances booked at local clubs as well.

But Royston believed they'd only be able to draw the core Mt. Hood fans if they had a big-name headliner. "Wayne Shorter was the one everyone felt we should have," board member Wayne Thompson remembered, "but his price tag was way bigger than we could dream about." Royston was ready to scale back, until Thompson offered to pony up the difference needed to bring Shorter. Then Thompson raised another sixty thousand dollars from local corporate donors—enough to lure new sponsors on a long-term basis and add other artists to the program.

Influential backers and large donations in hand, it seemed to be working. The 2006 festival generated 1,500 hotel stays, and based on Destination Marketing calculations, the projected economic impact of the 2007 festival was $1.3 million. By that time, it had been named one of the top jazz festivals in the country. That reputation was in part the result of Royston's marketing strategy, which included inviting writers and critics to attend as guests. He put them on panels and in

The Portland Jazz Festival debuted in 2004 and put the local jazz scene on the national map with bold programing and community partnerships. Pictured: The Afro-Cuban Allstars at the 2011 festival.

public "Jazz Conversations" with the headliners. The reviews reflected their positive experiences.

Royston got a national reputation for bold programming, too. After all, who else was presenting iconoclasts such as Cecil Taylor and Ornette Coleman? And in Portland no less. But it worked: an average of seven out of ten headliner shows sold out each year, and it became a model for the well-managed festival. It has increasingly hired local musicians as well, so despite high ticket prices for headliners, many festival shows are accessible to a wider audience. But they aren't the patrons the festival really needs.

"You want people who can afford the tickets and buy the merchandise," observed Thompson. "It's important for survival. I hate to say it, but this is a rich person's thing."

In Seattle, there was no shortage of such deep pockets.

Greta Matassa: "The best of all worlds"

Paul Freeman, *San Jose Mercury News,* January 16, 2015

Seattle-based jazz vocalist Greta Matassa's father was a visual artist, a painter. And a serious jazz buff.

"My dad and I used to stay up until three in the morning, talking about the parallels between jazz music and abstract art," Matassa tells the *Daily News*. "They are very similar in the spontaneity of the way they're put together. You start with a structure in a piece of music. Or a subject matter in art. And then the act itself of painting it or singing it is the point. It's not the end result, but the in-the-moment that I find so fascinating."

Her father and her scientist mother listened to jazz devotedly. "I was born in 1962, so they had a bunch of great jazz records," Matassa says.

Knowledgeable jazz publications find Matassa to be among the best at her art. "Greta Matassa is one of America's finest singers, and stands firmly among the best in today's jazz," said *Jazz Review*. Earshot Jazz, which has named her "Northwest Vocalist of the Year" seven times in fifteen years, declared, "Her scatting is as confident, nimble, and energetic as Ella's, and her phrasing is hip like Nancy Wilson's."

Tours have taken Matassa to Hawaii, Singapore, Japan, and Russia. Now that her kids are grown up, she spends as much time as possible on the road, teaching and performing. Often accompanying her is her husband, Clipper Anderson, a notable bassist. An outdoorsy person, Matassa wouldn't dream of changing her base from the Pacific Northwest to New York or Los Angeles.

"I travel all over the place. I come home and I still think, 'God, I live in the most beautiful place in the world.' And Seattle has quite a thriving jazz scene. It's the best of all worlds."

Matassa is one artist who's neither starving nor tortured. In fact, she's downright happy. "I've sung all kinds of music. I've made a living singing rock, pop. I was in a heavy metal band for a while. Living hand-to-mouth, being self-employed could be viewed as challenging. But what it did for me was build a sense of personal responsibility. You have your fingers in a bunch of different pies. It's a challenge, but I like it."

"HONEST MUSIC" IN THE NEW ECONOMY

By 2000, the economies of the region's sister cities were diverging dramatically. While Portland built its reputation on a "small is beautiful" image, in twenty-first century Seattle, big is beautiful.

In the 1990s, almost a half-million new residents poured into the Puget Sound, and Seattle was riding an economic boom fueled in large part by the city's high-tech industry. Not everyone had a seat at that feast, though, and the working class was being priced out of close-in housing. The old maritime and industrial economy, with its low-rise central city of dark taverns and small coffee shops, was being replaced by the new order.

In a progressive city with a strong labor tradition where politics had been characterized by compromise and consensus, public discourse was changing. The "community policing" approach practiced during the 1990s was giving way to a militarization of local law enforcement that was accelerated by the events of September 11. People of color were still arrested disproportionately by police, and the racial education gap widened. Gentrification further changed historically

Seattle was transformed by big money and half-a-million new residents into what's been called a "San Francisco on the Sound."

Southwest Washington native Clay Giberson of the Upper Left Trio believes their music reflects the environment where the band members grew up. With an impressionistic palette and smooth forward motion, it resembles the music of Seattle pianist Dave Peck.

African American neighborhoods that once sustained jazz, blues, and R&B. They were now home to specialty food shops, wine bars, day spas, and farmers markets.

Such changes were also going on in many other American cities, but in Seattle the process played out at warp speed. And rock, not jazz, was the soundtrack. The contrast between the buttoned-down suits of the neotraditionalists in jazz and the jeans and flannel shirts of grunge, shining trumpet versus fuzzy guitar, reflected the widening gap between audiences and approaches that occurred in the 1990s. By the turn of the century, rock and hip-hop had taken over the outsider image that had previously belonged to jazz.

So it was the grunge attitude, more than its sound, that influenced young jazz players like drummer Matt Jorgensen. His cohort, just entering their thirties at the end of the century, didn't consider the rock music they'd grown up with to be competition anyway, but rather a stimulus. "Musicians in Seattle were making honest music.... It had a huge impact on what I want to do as an artist," he said.[2]

Raised in Seattle, Jorgensen attended Shoreline Community College for two years before heading for New York City, where he spent the next decade. He always knew he'd come back, and in 2002 he returned to become co-owner of Origin Records with John Bishop, who had been his first drum teacher.

Jorgensen returned to a different city. Seattle had been transformed by money and a social climate that reflected the disputed presidential election of 2000 and the Patriot Act that followed the attacks of 2001. It appeared to have a chilling effect. Much of the jazz being made in the region and elsewhere during the Bush administration had no overt political or social content.

JAZZ AND POLITICS

In the past, major social changes were often reflected in jazz. Billie Holiday premiered "Strange Fruit," a bitter portrait of lynching in the South, in 1939, at the height of changes to the established order brought by New Deal social policies. Charles Mingus composed "Fables of Faubus" in 1959 in response to the racist acts of Arkansas governor Orval Faubus. John Coltrane recorded the tune "Alabama" after four African American children died in a Birmingham church bombing. And

Dave Peck: Pilot's Return

Paul de Barros, *DownBeat*, January 2006

"I'm the person and the player I am because of the community I have here," said Seattle pianist Dave Peck. "Back in the '70s, I might have thought about moving to New York. But when I started being house piano player at [the now defunct] Parnell's and Jazz Alley, I got to play with Sonny Stitt for a week, then I'd be playing with Chet Baker a couple of weeks later. That was the bird in the hand."

Peck still has no intention of leaving the Emerald City. But his sphere of influence is definitely expanding. Last June, he guested on Marian McPartland's *Piano Jazz* then signed up with ArtistShare, the online endeavor that has done so much for Maria Schneider. Peck just released his second trio album, *Good Road* (ArtistShare).

After many ups and downs, the fifty-two-year-old pianist has arrived at a personal lyric voice with regional resonance and he's ready to take it out on that "good road."

Raised outside Portland, Oregon, playing both piano and trumpet, Peck landed in Seattle in 1978 after a gig fell through in Canada. Soon, he was teaching at Cornish College and working as a sideman for Seattle vocalist Ernestine Anderson and saxophonist Bud Shank.

When touring musicians stopped picking up local trios, Peck became discouraged. He went back to school to study physics and wrote science fiction. His spirits picked up when Shank recorded *Tales of the Pilot: Bud Shank Plays the Music of Dave Peck* (Capri, 1990). But in 1995, Peck made another retreat, this time not by choice. Struck by Chronic Fatigue Syndrome... Peck was forced to take a year-long leave of absence from teaching.

"When I started to come back, it was all about making choices," said Peck, who turned his full attention to playing and recording with a piano trio. In 1998, he and his wife, Jane, started their own label, Let's Play Stella, and released *Trio*.

Seattle's reputation rests on rain, but folks who live there know it for the gentle contours of its clouds and mountains, its soft mists and almost mystical sense of natural intimacy. All that comes through in Peck's playing—lyrical and pastel, swinging and bluesy, with a ringing, crystalline touch.

---

in the Pacific Northwest, American Indian saxophonist and singer Jim Pepper made his political stance clear in the 1980s with provocative tunes such as "Custer Died for Your Sins."

Such direct use of jazz to comment on political and social realities was rare during the early 2000s, when jazz appeared detached from the broader culture and unable to connect with and make itself relevant to the concerns of its audience, even as a model for resistance. An exception was Wayne Horvitz's epic suite, *Joe Hill*, which attempted to address social and political issues head on.

"I have always had an aversion to the marriage of music and politics," wrote Horvitz in the program notes for the 2004 debut of his composition about a working-class hero that was funded, ironically, by the Rockefeller Foundation. However, he continued, "this piece has caused in me a transformation of sorts." A transformation, he added, that was the result of the political climate at the time.

Alternatively, a number of regional artists chose to reaffirm their isolation and make of it a virtue. The Upper Left Trio's first album, *Cycling*, from 2003, exhibits the joys of that isolation with original music that pays homage to the

Dawn Clement, who grew up in Washington and studied at the Cornish Institute, sat in on area jam sessions at age sixteen.

piano trio tradition while using fretless electric bass and keyboards in addition to grand piano. Written by Pacific Northwest natives Clay Giberson, Jeff Leonard, and Charlie Doggett, the tunes are complex yet the improvising feels calm. Their impressionistic palette and the smooth forward motion of their compositions resemble the music of Seattle pianist Dave Peck.

"I consider a sense of place in music very valuable," says Leonard. That influence can be heard in the music's textures and ensemble sound, not in a programmatic evocation of the natural world. "It reflects this environment where we all grew up," Giberson agrees, but not the natural environment alone: musicians in the region influenced them as well.

Jazz from the Pacific Northwest doesn't necessarily "sound like" the landscape, but it is made by musicians who have chosen to situate themselves here, and who are shaped by interactions with local artists. Naturally, the sound that results is different from jazz made by residents of New Orleans or Chicago. It's not another language, just a different dialect.

Many commentators contend that there are no regional styles anymore, as had previously been the case with Kansas City swing or Harlem stride piano. Once the music was widely disseminated and musicians were able to study with master players anywhere, they argue, geographical location no longer resulted in a cohesive and distinct regional approach. While that may be true for some kinds of music, jazz is different—it's intended to capture the moment and express an individual artist's unique voice. Musicians don't live in band rooms or earphones. The world they inhabit every day affects them profoundly.

Portland saxophonist and composer Rich Halley, for instance, situates his music directly in the region's natural areas. In 1998, in an open field atop an ancient volcano called Powell Butte just outside the city limits, Halley's Outside Music Ensemble held the first of its annual Outside Music concerts. The audience had to walk three-quarters of a mile to reach the site. Deer grazed in the meadow; at night, coyotes and skunks roamed. There was no electricity and no generator. The band used only horns and hand percussion.

"When you're on top of the butte, you're suspended above the city and you see mountains all around," he said. "I'm thinking what it will feel like to be up there and writing tunes that will really speak in that particular place."

Choosing to make music flavored by landscape and shaped by close association with like-minded artists does constitute a response to social and political conditions beyond an individual artist's control. The particular and the local may well be subversive of the depersonalized and mass-produced. And jazz is one arena where the idiosyncratic and highly personal are encouraged. Making art on the margins in twenty-first century America, where there's no chance of a hit, offers greater freedom. Some regional artists, like Seattle bassist Evan Flory-Barnes—"I'm as local as it gets!" he says—question the need for any outside approval at all.

It's a stance Floyd Standifer would recognize, one that captures the independent spirit of Jackson Street in the 1940s. And in twenty-first century Seattle, that spirit has been kept alive by an extensive support system.

Jazz activist Jessica Lurie cofounded the Billy Tipton Memorial Sax Quartet in honor of big-band pianist Tipton, a woman who lived as a man for more than fifty years in order to pursue a career in the male-dominated world of her day.

A FAMILY AFFAIR

Trumpeter Tatum Greenblatt was one of the high school musicians Paul de Barros had written about in the early 2000s. After graduating from the award-winning Garfield band, he went to New York for a master's degree from Juilliard and became a protégé of Wynton Marsalis. By 2015, Greenblatt had made several albums as a leader.

He'd been on that path from birth. His father, Dan Greenblatt, was a tenor sax player leading an octet at The New Orleans Restaurant in Pioneer Square during Tatum's formative years. With rehearsals and jam sessions in the living room, young Greenblatt—his father named him for piano master Art Tatum—picked up the trumpet when he was nine. He first worked professionally with his father when he was in fifth grade, and soon thereafter he and his dad were playing in the Edmonds Community College Big Band together. Dan coached musicians at Tatum's middle school while his son was in the jazz band there.

When Tatum moved to New York, the elder Greenblatt followed, taking a job at The New School. It wasn't a big jump. Greenblatt was a New York native with a doctorate in language and linguistics who had abandoned his academic career to raise a family and play jazz in Seattle—another immigrant during the pivotal 1990s. But he was never really happy there; he found it too "nice," he told de Barros.

"A lot of people found I was a pain in the ass," he said. "I was real critical, and not easygoing. Here in New York, I find that my approach is normal."[3]

He must have made a few friends, because the Greenblatts returned to play for a full house at Tula's in Seattle in 2004. It was a symbolic passing of the torch, and it put an exclamation point on a process that had been going on since his son was a toddler. They've repeated the show in Seattle several times over the years, calling themselves The Generation Band.

On piano with the Greenblatts that night in 2004 was young Dawn Clement, who had gone to high school in Vancouver, Washington, across the river from Portland. "It was a great place to grow up playing jazz," she remembered, "because there were sessions all the time, and they would let sixteen-year-olds come and sit in." A former classical player, she found jazz more congenial. "I never want to go back to that other world. Jazz is so free—you can be how you want to be, and have fun doing it...it's not about competition."[4]

WAYNE HORVITZ'S SEATTLE

Fresh out of Cornish, Dawn Clement was another distinctive new voice in the increasingly diverse Pacific Northwest jazz scene and another young Puget Sound musician riding the slipstream of the "Wayne Horvitz Express." Horvitz had come from New York in 1989, at the peak of its experimental music scene, for the lifestyle and environment. Once in the region, though, he discovered that it also had everything he needed artistically as well. Over the next twenty years, his work with local artists changed the Puget Sound improvisational music scene. And it changed him.

"My motivations for moving to the Northwest had a lot to do with just being very fond of this part of the world," he explained. "I figured I could make music anywhere. As it turns out, Seattle has a fantastic music scene. 'Jazz' scene, I wouldn't really know about—I don't really involve myself much in what I would term jazz, at least by the definition that is currently used in America.

"As for my world, Seattle has everything I need: lots of great improvisers and a strong interest in contemporary classical music."

Horvitz composes and performs chamber music, film scores, electronic music, and improvisational funk. On arrival, he started Pigpen, a kind of "rough jazz" sax-driven sound with young Briggan Krauss, fresh out of Cornish and eager to play. But he continued to work with Zony Mash, the signature ensemble he'd begun while still in New York, playing improvisational funk with a hard edge. In Seattle, he developed "unplugged" versions of that quintet—one he called American Bandstand, and the other, Sweeter Than the Day. Though that band's sound was mellower, it was still harmonically complex and challenging.

As was his chamber ensemble 4+1. And a strange chamber group it was, with Tucker Martine, a frequent Horvitz collaborator, mixing electronics with tracks from trombone, violin, viola, baritone sax, and drums. Another version of the quintet featured guitarist Tim Young. The personnel weren't as important as the effect Horvitz achieved with the mix.

He also debuted his Gravitas Quartet, with traditional chamber music instrumentation. In 2007, he released two albums of the same six tunes, one performed by Gravitas, the other by Sweeter Than the Day. But his greatest contribution to the community lay ahead.[5]

« Wayne Horvitz moved to Seattle for the lifestyle and environment, but soon discovered that the region had everything he needed as a musician, too.

Saxophonist Jessica Lurie, one of the Seattle's most active improvisers in the late 1990s, was working the same street as Horvitz, but on the other side.

With three women colleagues, Lurie started the Billy Tipton Memorial Sax Quartet in 1988 to honor the big band saxophonist and pianist who had worked most of his life in the Spokane area. After he died, it was discovered that Tipton was actually a woman who had lived as a man for more than fifty years. Many believe Tipton carried on the difficult masquerade in order to pursue a career in the male-dominated world of her day. Perhaps more than "honor" Tipton, the quartet's sometimes wild and raucous music unleashed a spirit repressed by the heavy wraps she always wore around her chest.

A Seattle native, Lurie was also involved in a variety of other boundary-crossing projects, most of them on the margins of straight-ahead jazz, including her punk-jazz groove trio, Living Daylights, with its repetitive, percussive sound. She also made three albums with New Music violinist Eyvind Kang, as well as several of her own, and started a record label. She financed some projects with grant funds, and she taught both privately and in workshops.

Lurie had constructed a life fairly typical for improvising musicians who were finding ways to pursue their individual visions. If they'd wanted fame and fortune, or projects that required grander resources, they might have relocated—like Lurie, who moved to New York in 2001. Or they might have curbed their quest for the most distinctive voice, and played more popular styles. And while some did, few crossed over to smooth jazz.

A SMOOTH AND SLIPPERY SLOPE

The popularity of smooth jazz exploded in the 1990s, the perfect soundtrack for corporate optimism and speculative earnings. It rode into the new century on a successful radio format that put KKJZ stations in many American cities, including Seattle and Portland, although it lasted much longer in Seattle. Smooth jazz artists came more frequently to Seattle, often playing Jazz Alley if not larger venues, some sponsored by KKJZ. That gave the style more visibility and helped it become the sound of "jazz" for many listeners—at least until 2011, when the last incarnation of smooth jazz radio in the region dropped the format.

But the popularity of smooth jazz in the Pacific Northwest reflected its stature on the national stage, not its infrequent local shows. It was primarily a radio phenomenon, but in concert, the crowd-pleasing performers made it a priority to provide what seemed to be lacking in straight-ahead jazz of the day—a direct, visceral connection with the audience: Rick Braun dashing into the crowd while still playing his trumpet, Dave Koz leading sing-alongs, Everette Harp opening his arms wide in appreciation after every song and calling out to the crowd. The headliners always signed autographs and shook a lot of hands after their shows.

Symbolically, smooth jazz is associated with Seattle because its most famous star is a native son. The career of Kenny G paralleled the rise of the high-tech corporate culture that was transforming the city during those years, even though he left his Lake Washington mansion for Malibu, California, in 1999. In fact, he was an early Starbucks investor. The former Kenny Gorelick grew up in the

Seward Park neighborhood, the center of the city's Jewish community, and started playing professionally as a sideman for Barry White's Love Unlimited Orchestra in 1973, when he was only seventeen. He majored in accounting at the University of Washington, graduated magna cum laude, became a member of The Jeff Lorber Fusion in Portland, then launched his solo career.

His work has drawn sharp criticism from jazz commentators and musicians. For instance, in 2000, guitarist Pat Matheny condemned G for a recording on which he overdubbed himself playing with Louis Armstrong on the song "What a Wonderful World." Matheny called for a boycott of G's music. "To ignore this trespass," he wrote, "is to agree that nothing in music has any intrinsic value." Yet the popularity of his simple, optimistic tunes, built on broad gestures and auditory slight of hand, is undeniable.

The shadow he cast across the Pacific Northwest was long, especially over fellow musicians and jazz fans; the greater his success, the more they seemed to distance themselves from smooth jazz. That caused problems for Portland saxophonist Patrick Lamb.

The son of a piano-playing science teacher, Lamb came to the region during his high school years and got his start playing blues with the Norman Sylvester Band; while with that group, Lamb won three awards from the Cascade Blues Association. Then he began touring with Tom Grant, who for a time ranked as high in the smooth jazz pantheon as Kenny G's former employer Jeff Lorber. Lamb moved on to playing with vocalist Diane Schuur, a Tacoma native who had built an international reputation in straight-ahead circles. Next he worked with smooth jazz singer and guitarist Bobby Caldwell, playing high-profile concerts and appearing on the *Today Show*.

Smooth jazz star Kenny G is a Seattle native who got his start with Barry White's Love Unlimited Orchestra and later played with Jeff Lorber in Portland. In 1992, his album Breathless sold twelve million copies.

At home, Lamb found himself pigeon-holed. "For an instrumentalist in the modern marketing world, you only have two choices: traditional mainstream jazz or the contemporary zone. Each has its stigma, especially contemporary or smooth jazz." And so he was stuck. He wasn't playing the music closest to his heart. "I began to feel like a mercenary," he said.

By the time he got on stage at the 2005 Waterfront Blues Festival, however, he had discovered a way out. Surrounded by R&B, gospel, jazz, and blues players in a tribute to Ray Charles, the blonde-haired saxophonist was smiling and in love with music again.

"It was about reinvention," he said. "I was really getting tired of what I was doing, though I was grateful for the work. We become comfortable, forget to keep trying something new, to reach out to people we wouldn't normally play with. You create magic by getting out of your comfort zone." He didn't find many Portland musicians doing that.

"If it's gospel they're in the church, if it's jazz, they're in their own circles. Blues people don't usually play with jazz people; they all stay within their own circles. That's not a good thing." Lamb decided the Ray Charles Tribute would be a way to break down those walls and follow his heart. What he found went beyond music. "When you're doing what you love, you can build your life around it," he said.

He expanded the project, hired the nationally known Charles Floyd to conduct and write the arrangements, and staged it as part of the Oregon Symphony Pops

Left: Patrick Lamb's Ray Charles Tribute project was a way to break down the walls between the region's blues, jazz and gospel performers. Pictured here in collaboration with the Oregon Symphony.

Right: Patrick Lamb, who came to Portland as a teenager, felt confined by the smooth jazz label he'd earned but managed to reinvent his sound by incorporating elements of R&B and gospel.

series at great financial risk. The album Lamb made after that event was titled *Soul of a Free Man*. Tough Motown backbeats, Tower of Power horn arrangements and a smooth Earth, Wind & Fire patina supported his upbeat, sunny melodies. It was Tom Grant filtered through the black church. And though he still tours with pop jazz star Gino Vanelli, Lamb has built a regional fan base that enthusiastically turns out for his shows. And they don't call it smooth jazz anymore.

The smooth jazz festivals that used to come every summer to the Pacific Northwest gradually disappeared in the new century, although smooth jazz acts continued to take the stage among the pop, funk, and straight-ahead styles that headlined outdoor jazz festivals in the early 2000s. The Vancouver Wine and Jazz Festival was among those that hosted them.

JAZZ IN CONTEXT

The Vancouver Wine and Jazz Festival staged its first edition in 1998. With almost two decades of outdoor jazz in the region to guide them, organizers recognized a key fact: presenting jazz in the context of related music and other activities draws a larger audience.

Wynton Marsalis spoke for those who believed the direction was wrong: "The promoters of these festivals readily admit most of the music isn't jazz, but refuse to rename these events... attempting to piggyback on the achievements of others, and duping the public."[6] But the public wasn't complaining.

The mix at the Vancouver Wine and Jazz Festival became even more eclectic as the years passed and attendance grew. Eventually it included blues acts like Elvin Bishop and the Fabulous Thunderbirds as well as smooth jazz saxman Boney James and even roots acts like Mavis Staples. The lineups continued to evolve, however, and by 2015, Latin jazz had taken the place of smooth jazz as the festival's preferred party music. More than twelve thousand people participate in the three-day event each year, according to organizers. And the Festival chooses its music with a close eye on the target demographic.

On the Road with John Stowell

Interview with Lynn Darroch, July 2014

On the margins, only the nimble survive.

Portland-based guitarist John Stowell has built a life based on staying nimble. It's the key to jazz improvisation and to managing the career he's stitched together out of performing, teaching, recording—and travel. He was on the road for nearly eight months in 2014, a typical year. It started in 1976, when he first came to the Pacific Northwest and began touring with bassist David Friesen; that partnership culminated in a 1983 tour of the former Soviet Union; he subsequently made three trips on his own in the '90s and another in 2012. He's traveled in Argentina ten times, and music has taken him to Indonesia, Europe, Australia, and all around the US.

This is how it works.

It's a sales job—a lot of follow-up, and lots of things that you pursue don't happen. You have to have a pretty thick skin to deal with the rejection and the fact that if you're not famous, there are very few good paychecks. Very often trips are breakeven or even situations where you might lose a bit, but you go to establish connections and put your name out there. If you're enjoying the work, you do it.

I met a guy in '93 in LA who was teaching at a small private school in South Germany.... He said, "We'll be doing some residencies, would you be interested in coming?" It was a gamble because they weren't able to give me a guarantee or pick up my airfare or cover my expenses, but I thought, "I'll just go and see what happens." I was there for six months, and it worked out fine, and I've been going back on a regular basis since.

I've got a friend in Constans, on a lake in Southwest Germany, and for the last two years he set up ten to twelve little gigs.... I stay with him and his wife and daughter, and we do little runs out from Constans. We did a recording last year, so we have a CD out, and he plays well and he's a nice guy. I have that kind of an arrangement with a few people, but I'm grateful to come for one gig.... If it involves a long train ride, or a flight or whatever, if I can make something, I'll come.

I play with guys all over Europe, many of whom play really well, and in some cases write interesting music, and they're very kind to me. Typically in a year I might travel 230 to 260 days, and between five and ten nights are in hotels, so all the rest someone's accommodating me. It wouldn't happen otherwise.... I enjoy traveling from friend to friend.

I could make a living just staying [in Portland].... There are people doing just fine here. Either they're playing a variety of styles or they're playing and teaching or they have another job. And where we live is a nice place; I don't want to be on the road constantly. But I would miss the variety.

If you're comfortable living simply and your overhead is low, it's possible to live a creative life.... I rent two rooms, I have no debt, credit cards paid off every month, paid cash for the car, and I'm able to save a little money each year.

Most people would not want this life. [But] I don't want to be a versatile player, I just want to do what I do. I don't mind doing that in a variety of situations ... as long as I have some space where I can be creative, I'll try just about anything. Basically I just want to play with my friends and have a good time. I think we're all just trying to create a small audience for what we do.

Vancouver sits on the north bank of the Columbia, the hub of Portland's sprawling southwest Washington suburbs. Its downtown has been refurbished with hanging baskets, banners on old-fashioned lampposts, and other amendments to make little shops more pedestrian-friendly and inviting than they once had been.

After a few years, the festival moved to a beautifully rehabilitated park right in the heart of downtown. There, attendees picnic on the grass in leafy glades near a covered bandstand, and children frolic in a cleverly designed fountain. The whole park is fenced off to create a gated community, and the festival surrounds the music with crafts and fine arts booths that add a gallery-hopping, shopping component; wine tasting booths are busy, and fine dining restaurants offer picnic menus. It's a summery, suburban experience. The majority of the audience appears to be over forty. Ticket prices are high, and the wine, art, and food are expensive.

Successful festivals of this kind, like jazz cruises, which also became popular during this period, present jazz in places where people with disposable income want to be, pair it with related music that appeals to the same demographic, and surround it all with activities they enjoy. But cruise ships and festivals don't keep a resident jazz scene alive. And lack of work damages more than a musician's bottom line.

"Advice for musicians considering a move to Portland? Get a teaching position or a day job, so you don't get bitter over not having enough gigs or enough money in your pocket," says saxophonist Katarina New, who came to the region from Palm Springs. "I've seen and met too many bitter musicians—including myself—and learned the lessons. Let the music be the love and happiness it's supposed to be when you play it!"[7]

MY KINGDOM FOR A STAGE

Despite the economic prosperity of the period, venues still came and went with gut-wrenching unpredictability for the musicians who depended on them. And most jazz players did. "Anyone in my trio could make the same money in one and a half hours of teaching as he could from five hours for a club gig," explained guitarist Dan Balmer. "But we do it to develop our music, to increase our skill and to bring it to the people. This is what musicians do."

So they reacted strongly when one of Portland's iconic clubs, the Jazz de Opus, closed in 2003. More was lost, they felt, than simply performance opportunities. Opened in 1972, it once hosted touring jazz legends as well as frequent local music. Both literally and symbolically, it was a pillar of Portland's jazz scene. "The quintessential jazz club," said Alan Jones, whose sextet worked there every Thursday for two years. "It had a reputation as *the* place to play. We used to hang out there even when there wasn't any music."

The older players had seen major clubs close before, and they'd always found ways to present their music. But history can be lost. The Jazz de Opus had contributed to the community's sense of place, to the image of Portland—it meant something to hear and play jazz in the same room where legends like Dexter Gordon once performed. And when a visible landmark is lost, vital connections to the past also vanish. The demise of Parnell's in Seattle's Pioneer Square was another such blow.

The loss of elders in the jazz community had a similar impact. Floyd Standifer, Don Lanphere, Leroy Vinnegar, and a number of other leading elders died during the early years of the new century. In the spring of 2007, musicians, family, and friends laid Williams Avenue trombonist Cleve Williams to rest with a jazz funeral. Ten days later, pianist Eddie Wied passed away in the same bed Williams had occupied at Hopewell House Hospice.

TURNING POINT

Those deaths marked the end of an era and coincided with another turning point; in 2007, the global financial crisis set in motion forces that would change cultural life in the Pacific Northwest as much as it altered economic conditions. The federal government bailouts prevented the collapse of large financial institutions, but in the Pacific Northwest, as in many other regions, the crisis eventually produced high unemployment, evictions and foreclosures, the failure of businesses, and declines in personal spending. And the jazz community felt all of those effects.

What little private sector support there had been for jazz was greatly diminished. And the City of Portland had to do some bailing of its own when it granted the Portland Jazz Festival $100,000 to ensure its 2008 edition went on as planned. It was the first time a jazz event had become so important to the culture and economy of the city that it couldn't be allowed to fail. But the larger jazz community had no such patrons. Just a few years earlier, jazz had been enjoying a new golden age, but for the music, as for the country as a whole, there were hard times ahead.

Left: Eddie Wied and Cleve Williams died within ten days of one another, marking the end of an era.

Right: Organizers of the Vancouver Wine & Jazz festival recognized that presenting jazz in the context of related music and other activities draws a larger audience.

"My hypothesis was that music is shaped by a connection to the terrain—both the physical place and the community from which it springs," says Darrell Grant. Pictured: Portland's Steel Bridge on the Willamette River.

Darrell Grant: A Jazz Ecology

Interview with Lynn Darroch, June 2013

When Darrell Grant was preparing a talk called "A Jazz Ecology" for the Walters Cultural Center in Hillsboro, Oregon, he shared his thoughts about landscape and art, sustainable culture, and what it means to think about a jazz scene as an ecological community.

I've been thinking and writing lately using the metaphor of the jazz scene as an ecology... It was clear on my first visit to Portland, that its territory allowed for different realities—different ways of living and thriving. How else to explain that musicians I had never heard of (insular East-coaster that I was in 1995) owned homes, when I, touring half the year, could barely keep up with rent. How was it possible for them to so visibly thrive as "local" musicians?

My hypothesis was that music is shaped by a connection to the terrain—both the physical place and the community from which it springs. Seeing how people choose to live here and the decisions we make regarding land use and community engagement, it seems unlikely that all of those decisions don't impact the art.

The Willamette Valley, more specifically Portland as its cultural locus, is known for scenes and subcultures: the indie music scene; the DIY Maker scene; the foodie culture; the artisanal coffee scene; food carts, craft brewing, pinball; locally grown food, pedestrian and bike and outdoor culture. There is a sense of abundance in this plethora of scenes. There is a feeling of the possible in this part of the world that I think seeps out of the verdant landscape into the politics, the urban planning, the ways of living on the land.

In the ongoing dialogue about sustainable environment, sustainable development, sustainable economic growth, where might something like music fit in? Can we come up with the answers by considering what makes a healthy ecology? While we necessarily focus on the basics of our survival—food, clean air, and water, livable land—how do we value the culture that gives our lives meaning? Is music as we know it sustainable? What, among its many traditions, institutions, practices, and works do we want to save?

What makes a healthy jazz scene? What does thriving mean? Does it mean always growing? Does it mean it's robust enough to withstand a crisis?

At some point, these things are outside human control. We cannot make it happen. So if we're willing to let jazz go, to see what it will become, it may continue to live, or live in a different form, or it may spring up somewhere else. Are we okay with that? Are we okay with jazz, in fifty years, being completely unrecognizable because it serves a different function than it did?

8

Freedom on the Margins: 2008-2015

"A shrinking audience, coupled with recent economic hardships, has not been kind to most professional jazz musicians. A dwindling number of venues and festivals has left many scrambling for work, rethinking their careers, and turning to other occupations for steady income.... Confusion, frustration, financial peril, and self-doubt often overshadow the most basic desire to simply play for an audience."

Tim Willcox

"There's no money in it anymore, and that's created a lot of freedom. The illusion of success has been taken away, so we might as well do what we care about."

Darrell Grant

A JAZZ ECOLOGY

The repercussions of the financial crisis took a while to trickle down to the jazz community in the Pacific Northwest. So as late as 2009, it looked to Darrell Grant like the region's thriving scene just might be sustainable. "What if we think about the jazz scene as an ecology?" Grant wondered. "If we apply the same principles as we do when analyzing the natural world, it might help understand what's needed for a healthy jazz ecology."

And at that moment, the Pacific Northwest jazz scene appeared to be the picture of health. Like a sustainable forest, with its mix of emerging and ancient trees webbed together at the roots, it appeared to be connected to its past and nurturing its future. All the elements were in place to disseminate and publicize the music. The cost of living was still low enough to accommodate an artist's lifestyle, the abundance of natural beauty was an attraction, the cities were perceived as "green," and there were recording and performance opportunities to be had.

When saxophonist David Valdez moved to Portland from New York before the crash, it looked like the best decision he'd ever made.

"I was amazed at the level of the players here and the amount of nice jazz rooms," he said. "It just seemed like Portland had a long history of being a jazz town. There was a regular jazz audience who actually liked to go out and pay money to hear good music! Everyone also

David Valdez moved to Portland from New York after being impressed by the quality of musicians and enthusiasm of the audience. "After just a few days, I called my wife and told her to start packing."

seemed much friendlier here. After just a few days I called my wife and told her to start packing."[1]

As Valdez recognized, a sufficiently large group of skilled players had clustered in the area. Competition encouraged high-level performance. Jazz organizations were active and visible, and—despite budget cuts—the jazz education system was strong and connected to the professional scene.

In addition to the region's award-winning jazz radio stations, a number of independent record labels were dedicated to disseminating the work of the region's jazz artists. World-renowned musicians consistently appeared at festivals and other high-visibility concerts and at the region's major clubs. And even in an era of reduced arts coverage, the largest newspapers still reported on some jazz events. Several specialty publications, although with much smaller subscriber bases, also promoted the music.

And maybe that was the tip-off. Those small subscriber numbers pointed to the weakest element in the system: the audience, the very soil from which those jazz trees grew. In part, its increasingly smaller numbers reflected a shortage of performance venues for the region's many prolific artists. And by 2011, things were looking pretty bleak to saxophonist Tim Willcox.

"A shrinking audience, coupled with recent economic hardships, has not been kind to most professional jazz musicians," he wrote. "A dwindling number of venues and festivals has left many scrambling for work, rethinking their careers, and turning to other occupations for steady income. NPR recently reported that the average annual income of an independent jazz musician is $23,000. Confusion, frustration, financial peril, and self-doubt often overshadow the most basic desire to simply play for an audience."[2]

Still, high-level musicians continued to arrive in Portland, including Chuck Israels.

CLUSTERING—THE NEXT WAVE OF JAZZ IMMIGRANTS

When he retired from Western Washington State University, Israels was looking to move—specifically, to a place with a pool of like-minded musicians large enough to staff an eight-piece group to play his arrangements of Bill Evans's music. His work in the Bill Evans trio from 1961–66 established Israels's reputation. After taking refuge in the academy for nearly twenty-five years, he was eager to get out and play again.

He chose Portland.

Israels had recorded with Stan Getz and Herbie Hancock and worked with other jazz legends, from Billie Holiday to John Coltrane. He directed the National Jazz Ensemble in Washington, DC, and recorded with the Kronos Quartet, too. And yet Portland was the affordable city where Chuck Israels, a leader very particular about sound and approach felt he'd find musicians appropriate for the band of his dreams. By the end of 2015, the Chuck Israels Jazz Orchestra had made two albums and was performing monthly.

Contrary to Israels' deliberate decision, it took Hurricane Katrina to get Devin Phillip to town—as well as an innovative program called the NOLA to PDX Initiative, conceived by Portland Jazz Festival artistic director Bill Royston.

"I didn't choose Portland, Portland chose me," Phillips recalled. "Immediately following the hurricane, I found a link on the WWOZ New Orleans website from the Portland Jazz Festival to help musicians who were dislocated. I made a phone call, and three days later I was here.

"I found instant family. For the first few years I felt like a welcomed outsider; then over time, you have kids and establish yourself. Now I feel like it's my home."

But Phillips brought his heritage and New Orleans musical traditions with him. One Sunday, nearly ten years after he arrived in the Pacific Northwest, he carried a pan of his homemade jambalaya to a rehearsal. His grandmother had always made jambalaya on Sundays. Nevertheless, the relocation changed him. In New Orleans he had been a sideman. In Portland, he became a leader.

First, Phillips led his quartet, New Orleans Straight Ahead, on a 2007 tour of West African countries sponsored by the US State Department. He made an album, performed the complete *A Love Supreme* by John Coltrane several times, and has led various other groups as well as worked as a sideman. And in Portland, Phillips got to play with his boyhood hero, Coltrane collaborator and legendary saxophonist Pharaoh Sanders.

Phillips had been asked to introduce Sanders from the stage at the Portland Jazz Festival, and after his heartfelt introduction, when the band was into its second tune, Sanders called Phillips up for a solo. The elder saxophonist even kept him on stage for a few more numbers.[3]

In 2015, a decade after he'd arrived, Phillips was inducted into the Jazz Society of Oregon Hall of Fame. At age thirty-three, he was the youngest ever admitted.

Other jazz immigrants with established reputations began to arrive in the region, including drummer Todd Strait, from Kansas City. He had been touring with such notable artists as the singer Karin Allison and the pianist Eldar. He'd been Marian McPartland's drummer for nine years in New York, and then, in Kansas City, he worked with the singer Kevin Mahogany for thirteen years. He didn't stop until 2007.

Portland was the affordable city where Chuck Israels, a leader very particular about sound and approach, felt that he would find musicians appropriate for the band of his dreams.

"When I decided to get off the road, I knew what I was doing," he said. "You're either in or you're not." Strait was not; that part of his life was over, and he was quickly absorbed into the region's jazz community, where he performed frequently, did a little teaching, and watched his son grow.

Former Robert Palmer guitarist Eddie Martinez also found a congenial scene in Portland for his brand of jazz, blues and Latin music; Spanish pianist Chano Dominguez settled in Seattle; and the pianist and composer Weber Iago, a native of Brazil who had been living in California, brought compelling original work to Portland stages. Iago (later known as Jasnam Daya Singh) has several albums as a leader and tours frequently.

The return of native son Cuong Vu in 2007 was precipitated by the offer of a position at the University of Washington, where he became chair of the jazz studies program. He had wanted to return to the Pacific Northwest for years, and, after establishing himself as one of the leading avant-garde trumpeters in New York, he has helped expand Seattle's improvised music scene. Vu currently advises the Improvised Music Project, a UW-based advocacy group comprising many of his former students; they regularly host performances at Café Racer in Seattle's University District.

Chuck Israels aimed to put together a large ensemble to play his arrangements of Bill Evans's music.

Vu likens the energy of Seattle's current artistic climate to the 1990s "downtown" New York scene. When added to the avant-garde tendencies of the UW's jazz faculty, Vu's activities helped elevate the Puget Sound's improvisational music to greater prominence. He received the University's Distinguished Teaching Award after his third year, and was credited by the *Seattle Times* with revitalizing the school's jazz program.[4]

The melding of avant-garde jazz, experimental and contemporary classical music, and their increasing distance from the dancing and dining experience, appeared to grow hand-in-hand with Seattle's new economy, which produced millionaire arts patrons and a number of concert series and other music projects sponsored by arts agencies and private businesses. It appeared that jazz had found a new niche in a booming city transformed by gleaming towers, glowing domes, and sculptural museums.

Or several niches, according to saxophonist Bryan Smith, a Portland native who attended the University of Washington and worked in Seattle for a number of years.

"In Seattle, there are many players and many different focuses within music. This causes smaller communities of musicians. Much of the time, these musicians rarely go outside of their community to experience the variety Seattle can offer."[5]

The region's major cities had grown apart. As opposed to the situation in Seattle, it was still possible to work with a variety of musicians and for a single individual to have widespread impact in Portland's smaller jazz community. And no established artist who arrived in the Rose City after 2007 has made an impact as significant as George Colligan. His instrumental mastery, sheer energy—both on and off the bandstand—and willingness to bring student musicians onstage with him helped Colligan quickly become part of the local scene. He arrived from New York by way of Winnipeg in 2011 for a faculty position in Portland State University's Jazz Department. He had already appeared on more than one hundred albums as a sideman and thirty as a leader, and he was touring with celebrated drummer Jack DeJohnette.

Left: Portland native Bryan Smith has also lived and worked extensively in Seattle.

Right: George Colligan's instrumental mastery, sheer energy, and willingness to perform with student musicians quickly made him a part of the local scene when he took a faculty position at Portland State University in 2011.

Playing piano—his primary instrument (he also plays drums and trumpet)—Colligan started bringing bands to every venue he could find, from Eugene to Bellingham. He continued world tours with DeJohnette and jazz-rock drummer Lenny White; he returned to the East Coast frequently to lead his own bands; he taught full-time; and he maintained his weekly blog, *JazzTruth*.

Such a whirlwind is bound to create a stir, and as a role model alone, Colligan raised the bar even higher for musicianship and bandstand verve. He became a catalyst, especially for younger players, and even played drums with two of them on the album *Theoretical Planets*.

At first, Colligan thought Portland could become a viable alternative to New York, that the lack of competitive intensity in the Pacific Northwest might be an advantage to local musicians. And though he may be right about that, his optimism faded after half a dozen key venues closed in 2014. "Yes, we have a scene, which is more than can be said for most cities in the world. Portland is cool...I mean, where are you gonna go—Cincinnati? But I think it can be better."[6]

The Cave, located near Portland State University, was closed after less than a year for its low ceiling and inadequate exits, but it felt like "a real jazz club" where the music was connected to a living culture. Seattle's Tractor Tavern served a similar function.

A CANDLE IN THE DARKNESS

Before the club scene in Portland turned bleak, a few flares of hope briefly blazed. One of them was kindled in a low-ceilinged basement near the Portland State campus called the Cave. Drummer Alan Jones booked the music there, and he also put together a band he called The Cavemen that included former Seattle saxophonist Rob Davis as well as Jones's former collaborator, Randy Porter. The music was similar to what Jones's earlier sextet had played, too. But this time, the musicians were fifteen years older than the university crowd drawn to the club. The students had come for the scene rather than jazz itself. They liked the funky decor and low cover charge at the all-ages place just steps from dorms and classrooms.

The Cave was open for less than a year, closed by order of the Fire Marshall for its low ceiling and inadequate exits. But it felt like a "real jazz club," where the music was connected to a living culture and the audience included older fans as well as young. Seattle's Tractor Tavern served the same function in its heyday.

Those diverse audiences were becoming increasingly rare: a survey by the National Endowment for the Arts, conducted in 2008, showed that the average age of a jazz event attendee was forty-six; in 1982, it had been twenty-nine. The audience was aging faster than the years were passing, and shrinking too: in 2002, 10.3 percent of Americans attended a jazz event; in 2012, that figure had dropped to 8.1 percent. The national sales figures for jazz recordings were even more dismal. In 2011, a total of eleven million jazz albums were sold, according to BusinessWeek—2.8 percent of all music sold in that year, falling to 2 percent in 2014.[7]

Such statistics are somewhat misleading because many jazz musicians sell their albums personally, and those sales aren't recorded. Often, self-produced albums are not reported to national databases. And national figures may not accurately reflect attendance and sales in the Pacific Northwest. Even so, there was no doubt that an aging audience was getting smaller. In Seattle, there were barely a dozen full-time jazz clubs. Irregular performances were going on in a number of coffee shops and other small venues around the Sound, however, and in 2010, the city's new mayor announced the city's new Seattle Night Life Initiative that would allow nightspots to remain open and serving alcohol after 2:00 a.m. But hungry young artists far outnumbered places to perform.

Faced with that reality, they played house concerts and they knocked on the doors of restaurants, taverns, and coffee shops, looking for new venues. They organized loose collectives to support the performance of each other's original work. The situation was similar in other major cities too, as musicians everywhere realized what had been clear all along to artists in the Pacific Northwest—they were on their own.

In Seattle, they saw that as an opportunity.

SEATTLE IS BOOMING

The Emerald City's prolific avant-garde community responded by banding together in organizations whose projects have used sounds and techniques that range from chamber music to rock. A number of them came out of Monktail Creative Music Concern. A composers' and musicians' collective, it gained visibility in 2006 when it began producing the free, multiday, all-ages Sounds Outside concerts at Cal Anderson Park. But in 2011, in a move that reflected the continuing recession, the Collective cancelled the series. The group continued its regular member performances at the Chapel Performance Space, however—a beautiful multiuse hall that lends seriousness and dignity to the music, an experience different from encountering their music at the bars and coffee shops where they also hosted shows. The collective also started its own record label.

Monktail member Beth Fleenor's projects illustrate one facet of the Puget Sound scene during these years. She developed several bands to perform her work, including Crystal Beth, whose sound she describes as "metal and lace."[8] A clarinet player, singer, composer, and 2004 Cornish graduate, Fleenor's goals were personal rather than commercial. She wanted to explore her authentic voice, no matter the cost. Fleenor's priority was to get her work out—she would worry about assessing it later. In the Pacific Northwest, it was still possible to take that approach and survive. In fact, a number of Monktail members' projects have been supported by grants from regional arts agencies.

Cafe Racer: Seattle's Famously Quirky Dive

Peter Bletcha, HistoryLink.org, October 7, 2012

Easily one of Seattle's all-time quirkiest and best-loved neighborhood dives, the Café Racer Espresso has since 2005 offered up good coffee, simple food, cheep beer, and fun music to an eclectic clientele comprising an ongoing parade of outsider artists, actors, writers, motor-scooter enthusiasts, neo-vaudevillians, musicians, hippies, steampunks, stray dogs—all sorts of social misfits—and even a few "normal" college students and neighbors.

Overseen by owner Kurt Geissel, the cozy venue . . . is a comfortable, inexpensive, and very inviting spot where everyone is welcome, conversation is spirited, live music is energizing, and creative sparks fly.

[It opened in 2005, and] Café Racer quickly attracted a broad array of people who began making it their second home. . . . Numerous informal social clubs and subcultural interest groups also began holding meetings there . . . perhaps most notably, Seattle's famed graphic-novelist Jim Woodring, who began leading drawing classes in a back room and helped found an associated cartooning group.

"I think that what is unique about this place," says Geissel, "is that so many different groups of people feel at home here. . . . It really does have an impact on people and their lives."

In 2010 a cluster of University of Washington music department students began holding experimental/improvisational jazz jams at the Café on Sundays—events that eventually took shape as the Racer Sessions, and even a couple of Racer Session Fests. Along the way, the idea for a new record label, Table & Chairs, was sparked there.

"I just always wanted a place where everybody could meet and get along, and be who they are. Non-judgmental, that's who we are. I think that pretty much sums it up. . . . The other night, when we first reopened, there was this woman singing and another playing the accordion. And they were doing it just for each other. Just because they needed to create it. Art for art's sake. And we need more of that in the world. I mean: it's not just all about money. And I think this place kinda shows it. I think people feel that that's what we're trying to do here."

Today, the Monktail Collective operates an internet radio station, records and archives many of its members' performances, and has released seventeen albums. And Monktail's record label is only one of a number of independents documenting and disseminating Seattle's avant-garde music. None of them rely on traditional record company/artist relationships; there's very little money in it anyway.

At Pony Boy Records, Origin Records, and Portland Jazz Composer Ensemble Records, each project is considered a partnership between the artist and the label. In return for the artist's help in funding production, they often receive a higher percentage of sales revenue than at traditional record companies. Other indie labels, like Table & Chairs, cofounded by drummer Chris Icasiano, also stage live shows of the music they record; in both 2012 and 2013, Table & Chairs won the Earshot Jazz award for Concert of the Year.

Icasiano also cofounded The Racer Sessions, a weekly composition and improvisation workshop which, according to Paul de Barros, is the most exciting thing going on in Seattle. The sessions are held at Club Racer, a casual place where young people feel comfortable and the music reflects the influence of the University of Washington's jazz program. But they weren't exciting enough—the Racer Sessions only reached de Barros on an intellectual level; it wasn't the serious emotional experience he was seeking. That's a more general problem with Seattle's New Music and avant-garde scene, he believes.

"When I listen to John Coltrane play 'Naima,' that's a serious emotional experience; not just because it's old and classic. I don't care if you call it jazz," he says. "Play me some music that does what *that* did to me!"

Maybe he's longing for musicians who play four or five hours a night, as Coltrane and his mates did, working ensembles rather than loose collections of freelance improvisers. Maybe he's longing for musicians who perform more than they teach—longing for another era. The jazz scene, as it was configured for many years, had partially unraveled in Seattle by the time the Racer Sessions took off. The music was bleeding out into rock, hip-hop, and contemporary classical configurations. That helped jazz artists find new audiences, but their work in those contexts was no longer perceived as "jazz." It appeared that the core traditions at the center could no longer hold—except maybe in the schools.

The Pacific Northwest was by this time well stocked with musicians trained at colleges and universities, many with postgraduate degrees. So it's no surprise that Icasiano and his credentialed peers have become educators as well as performers. Nearly every jazz artist's website advertises teaching experience, and classroom jobs as well as private instruction had become another indispensable piece of the jazz performer's income stream. Supplementing performance and recording work with part-time teaching enables many nontouring jazz players to eke out a living.

In a way, it's remarkable how many manage to make it work, especially musicians whose audience would appear to be limited. But more young players continue to rise up, like the Sequoia Ensemble. They draw inspiration from the landscape and describe their sound as "filled with earthy, lush textures and organic, colorful undertones…that capture the beautiful, powerful, awe-inducing natural world." It's a common theme in the region, but the chamber jazz group's soundscapes often feature circus horns leaping out of the forest, and at times those colorful undertones clash.

And speaking of the natural world, beginning in 2007, native people finally had a visible—though infrequent—presence in local jazz with Khu.éex' (Tlingit for potlatch), an all-star band playing funk and jazz versions of traditional Tlingit music. In 2014, the seven-piece group included Puget Sound glass artist and bassist Preston Singletary. Not all the band personnel are tribal members; Seattle saxophonist Skerik is also in Khu.éex', and he brings to it that punk-jazz energy of the 1990s—a strain as deeply embedded in the region as the pastoral.

And the traditional, too. Seattle is home to an ambitious and forward-looking all-star big band, the Seattle Repertory Jazz Orchestra. The crown jewel of straight-ahead jazz, its programs are thoughtful and instructive. Some are devoted to groundbreaking recordings like Miles Davis' *Birth of the Cool*, while others have included movies, the Harlem Renaissance, and dance music. The SRJO brings in a range of guest soloists, from National Endowment for the Arts Jazz Masters to local artists such as clarinetist Bill Smith, pianist Jovino Santos Neto, and singer Ernestine Anderson. The band has made three recordings, and its educational programs, Jazz Scholars and Jazz4Kids, bring jazz to the classroom and children to the concert hall. The ensemble has included veteran straight-ahead players such as Randy Halberstadt, Jay Thomas, Phil Sparks, and Clarence Acox.

And the Seattle area has an impressive pool of straight-ahead artists to choose from for such a band, including singer Greta Matassa; pianists Bill Anschell and Darin Clendenin; bassist Chuck Deardorf; guitarist Milo Petersen; drummers John Bishop and Mark Ivester; and saxophonists Richard Cole, Brent Jensen, and Hans Teuber—to name just a few.

At Tula's Restaurant in the Belltown neighborhood, listeners were likely to hear many of those players in one or another of the Puget Sound's many big bands. In 2012, at Tula's alone, ten different big bands performed. It takes a lot of musicians to staff those sixteen-piece units. Many are part-time players who donate their time and talent.

Though Jazz Alley is Seattle's best-known club, it has booked nationally touring acts almost exclusively, and they're not always jazz. So in Puget Sound, Tula's stands out as the quintessential jazz club, booking primarily regional artists since 1995. Wynton Marsalis listed Tula's as one of his top ten jazz spots in the nation. Yet it's always been a struggle to keep the one-hundred-seat restaurant open, says owner Elliott "Mack" Waldron. The customer base for jazz music is already limited, and business drops off with bad weather. Jazz festivals and other big concerts also take customers away.

Those are perennial problems for jazz clubs, of course, and it's still surprising that a city the size of Seattle, with so many high-level professional players, would have so few places for them to perform. Egan's Ballard Jam House, one of the city's principal jazz venues, seats fewer than thirty. The Triple Door opened in 2003 with Skerik's Syncopated Taint Septet, and in its early years the swanky 230-seat venue presented jazz acts regularly. That's changed; only a few regional jazz artists were performing there in 2015. And the closing of the New Orleans Creole Restaurant in Pioneer Square in 2013 left another hole in musicians' schedules. But that doesn't mean jazz—in all its guises—wasn't being heard. More venues were simply mixing genres, and a number of taverns, restaurants, and even a bookstore were hosting weekly or monthly jam sessions.

But Wayne Horvitz thought a different kind of venue was needed, so in 2011, he opened The Royal Room in Rainier Valley, an ethnically diverse neighborhood west of Lake Washington. The Royal Room hosts an eclectic range of styles, from singer-songwriter to straight-ahead and progressive jazz, electronica, and Horvitz's own project, the Royal Room Collective Music Ensemble. That multigenre approach is Horvitz's attempt at recapturing the more open and varied music policies of the New York clubs in the 1970s. It may be the most important among his many contributions to the region's music scene.

"He's making a difference," says Paul de Barros. "He's having local people playing music that has something to do with how we live and where we live and what we do." It's a noble effort, and not the first time a musician on a mission has taken on running a club. Elmer Gill tried it in the 1940s, and David Friesen in the 1970s, both with mixed results. Despite the shaky economics of such a plan, The Royal Room has stuck with a voluntary, sliding scale cover charge policy—and survived into 2015.

The all-star Portland Jazz Orchestra was a promising group that foundered on a shallow base of support.

SMALL IS PRECARIOUS

In contrast, clubs in Portland are even scarcer, and its big bands have faltered—in 2015, the city had no regularly working large ensembles. For years, however, there were several, including the Art Abrams Big Band and the Portland Jazz Orchestra, which was founded in 2005 as a way to preserve and extend classic big-band jazz. The all-star PJO offers an example of a promising group that foundered on a shallow base of support. During the financial crisis, while other arts organizations were cutting back, the band released an album of original compositions, increased its audience, doubled pay for musicians, and became the resident ensemble of the Portland Jazz Festival. In fewer than ten years, it was inactive.

Stable funding for such projects was more readily available in Seattle, and the Seattle Repertory Jazz Orchestra has continuing sponsors that include the Paul G. Allen Family Foundation and the Boeing Company as well as local arts agencies. It's also a membership organization, as is PDX Jazz, the producer of the Portland Jazz Festival.

In 2011, PDX Jazz added year-round programming in addition to its annual festival, and, by 2015, was producing more than fifteen shows per year featuring both national and local artists. Its members numbered more than five hundred.

But the organization almost didn't get that far.

A year after it received a $100,000 bailout from the city and was named one of the top five jazz events in the world by the Jazz Journalists Association, the Portland Jazz Festival was again on the brink of collapse. It would take a "miracle" to keep its 2009 edition alive, the board said. Then, on October 1, the miracle occurred: Alaska Airlines announced a multiyear sponsorship, and in the wake of that commitment, several other corporations with ties to Portland also pledged

Joe Doria's McTuff Trio has performed at the New Orleans Jazz and Heritage Festival three times and regularly draws crowds to Seattle clubs.

support. The donations were spurred by a new advisory committee, led by city commissioner Nick Fish and prominent businessman Sho Dozono. As is often the case with cultural activities, when elected officials and influential businesspeople get involved, money for the arts appears.

And that's more likely to happen when the arts organization is large. So PDX Jazz continued to grow, and as its activities increased, it came to rival Earshot Jazz, with its year-round concerts, annual festival, monthly magazine, and extensive educational programs. Earshot Jazz is also more deeply linked to the local community as well as to national jazz networks: it was one of twenty sites in the Lila Wallace–Readers Digest National Jazz Network, from which it received funding; and beginning in 2000, it joined eleven other groups to form JazzNet, which received financial support from the Doris Duke Charitable Foundation. Earshot Jazz has also arranged a number of productive partnerships, notably with the Seattle Art Museum and the Asian Art Museum. And in 2014, it added another concert series, "Jazz: The Second Century," that features Seattle artists.

The organization's Executive Director, John Gilbreath, is one of the most influential individuals in the Puget Sound scene. In addition to supervising Earshot Jazz activities, his programming vision extends throughout the area. He's artistic director of both the Bellevue Jazz Festival and the Anacortes Jazz Festival; he has programmed the Experience Music Project's "Jazz in January" concert series; and Gilbreath is on the radio, too: six days a week he plays a mix of jazz and international music on KBCS's morning show, and Sunday nights on KEXP, he plays more adventurous sounds. In 2012, he was named a Seattle Jazz Hero by the Jazz Journalists Association.

Top: Thara Memory's Superband performed soul and R&B hits, and often featured Janice Scroggins.

Right: Esperanza Spalding was named Best New Artist at the 2012 Grammy Awards, and in 2013 she shared another Grammy with her Portland mentor Thara Memory.

Esperanza Spalding: *Esperanza* Means Hope

Everybody loves a "hometown girl makes good" story. It validates the home folks and allows us to feel in part responsible for her success. And we are, Esperanza Spalding assured her fans on a recent visit to her hometown.

"It doesn't come from nowhere," she said. But her rapid rise to the top of the jazz world wasn't only due to musical knowledge gained in Portland. It was also about high expectations and on-the-job training.

"All the older musicians I played with here never treated me like a kid. I was treated with a lot of respect and the expectation that I could do the music well. So I left with a certain confidence that I had something to offer. I had the unique advantage of getting to play from the beginning."

That continued once she left to attend Berklee College of Music in Boston, where she earned the chance to play with a number of modern masters. Her most important lessons came from the years she spent in saxophonist Joe Lovano's ensemble.

"First of all, you get to see what the lifestyle is like. It's not just about how many hours a day you practice—he lives and breathes that music; he talks about it, thinks about it, reads about it, listens to it all the time. It's a way of living."

Spalding released her third album, *Chamber Music Society*, in 2010 and has become a jazz celebrity—the subject of a profile in the *New Yorker* and a fashion spread in *O, The Oprah Magazine's* "Women on the Rise" feature. She's appeared on numerous TV shows as well, received awards, and starred in a Banana Republic ad campaign.

Her major label debut, *Esperanza*, remained on the jazz charts for more than seventy weeks. But *Chamber Music Society* really boosted her stature. Some say she pushed the limits of jazz with it. Spalding doesn't agree.

"What I'm pushing limits of is what a record label will support ... and that's partially because I'm pretty and young. I'll use that to get away with musical things I want to do. So the record label thinks, 'We can sell this anyway, because we can sell her image.' Because of what the record companies see as my market potential, they put a lot of energy behind it, thinking they'll get a lot back. So two times in a row I've been given almost complete artistic freedom because they believed they could sell my image."

And so her upcoming album, *Radio Music Society*, is the next big challenge, both personally and in terms of the market. Her immediate task is clear: to figure out how "to format these elements of the music that I love in a way that people who are used to hearing commercial music will be able to enter the realm of improvised music."

Making jazz accessible: that's the goal. And there's a social dimension to her ambition as well.

"That process of being dedicated to a craft is missing in this culture among young people. Because it's relatively easy to emulate what you see these pop stars doing ... whereas, to be a great instrumentalist or a great singer, it takes a lot of responsibility and dedication and consistency. Working and exploring your craft are not incentivized in the music industry now."

Spalding hopes to change that. As we share in her success, we can also share that hope.

At the 2012 Grammy Awards, Spalding was named Best New Artist. In 2013, she shared another Grammy with her Portland mentor Thara Memory and his Pacific Crest Jazz Orchestra, for Best Arrangement Accompanying a Vocalist on her *Radio Music Society* album.

Steve Griggs developed a series of concerts in the Panama Hotel's tearoom that featured original tunes and narration explaining the building's rich history.

GET UP ON THE GOODFOOT

Funk was rarely heard at the Earshot Jazz or Portland festivals. But after 2008 it was alive and on the rise in several Portland bands and in the hands of Seattle organ player Joe Doria's McTuff trio. Featuring Doria on a Hammond B3, the group has performed at the New Orleans Jazz & Heritage Festival three times as well as up and down the West Coast. Their danceable, driving instrumentals never have trouble drawing a crowd to Seattle clubs like the Seamonster Lounge.

The city's leading jazz organist, Doria started on piano and studied at Cornish with straight-ahead keyboard artists such as Randy Halberstadt, Dave Peck, and Jerry Gray. Doria also worked with drummer Michael Shrieve in the avant-funk band Spellbinder.

In Portland in 2015, funk, soul, and contemporary R&B—modern-day versions of the jump blues and classic R&B that once animated Williams Avenue and Jackson Street—are played old-school. And during those years, there was more of it all the time. The Mel Brown B3 Organ Group released two albums in 2014. Activist and trumpeter Farnell Newton, who tours with funk master Bootsy Collins and contemporary R&B star Jill Scott, has contributed to the Portland funk scene by promoting the work of others as well as his own groups. In 2015, Newton released his third album, *Ready to Roll*—with Seattle's Skerik among the musicians contributing. Newton's bands often perform at The Goodfoot in southeast Portland. The large tavern-with-dance-floor has long been the city's most consistent site for funk and is another multigenre venue.

Thara Memory's Superband also performs soul and R&B hits; keyboard player and composer Janice Scroggins was often on piano with them until her untimely death in 2014. Her roots in blues and gospel made Scroggins a valued presence on a host of locally produced albums. Her longtime associate, vocalist Linda Hornbuckle, also moved easily between blues, gospel, soul, and jazz.

Hornbuckle also passed away in 2014, and no one seemed likely to fill her shoes. She started singing at age six in Portland's Grace and Truth Pentecostal Church, pastored by her father, and went on to tour and record with such nationally known Pacific Northwest rock and soul bands as Quarterflash and Nu Shooz. She was lead vocalist for the Motown revue band Body and Soul, and she fronted the No deLay Band in the 1990s while its leader was in prison. She was a member of the Oregon Music Hall of Fame.

Hornbuckle and Scroggins collaborated many times, but their only recorded work together was the 2009 album *Sista*, which inspired Grammy-winning jazz artist Esperanza Spalding. Scroggins had been her teacher when the bassist was a child, but, as Spalding remembers, "Janice Scroggins was, quite honestly, too deep for

me when I was eight years old." Only later did she realize how important the older woman's contribution had been in fusing gospel, blues, and jazz, Spalding admits.[9]

Scroggins was a member of the Cascade Blues Association's Hall of Fame and a consummate accompanist. When she died unexpectedly of a heart attack at age fifty-eight, Portland musicians lined up to sing her praises. "You know that trust game where you fall into someone else's arms backward? Playing with Janice was like that. You knew she'd catch," said bassist Lisa Mann.

Every year at the Waterfront Blues Festival, Scroggins and Hornbuckle performed together in Hornbuckle's "Old Time Gospel Hour." Once, just before the band was set to go, it started pouring rain. The power went out, the piano was destroyed, and an inch of water covered the stage. But Hornbuckle went on anyway, singing "Amazing Grace" a cappella. The clouds parted and the rain stopped. Artistic director Peter Dammann was waiting in the wings. Her performance brought him to tears.

"Janice Scroggins was, quite honestly, too deep for me when I was eight years old," recalls Esperanza Spalding.

Left: As Linda Hornbuckle sang "Amazing Grace" a cappella after rain caused a power outage at the Waterfront Blues Festival, the clouds parted and the rain stopped.

Right: John Nastos is a skilled performer and member of both the Mel Brown Septet and Brown's son Christopher's Quartet. He is also the creator of Metronomics, a metronome app for iPhone and iPad.

BIG PROJECTS

Thara Memory's album *Chronicle* credits Scroggins for "keyboards, piano, and advice." She was also part of several Soul-to-Soul concerts Memory staged with the aim of presenting soul music in its historical context, with high-level musicianship and jazz improvisation. They also worked together on Memory's collaboration with master drummer Obo Addy, "Africa Speaks, America Answers." Such themed projects have increased in the region over the years, and some have attempted to connect with the community's history. Among those was Seattle saxophonist Steve Griggs's Panama Hotel Jazz project.

He staged it at the historic Panama Hotel in Seattle's International District, which, Griggs wrote in program notes, "carries the memories of hope, hatred, and humility experienced by Japanese Americans before, during, and after World War II." His series of free concerts in the hotel's tearoom featured original tunes and narration explaining the building's rich history and tying it into Seattle writer Jamie Ford's historical novel, *Hotel on the Corner of Bitter and Sweet*. Griggs's band featured top Seattle straight-ahead players, and he produced an album of the music. Continuing his exploration of Seattle's jazz past, in 2015 Griggs was at work on a book about jazz artist and educator Joe Brazil.

What makes these big projects important is not their size but their mission to place jazz at the heart of the region's cultural identity, whether by using local history or collaborating with artists in other disciplines. Seattle bassist Evan Flory-Barnes wanted to bring together distant sectors of the local arts community in his piece *Acknowledgement of a Celebration*, which premiered at Seattle's Town Hall in 2009. Written for a large chamber orchestra, the nine-movement composition featured thirty-five musicians and ten dancers and was commissioned by a "meet the composer" program. In addition to the dance component, his music combined early twentieth century orchestral approaches with contemporary beats, reflecting his experience in both classical and hip-hop ensembles.

After that major work, people started asking Flory-Barnes why he wasn't moving to New York. His bandmate in the Industrial Revelation quartet, pianist Josh Rawlings, jumped in to answer: "I think Evan sees a profound amount of beauty right here and isn't ready to dismiss the talent, wealth, creativity, and opportunities that exist in his very place of birth. Why should he move away when everything he wants is right here?"[10]

The same has certainly been true for Darrell Grant. He hires New York musicians for many of his recording projects, but his heart now belongs to the Pacific Northwest. No other jazz projects have attempted to capture the landscape and history of the region like Grant's epic suite *The Territory*. Written for a nine-piece jazz band and a singer/narrator, its nine movements include a section depicting The Golden West Hotel, the first African American establishment in Portland, as well as paeans to the landscape. On a grand scale, it directly captures the sense of place that is expressed tangentially by most jazz made in the Pacific Northwest.

"My hypothesis was that music is shaped by a connection to the terrain—both the physical place and the community from which it springs," Grant says. He had already heard that connection in the work of Alan Jones. "As I've come to know Alan over the past twenty years, and lived in his environment and worked with him, I feel the ethos of this place embodies him—his choices and decisions. And his music sounds like that." And Grant heard it in the band Oregon, too: "When I got here, I was like, 'Oh, this music is like hiking in Forest Park.' Can I capture that sound? I've always been trying to get at it in some way in every piece.... If we can make ourselves sensitive to this place, then all the stuff that has happened here will affect us. I wanted to tap into that collective memory."

Perhaps the success of *The Territory* gave Grant a rosier view of the region's jazz ecology—even though the audience was getting thin, the scene did appear to be bursting with exciting projects and musical excellence. However, that delicate ecosystem was thrown out of balance as jazz became more widely accessible on the internet.

THE INTERNET CHANGED EVERYTHING

Early file-sharing services like Napster that shook the rock and pop industries had little impact on jazz players. It was the streaming services that finally squeezed off most of the meager earnings they had once received from album sales.

Left: "I give a lot of music, charts, or advice away for free. I'm more concerned with people hearing what I do than I am getting ninety-nine cents for it." Damian Erskine successfully crowdfunded his 2015 album, Within Sight.

Right: Ahamefule Oluo grew up poor in Seattle, became obsessed with music and art, and later branched out into standup comedy and writing. In 2012, he presented his musical drama, Now I'm Fine, at Town Hall Seattle. He is a member of the Industrial Revelation Quartet.

"It's a terrible, terrible model.... If you get one play on Spotify, that's .00048 cents, and if you get one hundred plays... you're still not getting a penny." John Bishop of Origin Records speaks for many artists. Streaming services have cut into his business, and that's not good for the hundreds of artists whose albums he carries. It's not just the artists who are harmed, either. As less money is returned from album sales, musicians are less able to record new material, diminishing the market for recording engineers and related contractors. It's a vicious circle. And streaming has cut into the already limited online sales of jazz albums and single-song downloads.

For some, however, this new paradigm was liberating.

"There's no money in it anymore, and that's created a lot of freedom," says Grant. "The illusion of success has been taken away, so we might as well do what we care about."

That could pass for a regional theme song. Whether that's a good thing depends on what each artist finds out here on the margins, where jazz is now located—liberation, or just another word for nothing left to lose. Money up front is still required to finance an album, so the internet's social media options made self-promotion— and the new bag of skills it requires—a necessity for most jazz musicians. Many albums that come out of the Pacific Northwest these days are financed in whole or part by crowdfunding campaigns.

"You've always had to play better than the next guy," observes veteran New York studio player Dan Wilensky, who moved to Portland in 2012. "But now, in addition to being a superior sight reader, doubler, and arranger, you have to master

Ahamefule Oluo: Now I'm Fine

Steve Griggs, *Earshot Jazz*, December 2012

"This place feels haunted at two in the morning," composer, musician, and comedian Ahamefule Oluo says. He sits center stage at a Steinway grand piano, under Town Hall's stained-glass cupola, surrounded by semicircles of original, century-old wooden benches that slope up and away from the stage.

On December 9, Oluo presents *Now I'm Fine* at Town Hall Seattle. Combining music and spoken word, the intimate and purposefully melodramatic work is the culmination of Oluo's three-month artist residency at the performance venue.

Now I'm Fine is an ambitious autobiographical piece with fifteen performers . . . [a] brass ensemble . . . [a] string ensemble . . . [a singer, and] rhythm section. Oluo will deliver spoken passages.

Now I'm Fine springs from a time six years ago when Oluo was definitely not fine. "Within six months, my dad died, my first marriage ended, I contracted bronchitis and had an autoimmune reaction to an antibiotic. I was diagnosed with Stevens-Johnson syndrome (progressive toxic epidermal necrolysis) and lost skin around my mouth, hands, feet, fingernails, toenails, and inside my eyelids. I took Dilaudid [a narcotic for pain]." From his illness came inspiration.

Alone in his apartment, Oluo reflected on the story of his life. . . . Born thirty years ago of an American mother and estranged Nigerian father, Oluo grew up poor in Seattle. "We never had electricity or a phone," he says. "For a while I lived in a Honda Civic with my mom and sister." Oluo experienced severe social anxiety. "I couldn't talk to people. I had no friends."

Oluo became obsessed with creating art. He drew. He attempted to make a guitar from found objects. "I would do anything to get out of that constant anxiety."

Before he found creative outlets, Oluo destroyed things. "I ate wood. I cut up a couch with a knife. Even now, I turn difficult when I don't have an outlet to express my demons. I have to find things that work."

Oluo continued to perform musically from his jazz roots while he branched out into standup comedy and writing. "Jazz is exploratory music," he says. "No matter what I do, there is a jazz person at the heart of it." After years of developing as a writer, storyteller, and musician, Oluo hit the rough patch that became the genesis for *Now I'm Fine*.

In an apartment upstairs from Oluo at that time, bassist Evan Flory-Barnes was developing his own autobiographical opus, *Acknowledgement of a Celebration*. . . . He would stop by to check in on Oluo, who would later perform in Flory-Barnes' piece and design packaging for his DVD.

For the five years following his illness, Oluo worked on the stories and musical ideas, adapting them for bands and standup comedy routines. Inspired by Flory-Barnes' success with *Acknowledgement*, Oluo sought institutional backing . . . [and] eventually was offered a three-month residency.

studio and computer skills, networking, self-promotion, and graphics, plus have a winning personality to get even a whiff of a career in music."[11]

How have jazz musicians adapted? Many are selling recordings, instruction books, and merchandise online and teaching via Skype. But more is required to promote an artist's work when every minute, forty-eight hours of video is uploaded to YouTube.

Portland saxophonist John Nastos, a skilled performer with a firm grip on the technology of self-promotion, is the creator of Metronomics, a metronome app for

It took a hurricane to get Devin Phillips to Portland from his native New Orleans. "I found instant family," he said. "Now I feel like it's my home." He was the youngest member ever admitted to the Jazz Society of Oregon's Hall of Fame.

iPhone and iPad, and he's currently at work on an ear-training app as well. In 2010, he and pianist Clay Giberson undertook a project they called Duo Chronicles, recording a new composition by one or the other each week for a year and posting videos of the performances online. "The videos have gotten thousands of views, and hopefully we've broadened our exposure base," Nastos says. "It has led to some nice performing opportunities and a couple of commissions." They did it again in 2012, this time recording one video per month.

Jazz players like Damian Erskine are adopting more of the audience engagement tools on social media that their peers in other genres have used. A virtuoso electric bassist playing around the globe in an ever-changing array of musical settings, he's also the nephew of former Weather Report drummer Peter Erskine. Saturation, he says, is the key to getting music to listeners.

"I have tried to have a presence in all of the major social networks as well as explore all of the new ones that pop up. I also give a lot of music, charts, or advice away for free. I'm more concerned with people hearing what I do than I am getting ninety-nine cents for it. Listeners have much more power these days. It has leveled the playing field in some regards, but also complicated it." He's adapted to the "music for free" model espoused by members of his generation who claim never to have purchased music. Erskine successfully crowdfunded his 2015 album, *Within Sight*.

THEY CAME FOR THE LIFESTYLE

Those who follow jazz are always looking for a new "jazz mecca" where the excitement and social relevance jazz once had will come alive again. For a while, some thought it might be Portland.

Even before a 2002 *DownBeat* article came out, proclaiming Portland the new jazz mecca, players had been moving to the city in droves. But musicians who came after 2008 might have been disappointed; performance opportunities were shrinking as the number of players grew. That didn't appear to deter them: unlike cities where established industries draw new aspirants, Portland's chief attraction seems to be the city itself.

They came, as did many young creatives, because their peers were moving to Portland, as Rita Rega observed while interviewing some of the newcomers for *Jazzscene*.

"They come because of their friends, or friends of friends. And it seems to me a lot of that generation know each other, they live near each other, they're constantly influencing each other."

Guitarist Storm Nilson moved to Portland from Southern California in 2011. He'd grown up in Alaska during the summers and in Carmel Valley in the winters; he attended grad school in Montreal. But he chose to settle down in Portland.

"I always liked Portland," he says. "I thought it was a cool place. And there are so many great players here. We get together all the time for sessions; they live just a couple of blocks from me."

Until he moved to London, England, in 2014, Andrew Oliver was a leader of those younger musicians. Blown back to his hometown from Tulane University by Hurricane Katrina, the cheerfully energetic Oliver was in the piano chair for Devin Phillips's New Orleans Straight Ahead on its West African tour. He went on to infuse the jazz scene with fresh musical and organizational energy, writing grant applications, composing music, forming bands, and leading them with energy and purpose. He believed the city had "a certain vibe," and he embodied it. One of Oliver's most enduring contributions to the local scene was bringing to life a new support group, the Portland Jazz Composers Ensemble, and its label, PJCE Records.

The Portland Jazz Composers Ensemble was originally a collective of writers and instrumentalists who got together in 2007 to try out new ideas. After some preliminary rehearsals, it was clear the group would be a performing ensemble, and by 2013 the PJCE was staging four concerts a year and had launched a record label. They'd become more than a group of musicians boldly creating new work; they were a bona fide arts organization receiving grant funds and donations—Portland's answer to Seattle's music collectives. And the city once again had a jazz label.

Oliver's other projects also enriched the scene.

He co-led a tango band; cofounded The Ocular Concern, a sextet with unusual instrumentation and an orchestral approach to composition; led and composed for a straight-ahead sextet; and played drums and sometimes cornet in a traditional jazz group. With kora player Kane Mathis and former Seattle trumpeter Chad McCullough, Oliver formed The Kora Band, a five-piece group combining

Mandinka folk melodies with jazz. And even after his move to London, Oliver remained part of the band Tunnel Six.

Composed of six diverse artists from distant cities, Tunnel Six has managed to continue touring and recording together since 2009, when its members first met at the Banff International Workshop in Jazz & Creative Music in Alberta, Canada. Their two albums of sweeping, impressionistic compositions capture the landscapes they've traversed together.

"Tunnel Six was born in the Canadian Rockies," Oliver explained, "so the music has definitely been shaped by the landscapes, big gigantic mountains and...just driving around [on tour] for five years, through a vast array of interesting landscapes." Oliver won an ASCAP Young Composer's Award for the title tune to their first album, *Lake Superior*.

Tunnel Six trumpeter Chad McCullough left Seattle for Chicago in 2014, when Oliver moved to London. A composer himself, McCullough has led several bands, including a productive association with Belgian pianist Bram Weijters. His move to Chicago was motivated by a growing disenchantment with his prospects in Seattle and the feeling that he could grow more rapidly as an artist with the opportunities offered by a larger market. Others arrived to take their places, but the kind of leadership and activity generated by the likes of Oliver and McCullough isn't easily replaced. Sometimes, however, necessity forces the issue, and leaders emerge.

That's how Mary-Sue Tobin found herself working behind the scenes as well as onstage.

In addition to her formidable musicianship, Mary-Sue Tobin is active as an organizer of jazz events around Portland.

HOMEGROWN LEADER

A teacher as well as an experienced performer on all four saxes, Tobin is a member of the Quadraphonnes, an all-female saxophone quartet, and has worked in many Portland groups, from the funky horn band Soul Vaccination to the avant-garde party ensemble, Industrial Jazz Group. It took her a while to get there.

She started playing saxophone in high school in Eugene, where the nearby University of Oregon ensured a supply of excellent teachers, including Carl Woideck. "[He] was the cool jazz teacher," Tobin recalls. "And he had the cool apartment right by the high school, and I'd go over there and he'd be eating artichokes and listening to Blue Note albums while writing liner notes. I said, 'Oh my god, I want to live in this cool jazz world.'"

Instead she joined a world beat band called Dub Squad that was playing around Portland, opening for Jimmy Cliff and Third World at festivals, and even traveling to Japan.

"I was nineteen, raising a child, and I decided to move to Portland. They asked me if I was twenty-one, and I said, 'Yeah,' and they asked if I played keyboards and sang, so I said, 'Yeah.' I had a little apartment off Hawthorne, my family was helping out, and I was pretty happy."

She was even leading her own bands. Then she had a second child and made a pop record called *Mary-Sue and the A-List*. But Tobin missed playing sax so much that, at the same time, she also joined the jazz-funk band Flatland—which

Members of the Quadraphonnes—Portland's all-female saxophone quartet, here augmented by bass and drums—were strangers when they met, but quickly became best friends.

led to a life-changing decision the night Flatland opened for Herbie Hancock and the Headhunters.

"The next day, I quit every band I was in," she recalled. "Herbie and those guys made me feel like I didn't want to BS anymore. I wanted to be the player I wanted to be, and I wasn't ready.... I wanted to go home and practice the saxophone." So Tobin got a job working graveyard at the post office, and after walking her son to school in the morning, she would practice for five to seven hours.

That lasted a few years, until she enrolled at Portland State University. "That's where I learned to be a jazz musician," she said. "I was hanging out with the other students, eating together, going to each other's houses. We loved each other." One year, her cohort included sixteen-year-old Esperanza Spalding, who sometimes carried her bass to class on a city bus. Tobin earned a Master of Music in Saxophone Performance, and so began her journey to the heart of the Portland jazz scene.[12]

Tobin hosted rehearsals at her place, prepared food for her colleagues, gave parties, and finally found her soul mates when she became a Quadraphonne. "We were strangers when we met," the four women say. "Now we're best friends." She organized a Sunday night jazz series at the Blue Monk, secured a sponsor, and kept it going for three years. She also helped bring jazz back to Williams Avenue at WineUp on Williams; she got her neighborhood group a weekly gig at the Starday tavern in another neighborhood; and she put her stamp on the Cathedral Park Jazz Festival as its volunteer talent coordinator for two years. She has also exercised her influence on the Portland Jazz Festival as a member of its programming committee. "We owe a lot to her," says fellow saxophonist Tim Willcox, "for this and as a spokesperson for our interests. Without her, our jazz scene would be a lot less vibrant."[13]

It's a good thing she had a full slate of students, though, because nightclub work was in short supply, and even the few venues still operating weren't drawing midweek crowds anymore.

Left: Seattle's median income continues to rise along with new Amazon and Microsoft towers, while the pay for jazz remains low.

Right: Third-generation Seattle musician D'Vonne Lewis has become one of the most sought-after drummers in the region.

THE ARTIST AND THE CITY

Historically, January is a slow month in the entertainment business, but to find fewer than a dozen tables occupied in early 2015 was unusual at Jimmy Mak's, Portland's top jazz club, where the Mel Brown Quartet was in residence every Wednesday. The music couldn't have been better—straight-ahead jazz at its highest level, played with skill and emotion by one of the city's most famous musicians leading a band of local all-stars. Streetcars stopped outside the big front windows, but no one got off.

Around the region, several jazz clubs had recently closed their doors, and scores of musicians were hungry for opportunity. But audiences were small, even at the few remaining venues. It was a precarious existence.

"It's a real tough, real hard world to be a jazz musician in, or a poet or a writer or anything," says saxophonist Phil Woods. "But that's where you separate the wheat from the chaff.... It's a burden for the artist—he just has to do better." Woods had known it wouldn't be easy, but he never felt alone; he was a member of a subculture that runs through American history, sometimes surging to the surface as an alternative and agent of change. The power of music can never be discounted, even under what appear to be adverse circumstances.

Take one sunny Sunday afternoon in Seattle's Ballard neighborhood, where three older men were playing bebop in a little tavern. On alto sax, Jay Thomas sounded fluid and at ease, fitting his sound into the talk and laughter in the crowded room. People weren't following the tunes, but everyone seemed happy, and jazz filled the air with possibility and the promise of adventure. It didn't demand their attention; the music affected them in the way temperature and quality of light do—it was part of the ambiance. That may not be the ideal listening or

D'Vonne Lewis: Deep Roots

Steve Griggs, *Earshot Jazz*, February 2012

Albums by his organist grandfather Dave Lewis lie on the coffee table. At twenty-eight, D'Vonne Lewis is young, but his musical roots in Seattle run deep. David Eugene Lewis (1939–1998), considered the father of Northwest rock, was signed by A&M Records after being heard by herb Alpert in a Seattle club. His 1964 single "Little Green Thing" was highlighted on Dick Clark's American Bandstand, exposing him to national audiences. Lewis's great-grandfather, David Eugene Lewis Sr., played guitar and gave musical tips to Jimi Hendrix and neighbor Quincy Jones. His great-uncle, Ulysses Lewis, was a partner in the Paramount Theatre, which hosted R&B shows in the 1980s.

Evan Flory-Barnes, bassist in Industrial Revelation, remembers the first close connection he had with Lewis: "I met D'Vonne at a jam session... and our rapport was instantaneous. The vibe, the good feeling, the smiles were there right away. He was sixteen years old."

Josh Rawlings, keyboardist with Lewis for the last eight years, echoes this recognition of talent. "His musicality directly transforms anyone who listens. All you have to do is go to a live show and see how people respond—from people dancing, to the guys hunched over bobbin' their heads at the bar, to musicians in the band yelling 'WHOA!'"

Many musicians were quick to heap praise upon Lewis, including trumpeter and KPLU DJ Jason Parker. "He has incredible touch and he knows the history of the music—not just jazz, but most popular music. He can convincingly play just about anything you put in front of him. He is also an attentive listener, both reacting to and propelling the other members of the band. But my favorite thing about playing with D'Vonne is the sheer joy he brings to every note he plays. It's like he's a kid who's just discovered the drums.... It's infectious, both for the band and for the audience. It doesn't hurt that he's the sweetest and most reliable guy around, either."

"D'Vonne is a musician of depth, humor, and character," Flory-Barnes summarizes. "He is deeply musical and open to serve whatever music he is playing. He will shy away from solos yet effortlessly lift a band to great heights... all in service of the music."

Lewis has worked so steadily since he attended high school that he decided to forgo college. "I started playing with [saxophonist] Hadley Caliman when I was still in high school. Then I went on a West Coast tour with singer Jennifer Jones and just kept getting gigs."

"I really don't know what I'm doing," confesses Lewis. "I try not to get in the way. I try to listen hard. I try to accompany what's going on."

---

performance experience, but without that little tavern, the power of jazz wouldn't be felt at all by casual listeners.

Weathering such slow times has become more difficult because of the rising cost of living, especially in Seattle, where the median income continues to go up along with new Amazon and Microsoft towers, while the pay for jazz remains low.

There's an argument to be made that the artist does best by sitting on the doorstep of the rich—after all, that's where the money is. So maybe Seattle is still a good place for jazz in 2015. But to many musicians and artists considering a move to the Pacific Northwest, the Emerald City isn't looking like such a nice place to live anymore, at least for those not employed in the new economy.

Christopher Brown: Always Thinking of Portland

Tree Palmedo, *Willamette Week*, September 10, 2014

"That's one thing I like about the jazz community: It represents our village," he says. "If you don't get what you need from your father, you can get it from this other guy, or this woman, or whoever."

Brown's musical education started with his father, legendary Portland drummer Mel Brown. Though he was around "enough to qualify as a dad," Chris Brown says, the elder Brown was divorced from Chris' mother and always gigging or on tour.

"I did watch a lot of his videos, though," Brown says of his father. "I watched tons of his videos to try to emulate everything he did, even the way he dressed, the way he walked." Now, when Brown takes the Jimmy Mak's stage after his father's weekly Wednesday night gig, he has his own sound, a fiery mix of Mel's swinging straight-ahead style and tight R&B grooves.

Brown's musical personality blossomed at Rutgers, where he studied for six years after a four-year tour with the Marines. He learned from heavyweights like drummer Ralph Peterson and saxophonist Ralph Bowen, and by night, he worked his way onto the New York scene. But even as Brown toured with Roy Hargrove . . . returning to Portland was always on his mind.

"The point of me joining the Marine Corps was to facilitate making it to the East Coast, to learn the things I can only learn there," Brown says, "and then bring that information back here so I could be a big fish in a small pond. That was always my plan."

But he didn't expect to be coming home so early: It was the death of his mother in late 2011 that prompted his return to Portland. Now that he's back, though, he's not going anywhere. In addition to his Wednesday night slot at Jimmy Mak's, he's working on a record with the Chuck Israels Orchestra, led by the Portland bassist who once played in the hallowed Bill Evans Trio. Even in Portland's smaller pond, Brown has found a [new] mentor.

In 2014, the *Seattle Weekly* ran a story on what it called "a citywide revolt against runaway growth." A building boom, it noted, that reflects "a demographic shift . . . turning [the city] into a 'monoculture' of rich, young tech workers."[14] Rents were going up, and the price of a single-family home in 2014 was almost double Portland's median home value. But that seemed to be changing, as the cost of housing climbed in the Rose City as well. Affordability had brought many new jazz players to the region. Would the jazz scene vanish along with affordable housing?

It hasn't as of 2015, even in Seattle. And with significantly fewer Fortune 500 corporations in town, it's hard to imagine Portland will ever resemble Seattle. Besides, other things keep young people around.

David Albouy, an economics professor at the University of Illinois, has created a metric he calls "the sacrifice measure." It charts how poor a person is willing to be in order to live in a particular city. Portland, he discovered, is near the top of the list. Even when college-educated residents do find jobs, they earn eighty-four cents on average for every dollar earned by their peers in other cities, according to Portland State University researchers. In forty-one of the country's fifty largest cities, young, educated people earn more than they do in Portland.[15]

Although Portland and Seattle have become very different, jazz musicians in both cities share the challenge of developing an audience. Some younger artists

Christopher Brown got his first drum lessons from his father, Mel Brown, who grew up learning from the older generation on Williams Avenue.

decided they'd need to leave jazz behind to find those listeners. But those with deep connections to the region's history have opted to stick with jazz, especially D'Vonne Lewis and Christopher Brown. Both are drummers and bandleaders, and they descend from two of the Pacific Northwest's most important musicians. Neither shies away from calling his work "jazz."

ON THE CUSP OF TOMORROW

The Lewis family goes back four generations in Seattle, beginning with the original Dave Lewis, an amateur twelve-string guitarist and barber who relocated to Bremerton during World War II from Fort Worth, Texas. When Boeing, under community pressure, opened jobs to African Americans, he moved to Seattle. His son, also named Dave, formed one of Seattle's first doo-wop groups, and while still at Garfield High School, he led a band that opened for such stars as Bill Haley and the Comets. In a few years, he had the city's top R&B jobs, and during the World's Fair he moved over to a jazz club called Dave's Fifth Ave.

Lewis had been playing piano, but took up the Hammond organ when soul-jazz became popular. He recorded a couple of local radio hits that influenced what came to be known as "the Northwest sound" in early rock 'n' roll by bands that included The Wailers.

"Dave Lewis was a pioneer in the Pacific Northwest," said his son, Dave Jr. "He crossed over into a white music realm, if you will—rock 'n' roll. He made the transition where a lot of musicians at that time in Seattle were afraid, or weren't allowed. He just kind of said, 'Here I am.'"

Dave Jr. left music and was absent during his son's childhood, so D'Vonne (born 1983), who was raised by his mother and stepfather, found inspiration in the career of his grandfather. As of 2015, Lewis has become one of the most sought-after drummers in the region. He didn't need to break as many barriers as his grandfather, however: as early as 2006, Lewis received the Golden Ear Award from Earshot Jazz. While he was still in high school, he started working with his mentor, saxophonist Hadley Caliman. He continued working after Caliman's death with such top straight-ahead artists as pianist Marc Seales as well as the funky and wild Skerik and Joe Doria of the grooving organ trio McTuff. Lewis leads Industrial Revelation. He has clearly made the most of his opportunities.[16]

His lineage is important because Lewis represents the continuation of the Pacific Northwest jazz tradition. Just as his grandfather rode the transition from Jackson Street to rock 'n' roll, the younger man is moving from straight-ahead to indie jazz and whatever may come next. But Lewis and his bandmates—Josh Rawlings, Ahamefule J. Oluo, and Evan Flory-Barnes—are bringing the blues along. They carry something from Jackson Street into hip-hop beats and free improvisation, and as a result they're making complex music that's accessible and audience friendly.

That's Christopher Brown's aim, too.

A Portland native who returned to his hometown from New York in 2012, Brown got his first drum lessons from his father, Mel Brown, who had absorbed local jazz history from the older men on Williams Avenue. That instruction often came via videos—during Christopher's childhood, his parents divorced and his father was usually on the road. The younger Brown was also a product of Portland school jazz programs, and he later received a masters degree from—and taught part-time at—Rutgers University. Brown completed his education on New York bandstands with the likes of national star Roy Hargrove.

All along, Brown planned to return to Portland. At first, he saw it as an opportunity to be a big fish in a small pond. The longer he was home, however, the more Brown realized the depth of those waters. He soon had a band good enough to carry out his agenda. They made their first album in 2015.

Every Wednesday night at Jimmy Mak's, he follows his father's quartet with a set by his own group, playing the music of his generation. He calls it "Rewind and Unwind: '80s Pop Hits in a Jazz World."

"A lot of the music I grew up listening to was radio music of the 1980s," he explains. "I like the challenge of taking... all this training and somehow [infusing] that into these eighties songs. I also want to win people to jazz music; I want people to be impressed by how much better a jazz musician can make songs... by what a jazz musician can bring."

No surprise that Brown is after something similar to what Portland native Esperanza Spalding was seeking with her 2012 Grammy-winning album *Radio Music Society*.

D'Vonne Lewis has also played occasionally with Portland's Trio Subtonic: musicians in their thirties, influenced, like him, as much by the pop and rock they grew up with as jazz. The pianocentric Trio Subtonic perhaps leans more toward rock than funk, especially when guitarist Dan Balmer joins them. But they're still playing jazz at venues for younger audiences where they're received with enthusiasm. In the public's mind, however, jazz has become so identified with swing, bebop, or the avant-garde that it presents a marketing problem for such bands, and leaves some of them longing for a post-jazz world.

Not Brown or Lewis. They're on a mission to make jazz culturally relevant. And that's the challenge all jazz artists face in an uncertain future.

9

An Uncertain Future

"Telling people we are a jazz ensemble is almost the worst thing we can do, unfortunately."

Barra Brown

LOOKING FOR AN AUDIENCE

Quo Vadis, jazz? Historian Gene Lees asked that question in 1987. Where is jazz headed? Nowhere, he answered; it's already arrived. His pronouncement fit the times, when Wynton Marsalis and the neotraditionalists were becoming the face of jazz and many of the greatest stars from the bebop era were still performing. For the straight-ahead style, it looked to Lees as if jazz would sail into the future with its identity intact.

But jazz is defined by what jazz musicians play, and of course it continued to change. Fusions with world sounds, hip-hop, rock, and contemporary classical music multiplied alongside traditional styles that were themselves evolving. It's more difficult than ever to define jazz beyond the narrow boundaries of a museum piece. And that is what jazz has become in the public's mind over the past twenty-five years.

Has the image of any other genre in American music gone through the dramatic change that jazz has experienced? From a youth music it has fallen into the old fogey ghetto along with the symphony and opera, but without the high culture status that brings those genres patrons and public agency funds.

New circumstances offer an opportunity for new directions, and two general approaches are beginning to appear. One strategy would abandon the jazz label entirely and have musicians simply make popular music using a jazz approach. The other would integrate jazz into

The Ballard Jazz Festival began as a one-day event in the Ballard neighborhood's commercial district, a boating center where the water has always been a vital part of physical and economic life. It is now a four-day festival. Pictured: the Ballard Locks leading to Lake Union.

the fabric of the cities at the neighborhood level, performing for primarily local audiences. For jazz artists who are not ready to jump ship and abandon their connection to the tradition, building a base from the ground up may turn out to be the most effective way to again become part of a living culture.

IN THE NEIGHBORHOOD

One of those neighborhood solutions takes listeners very near to some *real* ships. The Ballard Jazz Festival, founded in 2003 by Origin Records and supported by a host of business and community partners today, offers a model for situating jazz directly in a neighborhood at least once a year.

It began as a one-day "Jazz Walk," with performances at a number of restaurants, bars, and two halls in the historic Ballard neighborhood's commercial district near Salmon Bay. It's a boating center where water has always been a vital part of physical and economic life, a picturesque setting that recalls history while also affording views of new office and condo towers on the shore of Lake Union. Bicycle and pedestrian paths lead along the nearby ship canal to Shilshole Bay. The

The Montavilla Jazz Festival features cutting-edge progressive jazz in a formerly working-class neighborhood now being resettled by a younger, more progressive generation.
Pictured: Theoretical Planets at the 2014 festival.

air is fresh off the Sound, the event is held on a weekend in May in a charming, authentic-feeling corner of the city, and people pay to come listen. Now called The Ballard Jazz Festival, it is a four-day event, and with its recent nonprofit status—a must for these kinds of efforts—it is becoming a membership organization. Like the earlier concert series at zoos and wineries, this festival also situates jazz in an attractive setting with the one-stop convenience of a festival.

Taking its cue from The Ballard Jazz Festival, the Jackson Street Jazz Walk debuted in 2014, bringing listeners back to the site of the music's local history to hear contemporary sounds. It's a partnership with the non-profit neighborhood organization Jackson Commons, as well as area businesses. The sponsoring group calls it an example of "tactical urbanism." That kind of activity, new to jazz in the region, also includes pop-up cafes with music and other low-budget events like the Jazz Society of Oregon's flash-mob jazz choir, which materialized one December noon at an area mall. Such events almost always hinge on a dedicated and sustained volunteer effort.

A small group of activists and musicians in a Portland neighborhood are also pursuing a variation on that model, holding the first annual Montavilla Jazz Festival in 2014. One of the founders was the president of the neighborhood association, and the festival became an association project. Located on the outer edge of the central city, Montavilla offered few cultural resources, and at first glance a two-day program of cutting-edge progressive jazz seemed an odd fit for the working-class area. But its affordable homes and commercial spaces have attracted younger residents unable to afford inner-city neighborhoods. The jazz activists were simply following their peers.

Barry Johnson Sees the Future

John Pomietlasz, *Jazzscene*, April 2012

In April 2010, Jazzscene asked members of the jazz community what it would take to promote the Portland jazz scene. ArtsWatch editor and former arts editor at the Oregonian, Barry Johnson, suggested an audience development strategy.

What I want to create is... a Portland scene. We have the beginning now: players that go from established icons like Mel Brown and Nancy King and other... masters, to mid-career and younger players; students; clubs and concert venues for them to play in; recordings; and they are making a living. If we were able to put all those pieces together, including that last part, we wouldn't have to sell Portland jazz, it would sell itself.

We are starting to assemble some of the pieces.... It gives me optimism that something important and sustainable can happen here. Mainly because they are smart about it, the younger guys especially. They get the environment now, when everybody's asking, "How do you make money playing music anymore?" I have some confidence that they'll manage. Ultimately a successful scene gives the audience what it needs.

[The] problem for younger guys is, there are a whole lot of people their age who don't think jazz is where they are. This is the same problem ballet and classical music have. These guys are out trying to solve that problem as best they can. Last fall, when Oregon Ballet Theater furloughed its dancers, the dancers said, "We want to keep dancing," so they staged a show in Mississippi Studios with the acoustic indie band Horse Feathers. It was jammed. And they loved it. And the dancers loved it because they were performing for their peers. Portland Cello Project has also adopted this tactic.

So jazz has the same solution—if people aren't listening to what you do, go to where the people are and play for them. And maybe they'll still tell you, "This isn't what I want to hear." But if you're good, I don't think you have to worry about that, because people are going to be interested in listening to you.

Once you have them listening, you can do anything you want. Part of it is just breaking through. Most of it is social rather than having anything to do with the actual content of the music. That's why it should be performed at places where younger people hang, like Mississippi Studios.

If I had my way, when the Andrew Oliver Sextet played at Doug Fir, say, they would save a song for Nancy King, and she'd come sing for these kids, and they would love her. If they heard her sing, they'd say, "That's amazing!" It's been legitimized and socialized, because she has come to their place. They're comfortable, they're prepared to listen, there are no barriers between them and the music, and once they hear her, they'll say, "That's great." Because it is. And if she has a gig, Nancy should invite a young player to play with her. Unless there is that sort of respect going back and forth, that sort of respect for the form itself, it's just dog-eat-dog.

The arts in general are having a hard time connecting what they do to the world. How do we apply the arts to the rest of the world, how [do we] use the arts to be more creative and collaborative in our own lives? There are issues beyond just jazz at stake—how do you become and sustain yourself as an artist in American society is a big question.

Ben Darwish was an active jazz musician but found that he drew larger crowds with his Afro-pop dance band.

The potential of such ventures to make jazz visible and useful to a community hinges on the relationships and skills of its organizers, and the arts management experience on the Montavilla Festival team is extensive. They understand that collaboration with other groups is necessary to make both art and money, so in their second year they devoted proceeds to music programs in neighborhood schools. Such activists may help jazz artists reach new listeners.

And city governments may help them make more money while the musicians are playing clubs. In 2015, the Seattle city council passed "The Fair Trade Music Seattle Resolution," giving bands and venues templates for work contracts and offering classes to help owners and musicians learn to negotiate fair agreements. Tula's Restaurant and Jazz Club is one of twenty Seattle nightclubs pledging to treat musicians fairly. So far, it's all voluntary. But the first American city to pass the fifteen-dollar-an-hour minimum wage may do more in the future to assist musicians.

Some jazz artists are developing short-term private-sector partnerships. Patrick Lamb recruits small businesses to underwrite his R&B-infused shows. He and his wife, Amy Maxwell, started a successful ticket agency with lower fees for artists. Tom Grant regularly donates his fees for charity fundraisers. And Jay Thomas has helped set up cultural exchanges between Seattle and Japan. House concerts are also becoming more common as nightclubs close.

"I'm seeing this all over the world," says guitarist John Stowell, "Five to thirty people in a living room—it really just takes a friend with a room, and you call a few friends, and they call a few."

That may well be the role for jazz in the future. Contemplating that possibility has convinced some younger jazz artists to look for an alternative.

POST-JAZZ

Ben Darwish used to envy indie rockers. Not for the money they made, but for the respect they got from listeners.

"Their work is always received as art," said Darwish, who won an ASCAP Young Composer Award in 2010. "The whole room is really focused on the music. There's no question about what they're there to see.... They're not playing background where people are eating dinner and talking over the music."

Darwish gave jazz a good try, organizing concerts in alternative venues so the music would be seen as art rather than background. His "Notes from the Underground" series staged its shows at the Mission Theater, where patrons ate pizza and drank beer and wine at tables or in theater seats. The sound was good, a jazz-themed movie ran during breaks, and there was variety in the ensembles he booked. But Darwish drew larger crowds with his Afro-pop dance band, and he finally moved from jazz into pop and folk-rock.

Maybe that's why Portland's Blue Cranes call their music "post-jazz."

Built on simple melodies, often delivered slowly by alto and tenor saxophone over a soundscape of keyboard, bass, and drums, Blue Cranes tunes are constructed with subtle harmonic sophistication. Driven by rock beats, their music rises to cinematic sweeps, drops into off-kilter passages that veer briefly into free improvisation, and sometimes subsides into tranquility. It's evident they have collaborated with Wayne Horvitz; others, such as the Sequoia Ensemble, are entering similar territory.

But the five-piece group is actually doing what jazz has always been about: applying advanced harmonies and improvisation to the sounds of the day. And indeed, they are part of a trend among younger jazz players who are blurring genre boundaries as they freely follow their muse—and their listeners. "We wanted to play music that people from our generation would come listen to," says band member Reed Wallsmith.

Portland drummer and bandleader Barra Brown understands perfectly why they don't call it jazz: "Telling people we are a jazz ensemble is almost the worst thing we can do, unfortunately," Brown told *Willamette Week*. "If we tell people we play jazz, they have a very specific idea of what that is." So Brown aims, the paper reports, "to apply his jazz training to beat-heavy art music that doesn't require the listener to have a conservatory degree."[1]

Alternative newspapers usually depict jazz as "high-brow" music without relevance for their readers. That may be why the *Stranger* gave its 2014 Genius Award to Industrial Revelation—one of the few bands in the region not led by a musician with a conservatory degree. "People dance at these concerts!" the Seattle paper proclaimed, giving the quartet the highest compliment a young jazz band could receive.[2]

Branding profoundly influences consumer choice, and given the image of jazz as cultural artifact, Blue Cranes have tried to avoid being labeled a "jazz band" in the conviction that such a maneuver would allow listeners to experience their music free of prejudice. The co-op band appears at multigenre music festivals where their work is presented in the context of indie rock, folk, singer-songwriter and other acts popular with young eclectic listeners—like the Decemberists, whose bassist produced the band's latest album. Blue Cranes has collaborated with kindred

spirits such as Seattle guitarist Tim Young, a Wayne Horvitz associate, and they also perform at multigenre venues such as Portland's Mississippi Studios and Alberta Street Pub as opening acts for nationally known indie jazz bands.

Their sound reflects the Pacific Northwest as much as the bluesy hip-hop/funk-jazz of Industrial Revelation or the impressionistic straight-ahead sound of the Upper Left Trio.

"The Blue Cranes capture a sense of place," Darrell Grant says. "The unabashed sense of melody, the sincerity, the indie collective 'all for one' ethos, the unpretentious mix of rock, free improv, noise, and instrumental–singer-songwriter vibe, the tasteful use of penny-whistle and glockenspiel, all resonate [with] the place I call home."[3]

Barra Brown applies his jazz training to beat-heavy art music that is accessible to a wider audience.

CULTURAL RELEVANCE

Does Blue Cranes's music resonate with the concerns, lifestyles, and attitudes of significant numbers of their peers? Judging by audiences at their live shows, critical acceptance, and distribution by an East Coast label, Blue Cranes has succeeded—in a modest, Pacific Northwest kind of way—on their own terms. The band's tunes beat to rhythms people seem to recognize and speak an emotional language they share. The band successfully crowdfunded a tour by train and have been musical guests on the popular storytelling series *The Moth*. In the new economy, where most artists are marginalized and forced to be both creator and tout, when even venerable jazz label Blue Note is crowdfunding its releases, Blue Cranes seem to be as culturally relevant as anyone playing in a style associated with jazz.

Historically, jazz was a model for Americans coming together to negotiate differences and find common ground while fostering individual expression. It was a place where ethnic identities blended in a model for democracy and "the American way," an inclusive community of free individuals. In addition, its reputation as an exciting underground subculture once made jazz attractive to young people—especially its historical association with the African American community and the sexual connotations that still cling to the word itself. Its intellectual edge gave jazz the status of art, but it still pulsed with body rhythms and emotional directness.

Art forms are perceived as most relevant when they reflect the emotional life of significant numbers of people. And despite the quality musicianship and emotional power of jazz, today it's seen by many as stuck in the past.

Some of the most astute observers believe this is simply due to the way it is presented. As pianist Jason Moran points out, a model developed in 1938—picture the Duke Ellington Orchestra, impeccably dressed, sitting behind identical music stands—or even 1998, won't resonate with many listeners in a world where most everything else has changed. The quality of the music doesn't matter if it's not seen as part of the listener's life. So in 2014, as if to demonstrate, Moran released a reimagining of the music of Fats Waller that incorporates hip-hop beats and other radical rearrangements called *All Rise: A Joyful Elegy for Fats Waller*.

Alternatively, jazz may find a place for itself *within* hip-hop. Kendrick Lamar, D'Angelo, and other nationally known hip-hop artists made albums that are more jazz than soul in 2014; Lamar's featured young jazz saxophone star Kamasi Washington. So the revitalization may come from the integration of jazz into other genres. Seattle pianist and singer Darrius Willrich calls his version of jazz "sweet urban soul." But Willrich, a native of the Seattle suburb of Renton, says his goal is to bring listeners *back* to jazz. His self-produced albums follow the template laid down by Stevie Wonder, Prince, and Michael Jackson, and include contributions from hip-hop artists. They also feature the jazz piano he studied at Cornish.[4]

That may not be the recontextualization Moran had in mind, but it's a course other jazz players will likely pursue—not jazz that uses hip-hop beats but, more radically, hip-hop and soul that use jazz techniques. Will its identity be lost without those conventions that have previously defined the music—and perhaps made it a museum piece?

The "post-jazz" of the Blue Cranes captures the spirit of the region with their sincerity, collective identity, and unpretentious mix of various genres.

SO MUCH JAZZ EDUCATION, SUCH SMALL AUDIENCES

Those conventions are learned primarily in schools these days anyway, and that strong academic base for jazz may have increased its distance from the popular imagination.

In colleges and universities, student jazz musicians are, for the most part, playing for other jazz musicians and fellow students, and they have few opportunities to perform for nonmusicians. Even when they do perform in public, at Cafe Racer and other small venues, most of the audience is other young players.

In Seattle, the active and influential avant-garde scene is highly visible in part because of the efforts of Earshot Jazz. But the college-level jazz programs in the region are also responsible for the tilt toward experimental and new music,

The Westerlies: Landscape in Jazz

Composer and keyboard player Wayne Horvitz moved to Seattle in 1989, leaving New York's creative music scene for a new life out west. He found the nice place he'd come for, and compatible musicians as well as a new generation of artists hungry for his guidance. Several generations, actually—from the latest come The Westerlies, a quartet of brass players from Seattle who recently relocated to New York.

In a tribute to their Seattle mentor, the group's debut album featured their arrangements of Horvitz compositions, including jazz tunes, film music, and classical chamber pieces. A video from the album, "Sweeter Than the Day," shows the two trumpet and two trombone players on the rocky shore of Puget Sound. A wind-blown spruce is visible at dawn. It's staged as if they are borrowing sounds from and integrating the composition with the environment: the deep tones of the trombones evoke the depths of the inland sea, the trumpets herald the vast morning sky. Their arrangement combines American folk, classical chamber music, indie rock, and jazz in a beautiful paean to the landscape.

Horvitz, who played keyboard on one of the tunes, wrote the liner notes to that album, titled *Wish the Children Would Come on Home: The Music of Wayne Horvitz*. "They have the perfect name," he wrote. "Like Henry Cowell, Jimmy Giuffre, or any number of iconic Westerners who gravitated to New York City, they bring with them a subtle sensibility that I, myself a lover of the west, hear infused with an openness that is restrained and on fire at the same time."

especially at Cornish and the University of Washington. Historically, the audience for that kind of improvised art music has been limited.

And college faculty tend to approach jazz as art music rather than entertainment. It's understandable, given their circumstances and the uphill battle they've waged to achieve academic legitimacy. Employed in academia full-time, they have no need to rely on performance for income, and that's bound to change an artist's attitude toward their work.

A parallel process occurred with the growth of creative writing programs after magazine fiction ceased to offer a livelihood and publishers began the blockbuster strategy that poured resources into a small number of titles. Many of the graduates of those programs now find themselves in the same boat as jazz musicians, either teaching or alone on the internet, touting their work.

Apparently, the argument that jazz studies programs are training tomorrow's audience has not proved to be true. As those programs have grown, the audience for jazz has gotten smaller—especially among the young.

Still, while attendance for avant-garde jazz and other improvised music in Seattle may be small for individual performances, taken together those listeners represent a significant niche market in a city big enough to support it. The spirit of that community retains the flavor of old Seattle, too, where artists worked in an isolated setting and felt free to try anything, where self-satisfaction and independence were prized more than fame and fortune. Is this where jazz has gone? Or will it become just one of the many genres that professional, jazz-trained freelancers will be equipped to play?

ALL DRESSED UP WITH NOWHERE TO GO?

Seattle bassist-for-hire Farko Dosumov, an immigrant from Uzbekistan, is not in academia, so performance is his livelihood. He stays busy precisely because he is so versatile. "Today I'll be a blues bass player, because I'm playing a blues gig. Tomorrow I'm playing flamenco, so I'll be a flamenco bass player, and Saturday I'm playing with a zydeco guy, so I'll be a zydeco bass player! If I'm playing a lot of jazz gigs, I think, 'I'm a jazz guy.'" One Saint Patrick's Day, Dosumov played Irish jigs and fiddle tunes.[5] Such variety is also typical for Portland bassist Damian Erskine.

Caught between those two enduring poles of the jazz scene—art music and entertainment—perhaps straight-ahead jazz will live on in jazz parties and festivals and a few select nightclubs and concert series, where it will be celebrated as a valued historical treasure, a hobby for wealthy listeners and a labor of love for musicians. If that sounds like a description of classical music in America, it should be no surprise. Since the 1980s, influential voices have lobbied for jazz to be considered "America's classical music." And they've had an effect, too, pushing jazz toward museum status.

Ultimately, the jazz artists who survive will be those who find an audience and give listeners what they need. In that sense, the audience will determine the direction jazz takes—whether into the museum or the iPhone. Audience behavior is affected powerfully by social and economic forces, so in the near future, the audience for anything but museum-style jazz may even be priced out of Pacific Northwest cities, along with the musicians themselves.

Drip City Coffee on First Avenue in Seattle's Belltown neighborhood provides chairs with axe handles for legs and pitchfork tines for backs. They recall the area's past, now that it's become an upscale residential street of condo towers with majestic views of the Sound.

About a mile away, at the South end of First Avenue in Old Town, a bust of Chief Seattle sits atop a pedestal in a small fountain. All along the avenue, his image appears in bas-relief on manhole covers. A totem pole rises three stories above the stained sidewalks; across the street, a few sandstone and brick buildings remain from the 1900s; and down the street, a blues club from the early 1970s is still open. They too recall old Seattle, a darker and in some ways more vibrant place whose spirit still hangs on in the music.

Maybe in the future, after the jazz scene has found a more hospitable locale, a bust of Ernestine Anderson will adorn a pedestal at Twelfth and Jackson, in the shadow of new thirty-story towers, with posters from former jazz clubs blown into a pile at its base.

But there are still pockets in Portland and Seattle that feel like a village where artists might thrive, where casual collaborations and neighborhood synergy are as commonplace as they used to be, even though the small-town feel has diminished. In the comedy show *Portlandia*, they called that "the dream of the '90s."

"I was driving down the street," Seattle jazz immigrant Michael Shrieve told *5/4 Magazine* in the early '90s, "and I saw Bill Frisell riding his bicycle. I pulled over and said, 'Hey, let's do a record with organ, drums, guitar, and no bass.' And he said, 'I was thinking the same thing.' So I called up Wayne [Horvitz] and the label . . . and did it here in Seattle."[6]

That's the dream. Will conditions in the future provide artists the means to make it a reality? Will their neighbors park their bikes and listen? No jazz scene will thrive if it doesn't serve the listener's needs. That's where it started, and that's what jazz has to do in order to make *any* future a possibility—reflect the lives of those who live in this singular place.

ENDNOTES

Where more than one paragraph contains information from a single source, whether quoted directly or paraphrased, end notes have been placed at the end of the final paragraph. All unattributed quotes are from interviews with the author.

INTRODUCTION

1. White, Ryan, "High notes: A timeline of Esperanza Spalding's post-Grammy life," *OregonLive*, April 20, 2012.
2. Armbruster, Kurt E., *Before Seattle Rocked: A City and Its Music*, Seattle: University of Washington Press, 2011, 188.
3. de Barros, Paul, "Pilot's Return," *DownBeat*, January 2006.
4. Jones, Alan, liner notes for audio recording *Climbing*, 2010.

CHAPTER 1

1. de Barros, Paul, *Jackson Street After Hours: The Roots of Jazz in Seattle*, Seattle: Sasquatch Books, 1993, 9.
2. Dietsche, Robert, *Jumptown: The golden years of Portland Jazz: 1942–1957*, Corvallis: Oregon State University Press, 2005, 22.
3. de Barros, Paul, *Jackson Street After Hours*, 1.
4. Ibid., 20.
5. Ibid., 3.
6. Dietsche, Robert, *Jumptown*, 104.
7. Ibid., 102–104.
8. Armbruster, Kurt E, *Before Seattle Rocked*, 89.
9. de Barros, Paul, *Jackson Street After Hours*, 24–25.
10. Ibid., 24.
11. Ibid., 111.
12. Bletcha, Peter, "Bing Crosby and Mildred Bailey, Spokane's Jazz Royalty," Historylink.org Essay 7445.
13. Ibid.
14. Robinson, Jessica, "Search For Jazz Singer's Roots," *Northwest News Network*, May 2, 2012.
15. de Barros, Paul, *Jackson Street After Hours*, 5–7.
16. Ibid., 7, 145, 165.

17. Ibid., 45.
18. Dietsche, Robert, *Jumptown*, 15–16.
19. de Barros, Paul, *Jackson Street After Hours*, 43–44.

CHAPTER 2

1. de Barros, Paul, *Jackson Street After Hours*, 206–207.
2. Dietsche, Robert, *Jumptown*, 1.
3. de Barros, Paul, *Jackson Street After Hours*, 76–78.
4. Ibid., 78.
5. Ibid., 207.
6. Dietsche, Robert, *Jumptown*, 86.
7. Ibid., 153–156.
8. de Barros, Paul, *Jackson Street After Hours*, 111.
9. Dietsche, Robert, *Jumptown*, 87.
10. Armbruster, Kurt E, *Before Seattle Rocked*, 166.
11. Ibid., 167.
12. de Barros, Paul, *Jackson Street After Hours*, 107–110.
13. Ibid., 183.
14. Quotations include the author's interview with Charles as well as Ernestine Anderson quotes from de Barros, Paul, *Jackson Street After Hours*, 157–158.
15. de Barros, Paul, *Jackson Street After Hours*, 120–122.
16. Ibid., 69.
17. Ibid., 73.
18. Dietsche, Robert, *Jumptown*, 82.
19. Ibid., 84.
20. Armbruster, Kurt E, *Before Seattle Rocked*, 187.
21. de Barros, Paul, *Jackson Street After Hours*, 60.
22. Ibid., 168–169.
23. Dietsche, Robert, *Jumptown*, 94–104.
24. de Barros, Paul, *Jackson Street After Hours*, 188–190.
25. Dietsche, Robert, *Jumptown*, 116.
26. Ibid., 116.
27. Ibid., 47.
28. de Barros, Paul, *Jackson Street After Hours*, 194–195.
29. de Barros, Paul, *Jackson Street After Hours*, 171.
30. Armbruster, Kurt E, *Before Seattle Rocked*, 244.
31. Dietsche, Robert, *Jumptown*, 87.

CHAPTER 3

1. Armbruster, Kurt E, *Before Seattle Rocked*, 262.
2. Lee, Deborah, "Working Women" *Jazzscene*, January 1985.
3. Ibid.
4. Ibid.

5. Ibid.
6. Armbruster, Kurt E, *Before Seattle Rocked*, 237.
7. de Barros, Paul, *Jackson Street After Hours*, 198.
8. Ibid., pp. 198–199.
9. Griggs, Steve, "Justice for Joe," *Earshot Jazz*, April 2012.
10. Armbruster, Kurt E, *Before Seattle Rocked*, 264–265.
11. Griggs, Steve, "Justice for Joe," *Earshot Jazz*, April 2012.
12. Armbruster, Kurt E, *Before Seattle Rocked*, 265–267.
13. de Barros, Paul, *Jackson Street After Hours*, 203–204.
14. Ibid., 204.
15. Dietsche, Robert, *Jumptown*, 200.
16. Armbruster, Kurt E, *Before Seattle Rocked*, 199.
17. Love, Shannon, "Bluesman Isaac Scott," *Jet City Blues Review*, 1996.
18. Armbruster, Kurt E, *Before Seattle Rocked*, 276–278.
19. Ibid., 263–264.

CHAPTER 4

1. Gladden, Carolann, *The First Book of Oregon Jazz, Rock, and All Sorts of Music*, Portland: Self-produced, 1982.
2. Monaghan, Peter, "Don Lanphere," *Earshot Jazz*, November 2003.
3. Armbruster, Kurt E, *Before Seattle Rocked*, 292.
4. Ibid., 292–294.
5. Ibid., 292–294.
6. Ibid., 294.
7. Dietsche, Robert, *Jumptown*, 75–76.

CHAPTER 5

1. Campbell, Don, "On the Waterfront," *Vortex Music Magazine*, July 2, 2014.
2. Conklin, Ellis E., "Revolution Road," *The Seattle Weekly*, August 20–26, 2014.
3. Broadhurst, Judith, "Michael Bard," *Jazzscene*, November 1986.
4. Lacitis, Eric, "Jazz saxophonist Hadley Caliman, 78, dies," *Seattle Times*, September 11, 2010.
5. Ibid.
6. Bartlett, Andrew, "Coung Vu's Travels," *Earshot Jazz*, March 2002.
7. Barton, Chris, "Talking Punk Jazz," *Los Angeles Times*, July 15, 2011.
8. Ibid.
9. Uhl, Don, "Profile of a Northwest Jazz Fan," *Jazzscene*, November 1983.
10. Cline, Steve, "Jovino Santos Neto's 'Song of Rio'", *Earshot Jazz*, July 2003.

CHAPTER 6

1. Murphy, Joseph, "Bill Frisell: No Boundaries," *5/4 Magazine*, August 1995.

2. Ibid.
3. Seven, Richard, "The sound of one man dreaming," *Pacific Northwest Magazine*, The Seattle Times, April 22, 2001.
4. Marlin, Mike, "Violinist Eyvind Kang: Strung In," *5/4 Magazine*, February 1995.
5. Desmangles, Justin, "Face the Music," *5/4 Magazine*, November 1994.
6. de Barros, Paul, "Jazz saxophonist Bert Wilson dies at 73," *The Seattle Times*, June 8, 2013.
7. de Barros, Paul, "Bisio Presents Bisio," *5/4 Magazine*, February 1995.
8. Monaghan, Peter, "To the Beat of his own Drum," *Earshot Jazz*, December 2006.
9. de Barros, Paul, "Seattle's New Sounds," *Seattle Times*, April 26, 1998.
10. Smith, Deborah DeMoss, "John Bishop and the Story of Origin Records," *Jazzscene*, July 2012.
11. Hentoff, Nat, "Seattle's Jazz Master Of Five Horns," *Wall Street Journal*, April 19th, 2000.
12. Ramsay, Doug, http://www.jaythomasjazz.com/index.php/biography-of-jay-thomas-by-doug-ramsey
13. Mathews, Todd, "Big in Japan," *Earshot Jazz*, August 2004.
14. de Barros, Paul, "Seattle's New Sounds," *Seattle Times*, April 26, 1998.
15. Ibid.

CHAPTER 7

1. "Clarence Acox, Leader of the Band," *Earshot Jazz*, July, 2006.
2. Matzner, Franz A., "Seattle's New Sound," *All About Jazz*, May 6, 2004.
3. Staff, "Father and son who made mark on Seattle scene return," *Seattle Times*, December 24, 2004.
4. Monaghan, Peter, "Dawn Clement: Going somewhere of her own making," *Earshot Jazz*, January 2003.
5. Scigliano, Eric, "Wayne Horvitz Performs '55,'" Crosscut.com, July 4, 2014.
6. Marsalis, Wynton, "What Jazz Is—and Isn't," *New York Times*, July 31, 1998.
7. Scheps, Rob, "Jazz Immigrants," *Jazzscene*, May, 2015.

CHAPTER 8

1. Scheps, Rob, "Jazz Immigrants," *Jazzscene*, May, 2015.
2. Willcox, Tim, "Jazz in a Changing World," *Jazzscene*, September, 2012
3. D'Antoni, Tom, "Devin Phillips to JSO Hall of Fame," *Jazzscene*, March 2015.
4. Monaghan, Peter, "Professor Cuong Vu," *Earshot Jazz*, April 2007.
5. Scheps, Rob, "Jazz Immigrants," *Jazzscene*, May, 2015.
6. Ibid.
7. Wise, Brian, "NEA Report Arts Audiences," WQXR blog, September 26, 2013.

8. Gold-Molina, Jack, "Beth Fleenor: The Discipline of Being," *All About Jazz*, January 30, 2014.
9. Spalding, Esperanza, press release accompanying audio recording *Radio Music Society*, 2012, Heads Up.
10. Bias, Danielle, "Inheritance and Authenticity," *Earshot Jazz*, September 2009.
11. Rega, Rita, "Musician of the Month: Dan Wilensky," *Jazzscene*, December 2013.
12. Willcox, Tim, Mary-Sue Tobin," *Jazzscene*, August 2012
13. Ibid.
14. Shapiro, Nina, "Boomtown Brawls," *The Seattle Weekly*, September 9, 2014.
15. Schrock, Greg and Jurjevich, Jason, "Is Portland Really the Place Where Young People Go to Retire?" http://mkn.research.pdx.edu/wp-content/uploads/2012/09/JurjevichSchrockMigrationReport1.pdf
16. de Barros, Paul, "Family reviving the sounds of Seattle rocker Dave Lewis," *Seattle Times*, December 3, 2013.

CHAPTER 9

1. Staff, "Barra Brown," *Willamette Week*, January 7, 2015.
2. Mudede, Charles, "Industrial Revelation," *The Stranger*, October 22, 2014.
3. Grant, Darrell, "On the Territory" blog post, June 19, 2013.
4. Harvey, Schraepfer, "Darrius Willrich: There Is No How," *Earshot Jazz*, August 2012.
5. Cuthringer, Andrew, "Farko Dusomov: A Global Bass Traveler," *Earshot Jazz*, March 2015.
6. Atkins, John, "Michael Shrieve," *5/4 Magazine*, April 1995.

IMAGE CREDITS

INTRODUCTION

p14   Photo by John Gustavson, courtesy of Susan Gustavson
p16   Courtesy of Amateria1121 [CC BY-SA 3.0], via Wikimedia Commons
p19   Courtesy of Rich Halley
p20   Photo by John Gustavson, courtesy of Susan Gustavson
p22   Courtesy of US National Park Service [Public domain]

CHAPTER 1

p24   Courtesy of US National Archives and Records Administration
p26   (top) Photographer not credited, scanned from Oh, Mister Jelly by William Russell, JazzMedia Aps, 1999 [Public domain]
p26   (bottom) Courtesy Library of Congress, William P. Gottlieb collection
p28   Courtesy of Bede735 via Wikimedia Commons [Public Domain]
p31   Courtesy of Oregon Historical Society (Org. Lot 1274/ Acc.21853)
p32   Courtesy of Joe Mabel [CC BY-SA 3.0] via Wikimedia Commons
p34   Courtesy of Library of Congress, FSA/OWI Collection (UA 4831-E)
p35   Courtesy of Hans Bernhard
p36   Courtesy of Historic American Engineering Record

CHAPTER 2

p40   Courtesy of Seattle Municipal Archives Photograph Database 61074
p42   Courtesy of City of Portland Archives, Oregon, Historical Buildings. Record number AP/760, 1940
p44   Photo by Maurice Seymour, New York, courtesy of William Morris Agency
p46   Courtesy of the US Air Force
p47   Courtesy of John Tuttle Collection via The Oregon History Project
p48   Courtesy of James Benton
p51   Courtesy of Marion Post Wolcott for the Farm Security Administration
p52   Courtesy of William P. Gottlieb [Public domain], via Wikimedia Commons

p54   Courtesy of City of Portland (OR) Archives, A2004-002.6712

CHAPTER 3

- p56   Photo by Richard Bogle, courtesy of Nola Bogle
- p60   Courtesy of Hugo van Gelderen
- p62   Photo by Richard Bogle, courtesy of Nola Bogle
- p64   Courtesy of Ron Schwerin
- p66   (left) Photo by Richard Bogle, courtesy of Nola Bogle
- p66   (right) Courtesy of Phil Baker
- p69   Photo by Richard Bogle, courtesy of Nola Bogle
- p74   Photo by Rodney Dahl, courtesy of Jan Chciuk-Celt
- p76   Photo courtesy of Bernard Mayo Rivera, United States Coast and Geodetic Survey

CHAPTER 4

- p78   Photo by Richard Bogle, courtesy of Nola Bogle
- p80   Photo by Richard Bogle, courtesy of Nola Bogle
- p81   Courtesy of Phil Baker
- p83   Courtesy of Dianne Russell
- p86   Courtesy of Chuck Deardorf
- p87   Courtesy of Daniel Shen [CC BY-SA 2.0], via Wikimedia Commons
- p88   Courtesy of Steven M. O'Kelley [CC BY-SA 2.5], via Wikimedia Commons
- p92   Courtesy of Rich Halley
- p93   Courtesy of Dave Storrs
- p95   Courtesy of Patricia Caringella

CHAPTER 5

- p96   Courtesy of Another Believer [CC BY-SA 3.0 Unported], via Wikimedia Commons
- p98   Courtesy of Rich Halley
- p101   Courtesy of Finetooth (Own work) [CC BY-SA 3.0], via Wikimedia Commons
- p103   Courtesy of Joe Mabel. [CC BY-SA 3.0 Unported], via Wikimedia Commons
- p104   (left) Courtesy of Tom Grant
- p104   (right) Courtesy of Tom Grant
- p107   Courtesy of bradfordst219 [CC BY-SA 2.0], via Wikimedia Commons
- p108   Courtesy of Mike Horsfall
- p110   Photo by Richard Bogle, courtesy of Nola Bogle
- p113   Courtesy of Kotivalo [CC BY-SA 3.0 Unported], via Wikimedia Commons

p114   Courtesy of Svíčková [CC BY-SA 3.0 Unported], via Wikimedia Commons
p116   Photo by John Rudoff
p117   Photo by Ross Hamilton, courtesy of Rick Mitchell
p118   (top) Courtesy of Shirley Nanette
p118   (bottom) Courtesy of John Stowell
p119   Courtesy of John Stowell
p120   Courtesy of Phil Baker
p123   Courtesy of Susan Addy

Chapter 6

p126   Photo by Richard Bogle, courtesy of Nola Bogle
p128   Courtesy of Michael Hoefner [CC BY-SA 3.0 Unported], via Wikimedia Commons
p131   Photo by to Lars Topelmann, courtesy of Alan Jones
p133   Photo by Richard Bogle, courtesy of Nola Bogle
p134   (top) Photo by Richard Bogle, courtesy of Nola Bogle
p134   (bottom) Courtesy of Peter Gannushkin, downtownmusic.net
p137   Courtesy of Svíčková [CC BY-SA 3.0 Unported], via Wikimedia Commons
p138   Courtesy of Patricia Caringella
p139   Courtesy of Jim Semlor
p141   Photo by Carlos Pinto, courtesy of John Bishop
p144   Courtesy of Cacophony [CC BY-SA 3.0 Unported], via Wikimedia Commons

Chapter 7

p146   Photo courtesy of Eric Delmar [Public domain]
p148   Courtesy of Dusty York
p150   Courtesy of jseattle [CC BY-SA 2.0], via Wikimedia Commons
p152   Courtesy of Dave Storrs
p153   Courtesy of Rob Scheps
p154   Photo by John Rudoff
p156   (top) Courtesy of Rattlhed [Public domain]
p156   (bottom) Courtesy of Clay Giberson
p158   Courtesy of dawnclement.com
p159   Courtesy of Joe Mabel [CC BY-SA 3.0 Unported], via Wikimedia Commons
p160   Courtesy of Wayne Horvitz
p163   Courtesy of Sandra Alphonse
       www.flickr.com/photos/alphonsephotography/7772632746
p164   Photo by Norm Eder, courtesy of Amy Maxwell
p164   (right) Courtesy of Amy Maxwell (left)

p167 (left) Courtesy of Patricia Caringella
p167 (right) Courtesy of Dr. Michael Kissinger
p168 Photo by Andrew Parodi

Chapter 8

p170 Courtesy of David Valdez
p172 Courtesy of Charlie Porter
p173 Courtesy of Charlie Porter
p174 (left) Courtesy of Bryan Smith
p174 (right) Courtesy of George Colligan
p175 Courtesy of Alan Jones
p180 Courtesy of Damian Conrad
p181 Joe Mabel [CC BY-SA 3.0], via Wikimedia Commons
p182 (top) Courtesy of Dianne Russell
p182 (bottom) Courtesy of Andrea Mancini [CC BY-2.0]
https://www.flickr.com/photos/9473012@N07/3739997635/
p184 Courtesy of Joe Mabel [CC-BY-SA-3.0], via Wikimedia Commons
p185 Courtesy of Diane Russell
p186 (left) Courtesy of Diane Russell
p186 (right) Courtesy of John Nastos
p188 (left) Photo by Battista Photography, courtesy of Damian Erskine
p188 (right) Courtesy of Steve Griggs
p190 Courtesy of John Rudoff
p192 Courtesy of Mary-Sue Tobin
p193 Courtesy of Mary-Sue Tobin
p194 (left) Courtesy of Joe Mabel [CC BY-SA 3.0], via Wikimedia Commons
p194 (right) Courtesy of D'Vonne M. E. Lewis
p197 Courtesy of Christopher Brown

Chapter 9

p200 Courtesy of Doug Brown [CC BY-SA 2.0]
https://www.flickr.com/photos/49814332@N04/5655627929/
p201 Courtesy of Aaron Hayman
p203 Photo by Richard Bogle, courtesy of Nola Bogle
p205 Courtesy of Barra Brown
p207 Courtesy of The Blue Cranes

INDEX

Page locators in italics indicate photographs.

Accept No Substitutes (album), 94
Acknowledgement of a Celebration (composition), 187, 189
Acox, Clarence, 150, *150*, 151, 178
Adams, Tommy, 75
Adderley, Cannonball, 75
Adderley, Nat, *81*
Addy, Obo, 71, 121–122, *123*, 126, 186
African American communities: in the 1960s, 55–56; The Backyard, 49, 50; The Blue Note, 50; DePriest Project Family Jazz Concerts, 149; Golden West Hotel, 25–26; Pacific Northwest establishment of, 17, 23–24, 44, 46; regional godfathers, 26, 28–29, 51; self reliance of, 50; Williams Avenue, 53, 55, 75
African American orchestras, 24
Afro-Cuban Allstars, 154, *154*
Akiyoshi-Tabackin ensemble, 131
"Alabama" (song), 156
Alan Jones Sextet, 130–33, *131*
Alberta Street Pub, 205
Albouy, David, 196
Alcoa Aluminum, 36
Alexander, Aaron, 115
Allen, Paul, 103, 143
Allen, W. D., 25
Allison, Karin, 171
All Rise (album), 206
All We Are Saying... (album), 128
Al Pierre's Royal Knights, 33
American Bandstand quintet, 161
American Music Program, 15
Anacortes Jazz Festival, 181
Anderson, Clipper, 155
Anderson, Ernestine: and Bob Nixon, 124; career and family choices, 57; and Dave Peck, 157; Ernestine's club, 89; Garfield High School, 147, 151; *Hot Cargo* (album), 43; and Ray Charles, 45; and Seattle, 41, 43, 51, 110, 209; Seattle Repertory Jazz Orchestra, 178
Anderson, Ivie, 94
Anderson, Quen, 53
Andrew Oliver Sextet, 202
Anger, Darol, 118
Anschell, Bill, 179
Apollo Theater, 77
Armstrong, Louis, 30, 31, 86, 162
Art Abrams Big Band, 180
Art Blakey's Jazz Messengers, 78, 79
Asian communities, Pacific Northwest establishment of, 17
Association for the Advancement of Creative Musicians, 19
Atwater's Restaurant, 112
audiences: band and listener demographics, 118–19; global financial crisis (2007) and shrinking audiences, 167, 169–70; mixed-race bands and audiences, 38–40
avant-garde: defined, 21; market volatility (1970s–1980s), 91–92, *92*, *93*; Portland scene, 150, 152; Rich Halley, 18–19, *19*; rise of, 67–70; Seattle (1990s), 133–34, 136–38, *137*; Seattle (2000s), 176–79; Seattle punk-jazz, 115–18, *116*, *117*; The Way Out, 53
Averre, Dave, *108*

B3 Organ Group, 138–39
The Backyard, 49, 50
Bad Influence (album), 131
Bailey, Mildred, 16, *26*, 26, 30
Baker, Chet, 157
Baker, Phil, 18, *66*, 79, 81, *81*, 84, *120*, 124
Ballard Jazz Festival, 143, 200–201, *200*
Ballou, Monte, 30–31, *31*
Balmer, Dan, 91, *104*, 106–7, 117–18, 166, 198
bandleaders, women, 27
Bannister, Gary, 102
Bard, Michael, 108
Barrett, Dan, 140
Basie, Count, 34, 63, 108

Beach, Bill, *81*, *120*
Beat Generation Portland, 51
bebop, 21, 43–44, 51, 86
Bebop & Destruction, 136–37
Bechet, Sidney, 119
Bellevue Jazz Festival, 100, 181
Benson Hotel, 139
Benton, "Sweet Baby" James, 48, *48*, 49, 79, 138–39
Berg, Billy, 63
Bergsma, William, 89
Berk, Dick, 110, 114, 120
Berlin University of the Arts, 136
Between Two Worlds (album), 119
Biafra, Jello, 117
Bill Evans Trio, 67, 171
Billy Larkin and the Delegates, 70, 79, 138
Billy Tipton Memorial Sax Quartet, 159, 162
Birth of the Cool (album), 178
Bishop, John, 125, 139, 141, *141*, 156, 179, 188
Bisio, Michael, 134, *134*
Bitches Brew (album), 73, 74
Black and Tan supper clubs, 39
Black Art (album), 130, 135
Black Elks Club, 38, 45
Black Music Academy, 61
Black Power movement, 70
Blackwell, Bumps, 40–41
Blakey, Art, 78, 79
Blue Cranes, 204–6, *207*
Blue Lake Park, 102
"Blue Laws," 29
Blue Monk, 193
The Blue Note, 50
Blue Note Records, 91, 115
blues, 21, 72, 74–75
Blues Alley, 142
Boeing, 46, *46*, 48, 75
Boe, Peter, *66*
Bogle, Nola, 22, 132, *133*
Bombay Bicycle Shop, 88
Bonneville Power Administration, 36, *36*
boogaloo, 93
Booker, Sonny, 47
Boon's Treasury, 91
Bostic, Earl, 50
Botti, Chris, 16, 18, 84
The Boulder Cafe, 72

Bowen, Ralph, 196
Bracken, Warren, 36, 58, 62–63, *62*, 84
Bradford, Bobby, 16, 51, 79, 85, 129
Braun, Rick, 162
Brazil, Joe, 59, 61, 67, 70, 88, 134, 187
Brazil Music Academy (BMA), 61
Breathless (album), 139, 163
Brecker, Randy, 71
Brick Street Bar and Grill, 136
Bridges, Walter, 51
Britt Music Festival, 91
Brown, Barra, 199, 204, *205*
Brown, Christopher, 79, 196, 197, *197*
Brown, James, 74
Brown, Jim, 101
Brownlow, Jack, 44
Brown, Mary, 101
Brown, Mel: and Alan Jones, 131–33; Cotton Club, 70; James Benton's Backyard, 49, 50; Jimmy Mak's, 138–39, 194, 196, 198; and Leroy Vinnegar, 95, 112, 113, *138*; and Marianne Mayfield, 57; Mel Brown B3 Organ Group, 79, 184; Mel Brown's Drum Shop, 77, 79, 80; Mel Brown Sextet, 78–80, *80*; 1970s and 1980s, 75, 77–80, *78*, *80*, 84, 91; San Francisco, 71; Walter Bridges Big Band, 16, 51
Brown, Tom, 37
Brubeck, Dave, 55, 88
Bruce, Lenny, 43
Bud Shank Jazz Workshop, 87–88
Buford, Pops, 38
Bumbershoot Music Festival, 143
Bunce, Louis, 53
Bundy, Evelyn, 27, 40
Burdette, Tamara, 61–62
Burns, Ken, 145–46
Butler Hotel, 30

Cactus Setup (album), 140
Café Racer, 172, 177, 207
Caldwell, Bobby, 163
Caliman, Hadley, 113, *113*, 114, 127, 152, 195, 198
Calloway, Cab, 30
Cannon, Dyan, 68
Canto do Rio (album), 121
Cape Alava, Olympic National Park, *14*
Captein, Dave, 90, 112, 117

Caranto, Renato, 146
Carl Smith Big Band, 53
Carter, Betty, 97, 127, 135
Carter, Bruce, 94
Carter, Ron, 97
Cascade Blues Association, 163, 185
Cascade Mountains, 20
Cascadia: environment and jazz ecology, 168, 169; environment and local jazz communities, 17, 19–22, 23, 55–56, 89–90, 114–15; Jazz Tribe of Cascadia, xi, 90, 112, 127, 136
Castle Jazz Band, 31
Cathedral Park Jazz Festival, 91, 99, 193
Catlett, Buddy, 32, 84, 86, 142
The Cave, 175, *175*
Central Saloon, 74
Centrum Jazz Workshop, 87
Chamber Music Society (album), 151, 183
Chapel Performance Space, 176
Charles, Ray, 16, 38, 41, *44*, 45, 71, 100, 163
Cheney, Art, 72, 129
The Chris Brown Quartet, 79
Christofferson, Steve, 21, 84, 153
Chronicle (album), 186
Chuck Israels Jazz Orchestra, 171, *173*
Chuck's Steak House, 85
"City of Roses" Grammy award, 15
Clarke, S. P., 94
Clayton, Jay, 86
Clement, Dawn, 158, *158*, 161
Clendenin, Darin, 179
Climbing (album), 22
"Clouds" (song), 150
Clover Club, 25, 94
Club Maynard, 44
Cobb, Jimmy, *81*
"cocktail jazz" vs. jazz as art music, 59, 61–62
Coleman, Ornette, 65, 117, 154
Cole, Richard, 179
Colligan, George, 173–74, *174*
Collins, Bootsy, 184
Coltrane, John, 50, 59, *60*, 86, 111, 117, 127, 156, 171, 178
Columbia River, 36
community. *See* local jazz communities
Confer, Gene, 94, 105
Conklin, Ellis E., 97

Connick, Harry, Jr., 84
The Contemporary Group, 88
Cooke, Sam, 41
Cool'r (band), 94
Corea, Chick, 106
Cornish Institute of Allied Arts, 84, 85–86, 91–92, 112, 114, 121, 127, 136, 208
Coryell, Larry, 16, 61, 62, 64, 67, 71, 87
Cotton Club, 70
Cousin's nightclub, 108
Cray, Robert, 131
Creative Music Guild, 85, 92
Critters Buggin, 116, 136, 152
Crosby, Bing, 16, 28, *28*, 30
The Crusaders, 94, 97
Crystal Beth band, 176
Curson, Ted, 120
Curtis, King, 65
Curtis, Nancy, 134
"Custer Died for Your Sins" (song), 157
Cycling (album), 156–57

Dammann, Peter, 185
dams, shipyards, and musicians, 25, 36
Daniels, Dee, 124
Darensbourg, Joe, 26
Darwish, Ben, 146, *203*, 204
Dave Brubeck Octet, 88
Dave Brubeck Quartet, 55
Dave's Fifth Avenue, 53
Davis, Miles, 15–16, 44, 55, 73, 74, 75, 82, 105, 106, 145, 178
Davis, Rob, 143, 175
Davis, Sammy, Jr., 70
Davis/Taylor Project, 142–43
Deardorf, Chuck, 86, *86*, 179
de Barros, Paul: on Bill Smith, 134; on Cornish avant-gardists, 97, 115; on Dave Peck, 22, 25, 157; Earshot Jazz nonprofit, 102; on "the Generation of '79," 86; on Jackson Street (1940s and 1950s), 37–38; *Jackson Street After Hours* (de Barros), 25, 27, 149; on Jay Thomas, 141; on the Racer Sessions, 177–78; and the *Seattle Times*, 147; on Wayne Horvitz, 133, 179
DeJohnette, Jack, 173, 174
deLay, Paul, 74, 139
Delevan's club, 84, 108, 120

Del Tones, 49
DePreist, James, 118, 153
DePriest, Akbar, 149, 152
DePriest Project Family Jazz Concerts, 149
Desert Room, 49
Diana Ross and the Supremes, 77
Diatic Records, 146–47
Digger O'Dell's, 109
discrimination: 1940s and 1950s, 38–40, 44, 46–48, *47*, 50; jazz and race, 30–33; regional, 23–24
DJ's Village Jazz, 57
Doggett, Charlie, 147, 158
Dominguez, Chano, 172
The Doors, 112
Doria, Joe, 137, 181, *181*, 184
Dosumov, Farko, 209
DownBeat, 22, 191
Dozono, Sho, 181
the Dude Ranch, 39
Duke, Stanton, 39
Dunning, Brian, 119
Duo Chronicles, 190
Dust Yourself Off (album), 94

early jazz era (1800s), 23–24
Earshot Jazz, 86, 102, 108, 134, 155, 177, 181, 197–98, 207
Ebony Cafe, 71
The Ebony Five, 51
Eckstine, Billy, 36, 63
ecology, jazz ecology, 168, 169–70
economy: global economic crisis (2000s), 167, 169–70; 1970s decline of jazz, 75, 76; 1980s growth of jazz, 91–92; and Seattle jazz community (2000s), 143–44, 155–56, *156*
Egan's Ballard Jam House, 179
1800s era, 23–24
Eldar, 171
Ellington, Duke, 30, 34, 35, *35*, 94, 149, 206
environment: jazz ecology, 168, 169; Jazz Tribe of Cascadia, xi, 90, 112, 127, 136; and local jazz communities, 17, 19–22, 23, 55–56, 89–90, 114–15
Ecotopia (Callenbach), 80
Epistrophy (album), 115
Erickson, Eddie, 140

Ernestine's, 89
Erskine, Damian, 188, *188*, 190–91, 209
Erskine, Peter, 190
Esperanza (album), 183
Essentially Ellington competition, 149, 151
Eugene Hotel, 91
Evans, Bill, 67, 128, 171
Experience Music Project, 143, *144*, 181

"Fables of Faubus" (song), 156
Fabulous Thunderbirds, 164
Faehnle, Dan, 113
Failing, Bill, 122
"Fair Trade Music Seattle Resolution," 203
Fast Break (film), 71
"Father of the Walking Bass" (Leroy Vinnegar), 110, *110*, 111
Faubus, Orval, 156
Feinstein, Michael, 140
Fendel, Marc, 137
Ferguson, Swede, 33
file sharing and declining album sales, 187–88
Finch, Candy, 91
Finding Forrester soundtrack, 128
First Jazz concerts, 81
Fish, Nick, 181
5/4 Magazine, 133
Five Blind Boys of Mississippi, 72
The Flame, 53
Flanagan, Tommy, 72
flash-mob jazz choir, 201
Flatland, 192–93
Fleenor, Beth, 176
Flory-Barnes, Evan, 158, 187, 189, 195, 198
Floyd, Charles, 163
"folk poets," 47
The Folk-Type Swinger (album), 58
4+1 chamber ensemble, 161
"Four" (song), 82
The Four Tops, 77
Frat Hall, 33
Freda Shaw Band, 26
Freebop, 93
free jazz, 21
"free rock" bands, 116
The Free Spirits, 64

Friesen, David: at Digger O'Dell's, 109; *Gonna Plant Me Some Seeds* (album), 58; improvisation and avant-garde, 66–68, *69*, 70, 93, 118–19, 131, 134, 136; and Jim Pepper, 105; and John Stowell, 68, 118, 136, 142, 143, 165; Llahngaelhyn jam sessions, 117; *Three Sides of Elmer Gill* (album), 71
Frisell, Bill, 19, 110, 112, 125, 127, 128, *129*, 134, 209
Frishberg, Dave, 110, 112, 140, 146–47, 153
Fuller, Larry, 110
funk: defined, 21; funk-jazz fusion, 79; funk-rock, 116; growth of, 74–75; in Portland, 184; punk-funk, 117–18, *117*
fusion: defined, 21; funk-jazz fusion, 79; and future of jazz, 199; jazz-blues fusion and funk, 74–75; jazz-rock fusion, 64, 106; 1970s and 1980s, 93–94; rise of, 93–94

Gaillard, Slim, 63
Garage A Trois, 116
Garfield High School, 61, 108, 142, 147, 149, 150, 151, 159, 197
The Garfield Ramblers, 27
Garner, Erroll, 63
Gates, Bill, 103, 143
Geissel, Kurt, 177
The Generation Band, 161
"the Generation of '79," 86, 87
Geneva's, 108
geography. See environment
George, Pat, 85, 94–95
Getz, Stan, 66, 97, 112, 171
"Ghettos of the Mind" (song), 94
Giberson, Clay, 156, *156*, 158, 190
Gilbreath, John, 86, 181
Gill, Elmer, 71, 179
Gilles, Jim, 38, 47
Gillespie, Dizzy, 63, 82, 91
Gillgam, Harry, 95
G, Kenny, 17, 68, 75, 93, 139, 162–63, *163*
Golden West Hotel, 25–26, 28, 187
Gone, Just Like a Train (album), 127
Gonna Plant Me Some Seeds (album), 58
Gonzalez, Anita, 26
The Goodfoot, 184

Goodhew, Denney, 86, 131, 136
Goodman, Benny, 34
Goodwin, Jim, 112
Gordon Bleu (album), 79, 80
Gordon, Dexter, 59, 97, 166
Gorelick, Kenny (Kenny G), 17, 68, 75, 93, 139, 162–63, *163*
Grace and Truth Pentecostal Church, 184
Granelli, Jerry, 86, 136
Grant, Al, 66, 105
Grant, Darrell: on the Blue Cranes, 205; on jazz ecology and Pacific Northwest landscapes, 168, 169, 187; move to Portland, 18, 19, 134, *134*, 135; Portland State University, 129–30, 151; on streaming services and declining album sales, 188; *The Territory* (jazz suite), 16, 17; "Tribute to the Old Cats," 127, 129
Grant, Earl, 79
Grant, Malcolm, 135
Grant, Mike, 105
Grant, Tom, 66–67, 84, 104, *104*, 105, 164, 203
Gravitas Quartet, 161
Gray, Jerry, 58, 61, 95, 184
Greenblatt, Dan, 159, 161
Greenblatt, Tatum, 159, 161
Green, Walter Emmanuel, 29
Gresham Chamber of Commerce, 98, 99
Griggs, Steve, 186–87
Gross, John, 131, 147

Hahn, Jerry, 110
Halberstadt, Randy, 178, 184
Halley, Rich, 18–19, *19*, 92, *92*, 93, 157–58
Hall, Jim, 128
Hamilton, Scott, 101, 140
Hammon, Gary, 74
Hampton, Lionel, 39, 41
Hancock, Herbie, 74, 97, 106, 171, 193
Handy, W. C., 24
hard bop, 21
Hargrove, Roy, 196, 198
Harlem stride piano, 157
Harper, Geoff, 136
Harp, Everette, 162
Harris, Eddie, *66*, 149
Harris, Gary, 113, 122

Harrison, George, 77
Hart, Antonio, *81*
Haynes, Roy, 127, 135
Heathman Hotel, 112
Heck, Dan, 137
Heldman, Jerry, 67
Henderson, Fletcher, 31
Henderson, Joe, 66, 84, 105, 120
Henderson, Wayne, 94
Hendrix, Jimi, 16–17, 24, 74, 117
Hendrix, Nora, 24
Hendrix, Ross, 24
Henry, Ann, 35
Henson, Julian, 34, 50, 57, 79, 95
Hentoff, Nat, 141
Herbie Hancock and the Headhunters, 193
Herman, Woody, 44
heroin, 44, 45
Hickey, Al, 38
Hill, Andrew, 115
Hing, Kenny, 51
Hinton, Milt, 137
The Hobbit club, 78
Hobbs, Gary, 84, 124
Hoffman, Jeannie, 57–58, 93
Holden, Grace, 25
Holden, Oscar, 25, 26
Holden, Oscar, Jr., 75
Holden, Ron, 25
Holiday, Billie, 30, 68, 110, 156, 171
Holloway, Red, *138*
"Hometown Boy" (song), 105
Homowo Foundation, 122
Hood, Bill, 51
Hood, Ernie, 51, 53
Hooker, John Lee, 102
Hornbuckle, Linda, 184, 185, 186, *186*
Horn, Paul, 118–19, *119*
Horn, Ray, 122–23
Horsfall, Mike, 108, *108*, 124
Horvitz, Wayne: and Bill Frisell, 125, 136; and Briggan Krauss, 114; and Eyvind Kang, 143; *Joe Hill* suite, 157; move to Seattle, 110, 208; The Royal Room, 179; Seattle avant-garde scene, 133, *160*, 161
Hot Cargo (album), 43
Hotel on the Corner of Bitter and Sweet (Ford), 186

house concerts, 203
Hughley, Marty, 157
Hunter, Charlie, 116
Hutcherson, Bobby, 97, *120*

Iago, Weber, 172
Icasiano, Chris, 177, 178
improvisation: Alan Jones on, 15; David Friesen, 66–68, *69*, 70, 93, 119, 131, 136; Glen Moore on, 73; New Music, 127; Tom Grant Band, 106; Wayne Horvitz, 159, 161
Improvised Music Project, 172
Industrial Jazz Group, 192
Industrial Revelation quartet, 187, 188, 198, 204
In My Wildest Dreams (album), 106
Innovations in Modern Music Orchestra, 87
In Seattle (album), 134
Integrity (album), 122
the Internet and album sales, 187–91
interracial marriage, 47–48
Isham, Mark, 119
Israels, Chuck, 170–71, *172*, 173, *173*
Ives, Charles, 133
Ivester, Mark, 121, 179
"I Want to Be a Sideman" (song), 112
I Wish You Love (album), 140

Jackson, Archie, 32
Jackson, Carlton, *104*, 117, 118
Jackson, Michael, 41
Jackson-Mills Big Band, 113, 153
Jackson, Milt, 88, *88*
Jackson Street: during the 1940s and 1950s, 37–38, *40*; early jazz era in Seattle, 25, 26; and "Noodles" Smith, 26, 28; Savoy Ballroom, 40, 47–48, 52
Jackson Street After Hours (de Barros), 25, 27, 149
Jackson Street Jazz Walk, 201
Jacquet, Illinois, 41
Jamal, Ahmad, 97
James, Boney, 164
"jam grass," 118
jam sessions, 67, 77, 85, 91, 117, 120, 127
Jarrett, Keith, 119
jazz: arrival in the Pacific Northwest, 25–26; audience for, 175–76, 199–200, 207–10; "cocktail jazz" vs. jazz as art music, 59, 61–62;

definitions, 21; and early rock 'n' roll, 52; 1800s era, 23–24; future of, 209–10; jazz ecology, 168, 169; jazz-rock fusion, 64; neotraditionalism, 106, 145–46; new age, 118–19, 121; and politics, 155–58; post-jazz, 204–7; prankster bands, 116; punk-jazz, 115–18, *116*, *117*; and race, 23–24, 30–33; smooth jazz, 21, 106–8, 162–64
Jazz4Kids, 178
"Jazz After Hours" radio program, 89, 122
Jazz Alley, 81, 98, 124, 162, 179
The Jazz Arts (television show), 53
Jazz at Lincoln Center, 145, 151
Jazz at Newport festival, 101
Jazz de Opus nightclub, 113, 166
Jazz (documentary), 145–46
The Jazz Gallery, 75
Jazz Quarry club, 57, 85, 94, 108
Jazzscene, 97, 101, 151
Jazz Scholars, 178
Jazz Society of Oregon Hall of Fame, 68, 79, 113, 171
Jazz Society of Oregon (JSO), 81, 101, 104, 138, 153, 201
JazzTimes, 18
JazzTruth blog, 174
Jazz Workshop, 80
Jazz Workshop studio, 57
Jean Hoffman Sings and Swings (album), 57
The Jeff Lorber Fusion, 75, 163
Jensen, Brent, 179
Jimmy Cliff and Third World, 192
Jimmy Mak's nightclub, 79, 138–39, 194, 196, 198
jitterbug, 41, 51, *51*
Joe Hill suite, 157
"Joe's Basement," 61
Johnson, Barry, 202
Johnson, Palmer, 25
Johnson, Tom, 26, 28–29, 50
Jolly Roger Roadhouse, 74
Jones, Alan: Alan Jones Sextet, 130–33, *131*; The Cave, 175; *Climbing* (album), 21–22; Darrell Grant on, 187; on improvisation, 15; on Jazz de Opus, 166; *The Leroy Vinnegar Suite*, 113–14; *1-2-3* (album), 68
Jones, Hank, 72
Jones, Jennifer, 195
Jones, Lloyd, 74
Jones, Quincy: Garfield High School, 61, 108, 147, 151; *Hot Cargo* (album), 43; Seattle scene, 16, 27, 32, 40–41, 51; touring in Europe, 18
Jordan, Louis, 41, *52*
Jorgensen, Matt, 139, 156
jump blues, 41, 52, 72

Kaiser, Henry, 36
Kaiser Shipyards, 36, 51, 54, *54*
Kang, Eyvind, 125, 127, 143, 162
Kansas City swing, 157
Katz, Vera, 143
Kearney, David "Guitar Shorty," 74
Keller, Marilyn, 57
Kemp, Georgia, 45
Kennedy, Billy, 117–18
Kennedy, Tim, 37, 54
Kenton, Stan, 84, 87, 124
Keppard, Freddie, 25
Kerouac, Jack, 43
Keystone Investment Co., 29
Khu.éex' band, 178
Kilgore, Rebecca, 112, 140
King, B. B., 72
King, Freddie, 72
King, Nancy, 22, 57, 71, 80, 82, *83*, 84, 153, 202
King, Sonny, 56–57, 80
Kinsley, Michael, 103
Kirk, Rahsaan Roland, 149
Knapp, Jim, 85–86
Knauls, Paul, 70
Knights of Syncopation, 27
Knitting Factory, 115
Kool Jazz Festival, 98
The Kora Band, 191–92
Koz, Dave, 162
Krall, Diana, 113
Krauss, Briggan, 114, *114*, 115, 161
Kronos Quartet, 171
Ku Klux Klan in Oregon, 38
Kukrudu, 122

La Belle, Patti, 98
LaFaro, Scott, 67
L.A. Four, 87
Laine, Frankie, 63
Lake Superior (album), 192

Lamar, Kendrick, 206
Lamb, Patrick, 107, 163–64, *165*, 203
Landes Ordinance, 29
Lanphere, Don, 43–44, 84, 86–87, 124, 136, 167
Larkin, Billy, 79, 138
Larson, Gary, 125, 127
Lavezzoli, Peter, 59
Le Bon, 117–18, *117*, 152
Lee, Dorothy McCullough, 47
Lee, Ed, 61, 67, 74
Lee, Gordon: Diatic Records, 146; on Jim Pepper, 65; Mel Brown Sextet, 80; on music sounding like a place, 20, 21
Lee, Jof, 112
Lees, Gene, 199
Legacy Emanuel Hospital, 75
Legacy Quartet, 129, 139, 150
Legrand, Michel, 111
Leinonen, Pete, 52, 91–92
Leonard, Jeff, *104*, 158
The Leroy Vinnegar Suite (album), 113–14
Let Me Play My Drum (album), 122
Lewis, Dave, 16, 93, 195, 197
Lewis, Doug, 94
Lewis, D'Vonne, 16, 194, *194*, 195, 197–98
Lewis, Mel, 97
Lightfoot, Jack, 22
Lindberg, Mike, 102
Linegan, Jimmy, 38
Lionel Hampton Band, 41
Lionel Hampton Jazz Festival, 149
Little Richard, 40
Live in Seattle (album), 59
Living Daylights trio, 162
Llahngaelhyn coffeehouse, 67, 70, 91
local jazz communities: The Backyard, 49; Earshot Jazz nonprofit, 102; as ecological communities, 168, 169; environment and geography of, 17, 19–22, 23, 55–56, 89–90, 114–15; growth of blues and R&B, 72, 74–75; jam sessions, 67; "Joe's Basement," 61; regional godfathers, 25, 26, 28–29, 51; "small is beautiful" ethic, 149–50, 152–53; supportive nature of, 16–17, 124, 136, See also Portland; Seattle
Lombardo, Guy, 34
Lorber, Jeff, 75, 93, 163
Lost and Found (album), 136

Louis, Joe, 70
Love Unlimited Orchestra, 163
Lunceford, Jimmie, 31
Lurie, Jessica, 159, *159*, 162
LV's Uptown, 129

Madrona Records, 66
Mae, August, 40
Mahaffey, Chuck, 59, 61, 67
Mahara, W. H., 24
Mahavishnu Orchestra, 71
Mahogany, Kevin, 171
Makarounis, Jimmy, 79, 138, 139
Mango Tango (album), 106
Manne, Shelly, 57
Mann, Lisa, 185
Manolides, Jimmy, 89
Marable, Fate, 25
Marianne Mayfield Trio, 79
Marriott, David, Jr., 142
Marriott, Thomas, 142
Marsalis, Bradford, 97
Marsalis, Wynton, 84, 97, 106, 135, 145–46, *146*, 159, 164, 179, 199
Martha and the Vandellas, 77, 79
Martine, Tucker, 161
Martinez, Eddie, 172
Mason, James, 140
Mastersounds, 53
Matassa, Greta, 155, 179
Matheny, Pat, 100, 163
Mathis, Kane, 191
Maxwell, Amy, 203
Maybelle, Big, 149
Mayfield, Marianne, 50, 56–57, *56*, 58, 80, 112
Mazzio, Paul, 131
McCandless, Paul, 71, 73
McCann, Les, 84, 97
McClendon, Bill, 23, 29, 50
McCloskey, David, 90
McCullough, Chad, 191
McElroy, Burt, 39
McElroy, Cole "Pop," 39
McElroy's Ballroom, 35, 38, 39, *42*
McFarland, Gary, 72
McFarland, Lester, 93
McFarland, Tom, 72, 74, *74*

McKee, Garcia, 45
McNeely, Jay, 47
McPartland, Marian, 157, 171
McPherson, Charles, 131
McTuff organ trio, 137, 181, 184
media coverage of jazz in the 2000s, 147
Mel Brown B3 Organ Group, 79, 184
Mel Brown's Drum Shop, 77, 79, 80
Mel Brown Sextet, 78–80, *80*
Mel Lewis Big Band, 97
Memory, Thara: *Chronicle* (album), 186; Grammy Awards, 15; Mel Brown Sextet, 78; and Miles Davis, 15–16; move to Portland, 71, *126*; and Obo Addy, 122, 186; with Ron Steen, *66*; Superband, *182*, 184; teaching, 126, 151
mentoring: Buz Shank, 87–88; Chuck Mahaffey, 61–62; at Cornish Institute, 127; Eddie Wied, 94–95, *95*; at Garfield High School, 142–43; Jerry Gray, 95; Joe Brazil, 61; Omar Yeoman, 64; Portland scene, 127, 129; Warren Bracken, 36, 58, 62–63, *62*; youth movement (1970s), 83–88
Merchants Café, 88
Metcalf, Chuck, 58, 59, 75
Metronomics app, 186, 189–90
Microsoft, 103, 143
Milkowski, Bill, 18
Millander, Lucky, 41
Mingus, Charles, 124, 156
Minidoka internment camp, 22
minstrels and proto-jazz, 24–25
Mississippi Studios, 202, 205
Mitchell, George, 79, 84
Mitchell, Red, 110
Mitchell, Rick, 117, *117*
Modernaires, 72
Modern Jazz Quartet, 55, 89, 108
Monktail Creative Music Concern, 176–77
Monk, Thelonious, 114, 115
Montavilla Jazz Festival, 201, *201*, 203
Monterey Jazz Festival, 98, 99, 149
Montgomery, Buddy, 53
Montgomery, Monk, 53
Montgomery, Wes, 53
Moore, Glen, 22, 62, 66, 68, 71, 73, *83*
Moran, Jason, 206
Morrison, Van, 112
Morton, Jelly Roll, 25, 26, *26*

Mothers of Invention, 119
Mount Hood, *16*
Mount Rainier, 22
Mt. Hood Community College (MHCC), 84, 99
Mt. Hood Festival of Jazz, 57, 79, 84, 95, 97–99, 153
Mulligan, Gerry, 97
Mural Room, 57
musicians: adaptability of, 58–59; album sales, 187–88; arrivals in the Pacific Northwest, 17, 18–19, 36, 71–72, 109–15, 171–75, 191–92; bebop and African American intellectuals, 43–44; cost of living (2000s), 194–97; day jobs, 47, 53, 77, 80, 82, 129, 165, 166; departures from the Pacific Northwest, 16–17, 71; heroin use, 44, 45; local attitudes about, 78; mixed-race bands and audiences, 38–40; teaching positions, 61, 84, 85–86, 88, 115, 124, 127, 129–30, 173, 174, 178, See also local jazz communities; Portland; Seattle; specific names of musicians
Musicians Union Local 99, 51, 62
Musselwhite, Charlie, 74

Nanette, Shirley, 118, *118*
Nanking Cafe, 32
Nastos, John, 186, *186*, 189–90
National Jazz Ensemble, 171
Navarro, Fats, 44, 86
Negro Musicians Union in Seattle, 50
neotraditionalism, 106, 145–46
new age jazz, 118–19, 121
New, Katarina, 166
New Music, 127, 161
New Orleans Restaurant, 103, *103*, 129, 139, 159, 179
New Orleans Straight Ahead, 171, 191
New Seattle Three, 91
New Stories Trio, 124
Newton, Farnell, 184
New Traditionalism, 108
New York City, 18, 55
Night Charade (album), 106
Nightnoise, 119, 121
Nilson, Storm, 191
Nirvana, 115
Nixon, Bob, 124
Norman Sylvester Band, 163

"Northwest Mystics," 134, 136
Norvo, Red, 30
Now I'm Fine (composition), 189

Obrador, 134
The Ocular Concern, 191
O'Day, Anita, 59
Odean Jazz Orchestra, 32
Ó Domnaill, Mícheál, 121
O'Hearn, Patrick, 119
Okropong ensemble, 122
Oliver, Andrew, 151, 191–92
Oluo, Ahamefule, 188, *188*, 189, 198
Om (album), 59
1-2-3 (album), 68
Oregon (chamber jazz group), 22, 71, 73, 112
Oregonian, 147
Oregon Music Hall of Fame, 68, 147, 184
Oregon Symphony, 79, 118, 153, 163–64, *164*
Oregon Zoo, Your Zoo and All That Jazz concert series, 91, 100
organ trios, 75
The Original Creole Orchestra, 25
Original Dixieland Jazz Band, 26
Origin Records, 121, 139, 141, 156, 177, 188, 200
Oskay, Billy, 119
Otis, Johnny, 41
Otter Crest Jazz Weekend, 101, *101*, 137
Outside Music Ensemble, 157–58

Pacific Crest Jazz Orchestra, 151, 183
Pain, Louis, 138–39, *139*
Panama Hotel Jazz project, 184, *184*, 186–87
Parchman Farm, 57, 108
Parker, Charlie, 44, 51, 63, 86, 117
Parker, Jason, 195
Parks, Aaron, 16
Parnell, Roy, 89
Parnell's (Roy's Living Room), 81, *88*, 89, 124, 142, 166
Pascoal, Hermeto, 121
Pastorius, Jaco, 117
Paul deLay Blues Band, 138
Paul Horn Quartet, 68
PC&S Tavern, 85
PDX Jazz, 180–81
Peacock, Gary, 86

"The Peacocks" (song), 37
Pearl Jam, 116
Peck, Dave, 22, 87, 89, 157, 158, 184
Peck, Jane, 157
The Penthouse, 59, 61, 124
People's Observer (newspaper), 29
Peplowski, Ken, 101
Pepper, Gilbert, 65
Pepper, Jim, 22, 51, 62, 64–66, *64*, 71, 84, 106, 157
Pepper, Ravie, 65
Petersen, Milo, 179
Peterson, Oscar, 50
Peterson, Ralph, 196
Pete's Poop Deck, 53, 58
Phillips, Devin, 171, 190, *190*
Phillips, Nate, 94
piano tradition in the Pacific Northwest, 94–95, *95*
Pierre, Al, 33, 46, 102
Pigford, Major, 40
Pigmy (album), 79, 138
Pigpen, 161
Pike Place Market, 103–4
Pink Martini, 18, 113
Pink Pussycat, 53
Pioneer Square, Seattle, 103
Playboy Jazz Festival, 78, 79
players. *See* musicians
Pleasure (funk band), 93–94
Poindexter, Pony, 71, 82
politics and jazz, 155–58
Pony Boy Records, 177
pop-jazz, 18
Porter, Randy, 68, 130, 131, 151, 175
Porter, Sid, 22, 132
Portland: in 1890, *24*; downtown, *16*; the Dude Ranch, 39; during the Great Depression, 33, *34*; environment and geography of, 20, 23–24; future jazz scene, 202; Montavilla Jazz Festival, 201, *201*, 203; musicians moving to, 47, 191–92; and national jazz map, 153–54, *154*; 1990s revitalization of jazz scene, 102–3, 104–8; "small is beautiful" ethic, 149–50, 152–53; suburbs, 106; Waterfront Blues Festival, *96*, 97, 107, See also Williams Avenue
Portland Brewing Company, 112
Portland Center for the Visual Arts, 92
Portland Jazz Composers Ensemble, 177, 191–92

Portland Jazz Festival, 153–54, 167, 171, 180–81, 193
Portland Jazz Orchestra, 180, *180*
Portland State University, 115, 127, 129, 135, 173, 174, 193
Portland Trail Blazers, 71
Port Townsend Jazz Festival, 87
post-jazz, 204–7
post-Prohibition era, 33–34
Presley, Dan, *108*
Priester, Julian, 86, 127, 136, 152
Prima Donna club, 57, 77, 95
proto-jazz, 24–25
punk-funk, 117–18, *117*
punk-jazz, 115–18, *116*, *117*

Quadraphonnes, 192, 193, *193*

race and jazz: early jazz era, 23–24, 30–33; listener demographics, 118–19; mixed-race bands and audiences, 38–40; race relations in Portland and Seattle, 38–39, 40; riots (1960s), 70
Racer Sessions, 177–78
radio broadcasts of jazz, 122–23, 162, 181
Radio Music Society (album), 15, 151, 183, 198
Ralph Towner, 73
Ramsey, Doug, 44
Rand, Warren, 131
Rawlings, Josh, 187, 198
Ray Charles Tribute, 163–64, *164*
Ray's Helm, 58, 85, 93
R&B: growth of, 72, 74–75, 93–94; and Obo Addy, 122; regional influence of, 19
Ready to Roll (Album), 184
redlining, 44, 46, 56
Reed, Rufus, 67
Reeves, Martha, 77, 79
Rega, Rita, 122–23, 145, 151, 191
Reischman, Steve, 100, 102–3
Remo's, 108
Reprise Records, 57
Return to Forever, 71
Rhythm Room, 50
Richardson, Chan, 44
Rinker, Al, 30
Ritenour, Lee, 98
Ritz, Lyle, 140

Roberts, Howard, 57
Robinson, Joanne, 115
Robinson, R. C. (Ray Charles), 16, 38, 41, *44*, 45, 71, 100, 163
"Rockin' Chair" (song), 30
rock 'n' roll, 52, 53–54, 55
Rollins, Sonny, 44, 97, 112
Ronne, Jean, 94, 139
Roosevelt High School, 147, 149, 151
Rose City Blues Festival, 102
Ross, Diana, 18, 77, 79, 84
Ross Island (album), 150
Rouse, Charlie, 114–15
Rowles, Jimmy, 37
Royal, Marshall, 28
The Royal Room, 179
Royston, Bill, 153–54, 171
Ruff, Willie, 43
Rush, Otis, 74

"St. Louis Blues" (song), 24
Salgado, Curtis, 74, 93
Salon de Refuses, 152
Sample, Joe, 94
Sanborn, David, 106
Sanders, Pharoah, 59, 171
San Francisco Blues Festival, 74
Santana, 114, 172
Santos Neto, Jovino, 121, 178
Saunders, Jimmy, 152
Savage, John, 31–32
Savoy Ballroom, 40, 47–48, 52
Scheps, Rob, 111, 152–53, *153*
Schiff, Matt, 85, 94
Schlichting, Sam, 129
Schneider, Maria, 157
Schulte, Dan, 131
Schuur, Diane, 97, 107–8, *107*, 163
Scott, Isaac, 72, 74
Scott, Jill, 184
Scroggins, Janice, 71, 122, 149, 181, 184–86, *184*
Seales, Marc, 86, 124, 142, 198
Seamonster Lounge, 184
Seattle: avant-garde scene, 133–34, 136–38, *137*, 176–79; cost of living, 194–97; environment and geography of, 20, 23; "Fair Trade Music Seattle Resolution," 203; jazz scene

revitalization (1990s), 103–4, *103*, 106–8, 125, 127; local scene (2000s), 155, 172–73; "Noodles" Smith, 26, 28, 29, 33; Oscar Holden, 25; Pike Place Market, 103–4; punk-jazz, 115–18, *116*, *117*, See also Jackson Street
Seattle Black Musician's Union Hall, 50
Seattle Jazz Society, 59, 75
Seattle Repertory Jazz Orchestra, 178–79, 180
Seattle Times, 147
segregation, 38–40, 44, 46–48, *47*, 50
Selah coffeehouse, 67
Sequoia Ensemble, 178
Sessions Club, 38
Severinsen, Doc, 51
Shank, Bud, 86, 87–88, *87*, 157
Shaw, Woody, 66, 105, 120
Shearing, George, 50
Sheldon, Jack, *138*
Shepik, Brad, 115
shipyards, 36
Shorter, Wayne, 97, 153
Shrieve, Michael, 114, 125, 184, 209
Silverman, John, 115
Simon, Mark, 77, 84–85, 94, 95, 112
Singletary, Preston, 178
Sista (album), 184
Skerik (Eric Walton), 116–17, *116*, 121, 178, 194
Sky Trio, 85
Sly and the Family Stone, 94
"small is beautiful" ethic, 149–50, 152–53
Smith, Bill, 88, 89, 134, 178
Smith, Bryan, 173, *174*
Smith, Carl, 53
Smith, "Noodles," 26, 28, 29, 33
Smokin' Java (album), 130, 135
smooth jazz, 21, 106–8, 162–64
The Smuggler, 91
Sokol-Blosser Winery, 100
Solo Piano (album), 105
Souders, Jackie, 30
soul jazz, 21
Soul of a Free Man (album), 164
Soul Vaccination, 192
Sounds Outside concerts, 176
Space Needle, 76
Spalding, Esperanza: Best New Artist, 2012, *182*, 183; departure from Portland, 16; Grammy Awards, 15; on Janice Scroggins, 184–85; Mel Brown Summer Jazz Workshops, 79; Portland State University, 193; *Radio Music Society* (album), 15, 151, 183, 198; summer jazz camps, 151; on teachers and dedication to craft, 183; and Thara Memory, 15, 183
Sparks, Phil, 178
Spellbinder, 184
Spirit (album), 135
Springer, Dennis, 93
Spyro Gyra, 98
Standifer, Floyd: on Blackwell's Junior Band, 40; death of, 167; move to Portland, 18; 1960s, 58; 1970s, 84, 86; and Seattle, 37, 38, 51, 53, 142; on segregation and discrimination, 48
Stan Kenton Band, 84
Stan Kenton Orchestra, 124
Staples, Mavis, 164
Steel Bridge, Portland, *168*
Steen, Ron, 57, 62, 64, 66–67, *66*, 84, 105, 120, *120*
Stentz, Chuck, 134
Stentz, Jan, 57
Stitt, Sonny, 84, 157
Stone, Sly, 74
Storrs, Dave, 92, *93*, 150, 152, *152*
Stowell, John: and David Friesen, 68, 118–19, 136, 142, 143; at Digger O'Dell's, 109; *Gonna Plant Me Some Seeds* (album), 58; on house concerts, 203; improvisation and avant-garde, 93; touring schedule, *118*, 119, 165
straight-ahead jazz, 21, 163
Strait, Todd, 171
"Strange Fruit" (song), 156
streaming and declining album sales, 187–88
Strings for Industry, 118
Stubelek, Tyson, 151
summer festivals, 97–103
Superband, *182*, 184
The Supremes, 77, 79
Swampdweller, 137–38
Sweeter Than the Day quintet, 161
Sweet-Smellin' Eddie, 49
swing: defined, 21; jump blues and jitterbugs, 41; Kansas City swing, 157; roots of, 29–30
Swing Journal, 68
Sylvester, Norman, 72, 162
Syncopated Classics (Waldron), 32

Syncopated Taint Septet, 121, 179

Table & Chairs records, 177
Tacoma Art Museum, 133
Tales from the Far Side soundtrack, 125, 127
Tales of the Pilot (album), 157
Tall Jazz Trio, 108, *108*
Tatum, Art, 95, 111
Taylor, Cecil, 154
Taylor, Charles, 27
Taylor, Charles, Jr., 27, 40
Taylor, Mark, 143
The Temptations, 77, 79
Terrill, Steve, 105
The Territory (jazz suite), 16, 17, 187
Teuber, Hans, 121, 179
Tex, Joe, 126
Theoretical Planets (album), 174
Thomas, Jay, 55, 89, 141–42, 178, 194, 203
Thomas, Marv, 89
Thomas, William, 93
Thompson, Wayne, 97, 98, 99, 100, 153
Thornton, Big Mama, 70
Three Sides of Elmer Gill (album), 71
The Three V's, 57
Through the Listening-Glass (album), 68
Tipton, Billy, 159, 161
Tlingit music, 178
Tobin, Mary-Sue, 192–93, *192*
Todd Shipyards, 25
Tolles, Billy, 46, 52, 75, 93
Tom Grant Band, 93, 104, *104*, 106–7, 118
Tom Johnson's Chicken Dinner Inn, 29
Tower, Ralph, 66, 137, *137*
Towner, Ralph, 22, 71, 112, 136
Tractor Tavern, 175
Trianon Ballroom, 31, *32*, 40, 44
"Tribute to the Old Cats," 127, 129
Trio (album), 157
Trio Subtonic, 198
The Triple Door, 179
Truth and Reconciliation (album), 135
Tuck Lung Restaurant, 95
Tula's Restaurant, 179, 203
Tunnel Six, 192
Turnham, Edythe, 27
Turnham, Floyd, 27

Turnham, Floyd, Jr., 27
Tympany Five band, 41, 52
Tyner, McCoy, 61

Ubangi Club, 33
Uhl, Don, 118
Underground Blues Festival, 74
University of Oregon, 124
University of Portland, 149
University of Washington, 61, 85, 88, 89, 92, 116, 134, 143, 172, 208
Unsafe (album), 130
Unspeakable (album), 128
Upper Left Trio, 156–57, 205
Upstairs Lounge, 66

Valdez, David, 169–70, *170*
Vancouver Wine and Jazz Festival, 164, 166
Vanelli, Gino, 107, 164
Van Sant, Gus, 149–50
Vaughan, Sarah, 37
Vaughn, Leon, 38
Venetian Gardens, 30
Veterans Memorial Coliseum, 53, 55
Vinnegar, Leroy: and Alan Jones, 133; "Father of the Walking Bass," 110, *110*, 111; Jazz Quarry club, 85; and local jazz community, 129, *138*, 167; musical influence on Pacific Northwest region, 19, 95, 112–14, 122
Vinton, Will, 150
Vu, Cuong, 115–16, 172–73

Walcott, Colin, 71
Waldron, Elliott "Mack," 179
Waldron, Frank, 32
Waldron, Mal, 68, 114
Walker, Junior, 65
Walker, T-Bone, 47, 149
Walkin' the Basses (album), 112
Waller, Fats, 25, 206
Walter Bridges Big Band, 16, 51, 62, 79
Walton, Bill, 71
Walton, Eric (Skerik), 116–17, *116*, 121, 178, 184
Ward, Carlos, 67
"Warm Valley" (song), 35
Washington, Dinah, 63
Washington High School, 16

Washington, Kamasi, 206
waterfalls, *20*
Waterfront Blues Festival, *96*, 97, 104, 107, 163, 185
Waterfront Park, 104
"Watermelon Man" (song), 74
"Waterwheel" (song), 71
The Way Out, 53, 67
Weather Report, 55, 71
Webster, Ben, 94
Ween, 116
Weijters, Bram, 192
Wendeborn, John, 147
The Westerlies, 208
Western Washington State University, 171
"What a Wonderful World" (song), 163
White, Barry, 1623
White, Lenny, 174
Whiteman, Paul, 30
White, Michael, 143
Whitney, Larry, 89–90
W. H. Mahara's Minstrels, 24
Why Fight the Feeling? (album), 140
Wicks, John, 1376
Wied, Eddie, 71–72, 77, 84, 85, 94–95, *95*, 129, *138*, 167, *167*
Wilensky, Dan, 188–89
Wilke, Jim, 75, 89, 100, 122
Willcox, Tim, 169, 170–71, 193
Williams Avenue: 1940s and 1950s, 37–38, 49, 53–54; late 1980s, 108; and local jazz community, 18; and Tom Johnson, 28–29
Williams, Clarence, 47–48, 50
Williams, Cleve, 17, 51, 79, 85, 129, 167, *167*
Williams, Jessica, 110, 112, 115
Williams, Joe, 97
Williams, Tony, 104, 105, 106
Willrich, Darrius, 206
Wilson, Bert, 133–34
Windham Hill Records, 119
Winston, George, 119
Winter, Brad, 85
"Witchi-Tai-To" (song), 64, 65, 106
Within Sight (album), 188, 190
Woideck, Carl, 192
Wolfe, Ben, 84, 85
Womack, Bobby, 98

women: bandleaders, 27; and the jazz community, 56–58
Woodland Park Zoo, 100
Woodring, Jim, 127, 177
Woods, Phil, 44, 99–100, 194
world musicians in Portland, 121–22, *123*

Yamhill Marketplace, 104
Yeoman, Omar, 64
York, Dusty, 145, 146–47, *148*
York, Michael, 146–47
You Hardly Know Me (album), 105
The Young Oregonians, 22, 62
Young, Tim, 143, 161, 205

Zappa, Frank, 119
Zawinul, Joe, 86
Zony Mash ensemble, 161
Zoo Tunes, 100

ABOUT THE AUTHOR

Lynn Darroch has written extensively about jazz for the *Oregonian*, *Jazz Times*, and *Willamette Week*, and has contributed to the books *The Guide to United States Popular Culture* and *Jumptown: The Golden Years of Portland Jazz, 1942–1957*. His script for "The Incredible Journey of Jazz" is performed yearly in area schools, and his stories about jazz history—told to the accompaniment of live music—are collected in three albums: *Jazz Stories: Heroes of the Americas* (2006), *Beyond the Border—Stories of the Latin World* (2008), and *Local Heroes/American Originals* (2009). Currently, Darroch hosts a weekly jazz radio show called *Bright Moments!* and edits and produces the monthly magazine *Jazzscene*. Having lived up and down the West Coast, he has called Portland, Oregon, home since 1979.

OOLIGAN PRESS

Ooligan Press is a general trade publisher rooted in the rich literary tradition of the Pacific Northwest. Ooligan strives to discover works that reflect the diverse values and rich cultures that inspire so many to call the region their home. Founded in 2001, the press is a vibrant and integral part of Portland's publishing community, operating within the Department of English at Portland State University. Ooligan Press is staffed by graduate students working under the guidance of a core faculty of publishing professionals.

PROJECT MANAGER

Tyler Mathieson
Margaret Schimming

ACQUISITIONS

Brian Tibbetts (manager)
Meagan Lobnitz
Sabrina Parys

EDITING

Katey Trnka (manager)
Olenka Burgess (manager)
Brendan Brown
Bess Pallares
Kurt Spickerman
Cora Wigen

DESIGN

Erika Schnatz (manager)
Ryan Brewer (manager)
Olenka Burgess
Alyssa Hanchar
Julia Skillin

DIGITAL

Cora Wigen (manager)

MARKETING

Ariana Vives (manager)
Dory Athey (manager)
Maeko Bradshaw
Melissa Gifford
Andrew Fitzgerald
Jacoba Lawson
Kurt Spickerman
Amanda Taylor
Chris Thomas
MacKenzie Turner
Caitlin Waite
William York

RESEARCH

Andrew Fitzgerald
Kathryn Osterndorff
William York

COLOPHON

This book is set in TeX Gyre Schola, which is based on the 1919 typeface Century Schoolbook by Morris Fuller Benton. Captions and sidebars are set in Roboto by Christian Robertson, and titles are set in Oswald by Vernon Adams.

A steady soundtrack of jazz influenced the interplay of classic and modern letterforms.